THE FUTURES OF EUROPE

THE FUTURES OF
EUROPE

EDITED FOR PUBLICATION BY
WAYLAND KENNET
DIRECTOR OF THE EUROPE PLUS THIRTY PROJECT

BASED ON A REPORT TO THE
COMMISSION OF
THE EUROPEAN COMMUNITIES

CAMBRIDGE UNIVERSITY PRESS
CAMBRIDGE
LONDON · NEW YORK · MELBOURNE
FOR THE COMMISSION
OF THE EUROPEAN COMMUNITIES

Published by the Syndics of the Cambridge University Press
The Pitt Building, Trumpington Street, Cambridge CB2 1RP
Bentley House, 200 Euston Road, London NW1 2DB
32 East 57th Street, New York, NY 10022, USA
296 Beaconsfield Parade, Middle Park, Melbourne 3206, Australia

First published 1976

Printed in Great Britain
at the
University Printing House, Cambridge
(Euan Phillips, University Printer)

Library of Congress cataloguing in publication data
Main entry under title:
The Futures of Europe.
1. Economic forecasting – European Economic Community
countries. 2. Technological forecasting. I. Young, Wayland
Hilton, Baron Kennet, 1923– . II. Commission of the European
Communities.
HC241.2.F87   330.9'4'055   76-9541
ISBN: 0 521 21326 6

Contents

Preface by the Commission of the European Communities

The origin of this book is as follows. It began with an increasing feeling in the Commission and Council of the European Community, as it neared the third decade of its existence, that the Community should set fresh goals as it moved towards Economic, Monetary and Political Union, based on assessments of likely long-term developments. The feeling found practical expression in a resolution prepared by former Commissioner Ralf Dahrendorf and passed by the Council of Ministers of the Community in January 1974.[1] The resolution asked the following two questions:

(1) Should the European Communities undertake a study entitled 'Europe Plus Thirty' concerning the foreseeable or possible developments over the next thirty years which are likely to affect the progress of Europe; and, if so, will this study make it possible to create a forecasting instrument which can be constantly updated?

(2) Should the European Communities create their own Technology Assessment Office in an attempt to evaluate in advance the effects of scientific and technological development on the society and economy of the Community?

The Council instructed the Commission of the European Communities to undertake a study to answer these questions, and allocated half a million Units of Account[2] for the purpose. Wayland Kennet was appointed director of the study; it was carried out by a Project Board, supervisory and advisory, and a Project Team which made specific contributions to the drafting of the report, rewritten many times over.

The Europe Plus Thirty project was completed in about a year and a quarter. This period, which was stipulated by the Council of Ministers, is short for such a vast subject and imposed a particular method of work. It was impossible to ask a small number of highly qualified people to drop everything overnight and work together full-time. Therefore, the opposite method had to be chosen: a large number of highly qualified people working together part-time, making up the Project Board and the Project Team members listed below.

This book, *The Futures of Europe*, was once more edited and partly

---

[1] Resolution of 14 January 1974, annex: action programme as regards forecasting, assessment, and methodology.
[2] See n.1 on p. 16.

rewritten by Lord Kennet, who therefore accepts the responsibility for it.

The members of the Project Board and Project Team involved in this study were as follows.

PROJECT BOARD

Dr L. Bölkow	Director of Messerschmitt–Bölkow–Blohm GmbH, Munich.
Prof. A. Buzzati-Traverso	Senior Scientific Adviser to the United Nations Environmental Programme, formerly Assistant Director General for Science, UNESCO.
Prof. H. B. G. Casimir	President of the Royal Academy of Arts and Sciences, Amsterdam.
Prof. Umberto Colombo	Director of Corporate Research and Strategic Planning, Montedison, Milan.
Prof. R. Dahrendorf[1]	Director of London School of Economics, formerly a Member of the European Commission.
Prof. Bertrand de Jouvenel	Founder of Association Internationale des Futuribles, Paris; author, among other books, of *The Art of Conjecture.*
Lord Kennet, Chairman	Formerly Parliamentary Secretary for Housing and Local Government, U.K. Government.
Dr Alexander King	Chairman of the International Federation of Institutes of Advanced Study, Co-founder of the Club of Rome, formerly Director General for Scientific Affairs, OECD.
Dr H. Hermann Koelle	Professor of Space Technology and Systems Engineering. Founding President of the Centre for Futures Research, Berlin.
Dr Max Kohnstamm	Principal of the European University Institute, Florence.
Mr Keith Pavitt	Senior Fellow, Science Policy Research Unit, University of Sussex;

[1] From October 1974.

	member of Directorate for Scientific Affairs, OECD; former Visiting Lecturer at Princeton University, U.S.A.
Prof. P. Piganiol	Association Internationale des Futuribles, Paris.
Prof. I. Prigogine	Professor at the Free University of Brussels.
Prof. P. Nørregaard Rasmussen	Professor of Economics at the University of Copenhagen.
Senator Mary Robinson	Professor of Law at Trinity College, Dublin; barrister.
Prof. R. Saint-Paul	President of the Department of Economics and Management, Conservatoire Nationale des Arts et Métiers; Director of the Centre Science, Technologie et Societé, Paris.
Dr Ing. J. Seetzen	Arbeitsgemeinschaft der Grossforschungs-Einrichtungen.
Prof. H. Thiemann	Counsellor and R & D Coordinator, Nestlé Alimentana SA, Vevey; formerly Director General of the Battelle Institute, Geneva.
Prof. P. de Wolff	Professor of Econometrics at the University of Amsterdam.

PROJECT TEAM

Dr Bernhard Badura	Faculty of Sociology, University of Constance.
Dott. Ugo Businaro	Direzione Centrale Ricerca e Sviluppo, Fiat, Turin.
M. Bernard Cazes	Commissariat-Général du Plan, d'Equipement et de la Productivité, Paris.
Prof. M. de Cecco	Professor of International Economics at the University of Siena; Visiting Professor at the Royal Institute of International Affairs, London.
Dr Sam Cole	Science Policy Research Unit, University of Sussex.

ix

Prof. Dr Meinolf Dierkes	Adjunct Professor of Public Affairs at Carnegie–Mellon University, Pittsburgh; Head of Applied Social and Behavioural Science Research Division of the Battelle Institute, Frankfurt.
Prof. Dr H. Flohn	Meteorological Institute, Bonn University.
Sir George Godber	Formerly Chief Medical Officer, England.
M. François Hetman	Directorate for Scientific Affairs, OECD.
Prof. Dr J. de Hoogh	Landbouw-Economisch Instituut, The Hague.
Prof. Torsten Husén	Professor of Education at the University of Stockholm; Director of the Institute for the Study of International Problems in Education, Stockholm.
Mr Erling Joergensen	Danmark Statistik; President of Central Council of Education of Denmark.
Lord Kennet, Director	
Prof. Dr Beate Kohler	Professor of Political Science at the Technische Hochschule, Darmstadt.
Mr Gerald Leach	International Institute for Environment and Development, London.
Dr H. Paschen	Studiengruppe für Systemforschung, Heidelberg.
Prof. P. Piganiol	Association Internationale des Futuribles, Paris.
Mr B. T. Price	Secretary General, the Uranium Institute; formerly Director of the Defence Operational Analysis Establishment, U.K.
Prof. ir. O. Rademaker	Technische Hogeschool, Eindhoven.
Prof. Giuseppe Sacco	Professor of Industrial Economics and Policy, Department of Political Science, Florence University.
Dr Craig Sinclair	Consultant, Environment Direc-

torate, OECD; formerly Chairman of Faculty, International Institute for the Management of Technology, Milan.

Prof. Dr Kurt Sontheimer   Professor of Politics at the Geschwister-Scholl-Institut für Politische Wissenschaft, University of Munich.

M. L. Thiriet   Département des Programmes, Commissariat à l'Energie Atomique, Paris.

Mr J. M. Thomson[1]   Head of the European Intercity Transport Study, OECD, Paris.

Prof. Guillaume Wunsch   Department of Demography, Université Catholique de Louvain.

Mr W. Zegveld   Director of the Industrial Liaison Department, TNO (Netherlands Applied Research Organisation), The Hague.

The Administrator of the Project and Secretary of the Project Board was Brigadier C. T. Honeybourne, the Research Assistant was Charles Landry, and the secretaries were Anne Wood and Catherine Gaynor.

The report of the Europe Plus Thirty Group, comprising both Project Team and Project Board, was submitted in September 1975 to François-Xavier Ortoli, President of the European Commission, and to Guido Brunner, Commissioner for Research, Science, and Education. The Commission of the European Communities officially took note of the Report on 22 December 1975 and agreed to the publication of a version of it, namely this book.

The Report was an action document; it analysed the difficulties encountered by the Commission and Council of the European Communities in a detail which would not interest the general reader, and it advised them what to do in similar detail. *The Futures of Europe* omits much of this detail, but not all. It retains the main recommendations made to the Institutions of the Community (Council and Commission) since if the general reader is interested in the topic of long-term forecasting and assessment for the European Community, he is likely also to be interested in what has been recommended on his behalf.

The Commission does not identify itself with all the views expressed in the Report, which is essentially the result of a study entrusted to

---

[1] From March 1975.

an external group of experts under the direction of Lord Kennet. The Report, at the time of writing, is being analysed by the Commission, which will decide as to the nature of any future action to be undertaken by the Commission of the European Communities in this field. The Commission of the European Communities has expressed its appreciation to all contributors to the study for the way in which this broad and relatively new and complex subject has been tackled, and for the ensuing results. It is to be hoped that the publication of this version of the Report will encourage further discussion of the whole question of long-term forecasting at Community level.

H. G. SCHUSTER
Director General of the Commission
of the European Communities for
Research, Science, and Education

Acknowledgements

How this book came to be written is described in the Preface. As well as the Project Board and Project Team, the following have helped in various ways, and their help is gratefully acknowledged:

Melanie Archer
John Bibby
John Clark
Paul Cornière
David Fishlock
Professor Gareth Williams
Dorothy Haas
Krishna Kumar
E. J. Tuininga
Elizabeth Young

Introduction

The world is bursting in on us. It is less important that we are French, German, British, and so on than that we are Europeans, and less important that we are Europeans than that we are human beings. Because of the recent revolutions in transport, communications, and weaponry, it is world forces and world factors which shape our lives, and sometimes threaten them. But it is still as citizens of a single nation that we entrust power to those who must guide and protect us. Events are global, while political legitimacy remains national.

That this paradox makes it harder for us to control our fate and invent our future is well understood. We as Europeans, acting at the middle level, should therefore direct our ingenuity to finding ways of reducing the effects of the paradox. If we can achieve greater control of events by broadening political legitimacy, we should do so; this is the impelling logic of the European Community.[1] And if we can achieve greater control of events by thinking ahead, we should do that also; that is the impelling logic of forecasting.

The rapid political change and extreme economic uncertainty of the world today are forcing all our countries to take cognisance of trends, and of the interaction between them, which hitherto it was possible to ignore. At both national and Community levels we should develop whatever means we can for identifying necessary relationships between the policy sector and long-term planning and, in the light of these, for elaborating alternative policies and strategies. The object must always be to examine what is possible for Europe and what is impossible; the latter is generally easier to identify than the former

---

[1] In law there is no such thing as 'The European Community'; there are only the European Economic Community, the European Coal and Steel Community, and Euratom. At first, each of the three had its own Commission; but in 1967 the three Commissions were amalgamated, becoming the Commission of the European Communities, while the three Communities themselves remain legally distinct.

In political and social reality, on the other hand, there is certainly such a thing as 'The European Community'. The words will be used here as the context requires. 'The European Communities' are the three legally separate entities; 'The European Community' is the single socio-political entity.

'The Commission of the European Communities' is the full legal title of the famous body in Brussels. 'The European Commission' or 'the Commission' is the common name of the same body, reflecting the political and social reality. The adjective 'Community' (as in 'Community level' or 'Community system') will be used here to mean 'of or pertaining to either the single socio-political Community or one or another of the separate legal Communities', as the context shows.

and provides a welcome element of certainty in an activity where certainty is by definition scarce.

The interdependence of nations has long been accepted in a general and superficial way, but it has now reached a new intensity. The vastness of international transactions, especially the ever-increasing demand for energy and raw materials with all its payments, investment, and monetary consequences, has greatly increased the importance of factors external to each country, leaving strictly limited possibilities of initiative to all but the biggest.

The energy crisis has shown how a problem in one field can penetrate the whole economic, social, and political fabric. Rapid population increase, rising demand for food and especially for protein, changing expectations concerning economic growth, agricultural innovation, climatic change, and many other problems on the horizon may well have equally far-reaching and disconcerting effects, some of them quite soon. We have in fact reached a situation where the interactions are so important that it is difficult even to identify discrete problems, let alone to apply discrete solutions. Yet the machinery of our governments, designed for earlier and simpler days, is still organised sector by sector and can only with difficulty assess inter-policy conflicts, or synergisms, by interdepartmental committees or by coordination at the top. And the same is true of the European Community.

It seems to be generally accepted that a doubling of the population of the world in just over thirty years is inevitable. By far the greater part of this expansion will take place in the less-developed countries. In 1920 the present European Community countries contained 9.7 per cent of the world's population, in 1970 it was 6.9 per cent, and in 2000 it is unlikely to be more than 4.6 per cent.[1] This changing proportion cannot fail to have major political consequences for the whole world, quite apart from the direct effects of the increase, such as pressure on food and raw materials. The much smaller population increase probable in the industrial countries will also have a disproportionate effect on the demand for energy and materials, since per capita consumption in those countries is, today, between twenty and forty times that of the less-developed world.

The internal social effects of these changes would be very different in the less-developed and in the industrial countries. In the former, a doubling of the present population, of very young average age, would treble the workforce, with inevitable employment difficulties. In the latter, zero or very small growth rates would lead to a consi-

---

[1] EEC figure for 2000 from the OECD Report of 1974; for 1920 and 1970 from the UN Demographic Yearbook. Estimates of world population from various UN sources.

derable increase in the average age and hence to a gradual reduction in the active, though not in the consuming, population.

Neo-Malthusian doubts are now raised everywhere about the possibility of economic growth continuing indefinitely, because population-doubling and the development of the poor regions would add so enormously to the global demands for raw materials and energy. The problem in the decades to come will be not so much the absolute exhaustion of resources as greatly increased costs, including energy costs, for working the more difficult energy deposits, which are all that will be left. The energy crisis has given us a foretaste of difficulties which could become quite common. But – and here is the contradiction – we have allowed energy to become the key to continued material growth. The very great increase which must be expected in the demand for food can apparently only be met by a corresponding increase in the energy inputs, particularly for mechanised agriculture and the desalination of water. Similarly, nearly all substitution for scarce or expensive materials seems to require a large increase in the use of energy. Two trends are here on a collision course.

We can no longer maintain the simplifying distinction of 'the three worlds'. There is a continuous spectrum of societies, and the harmonisation of disparities within this one world is clearly not mainly a humanitarian or philanthropic problem, as it has so often been presented in the past; it is the world's major political issue. Already the OAPEC countries give more aid per capita than the OECD countries. Already there has been a call, within the General Assembly of the United Nations and in OPEC, for the creation of a New International Economic Order. This must be taken as the first sign of a movement likely to appeal to the sense of justice of the majority of mankind, one which the developed countries will find it unwise to ignore and impossible to repress.

Our political systems are ill adapted to face major discontinuity, and neither precedent nor the traditional indicators give much guidance. The democratic system, with its three-to-seven-year electoral cycle, concentrates political action upon immediate issues, and there is little opportunity or incentive to elaborate longer-term policies. Thinking about the future is therefore all too often relegated to party research groups, to academe, and to multinational corporations.

The time scales of the worlds of politics, of administration, and of science are greatly different: this is a fundamental fact of national and world development. Research and development are essentially (and increasingly) long-term processes. The time from the appearance of a new concept in the mind of a scientist to its generalised application in the form of a new product, process, institution, or industry can be thirty years or more. In such contemporary economic thinking as bases itself on the need to ensure uninterrupted economic growth, there is an implicit reliance on the 'technological fix' – that is, the assumption that economic forces will themselves summon up, from the cornucopia of science, a continuous flow of necessary innovations. It has been so, and it may continue to be so. But it is running a notable risk to assume that technology will always respond smoothly to increasing needs. Lead times are important, and a smooth 'fit' is not likely; the risk is of recurrent crises.

To meet all these dangers, then, democracy itself must be endowed with new tools in education, in participation, in communication, and in management. It is not our task to suggest what these might be. Our task is to suggest a new tool for democracy in thinking about these dangers, in understanding them, and especially in thinking about and understanding them all together. Mapping out alternative policies and delimiting the possible from the impossible can be regarded as a form of insurance against the uncertainties of a changing world. An individual who does not protect himself and his family by insuring against contingencies is regarded as irresponsible; on the national scale (except in the defence field) such foresight has too seldom been expected.

What we have said applies to all nations but particularly to those of the European Community. Western Europe today has relatively few natural resources but a highly skilled, educated, and enterprising population, abundantly capable of innovation in technology, in social evolution, and in politics. What we lack in *materia grezza* we make up in *materia grigia*. The European Community therefore not only must but can come to grips with the complexity of the situation and design the change it wants, rather than merely reacting belatedly to events.

But we cannot confine ourselves to a study of the Community as a system, since it is an 'open system' within the world. And as there are reasons to think that the major features of the period 1945–75 are now undergoing a fundamental change, it seems necessary to look back at least to the period 1914–44 if we are to understand our true context and our social momentum.

The period 1914–44 began and ended with great wars which shook the whole of Europe and through it shook the world. It was marked by the upsurge of new forms of government, communist and fascist, which, however important their differences, both stood in stark contradiction to the belief current in pre-1914 Europe, and apparently triumphant at the time of the peace treaties of 1919 and 1920, that every state was bound to repeat the parliamentary form of government developed in Britain. In the economic world the main event was the

Great Depression, the break-up of international trade and capital movements. The distress of unemployment gave rise to a new imperative which was to dominate the next period, 1945–75: the imperative of full employment. It also gave rise to social institutions which added a new dimension to public finance: the dimension of social welfare.

In 1914 there had been no distinction between the political and the geographical uses of the word 'Europe'. Nobody then would have thought of Europe in the narrow sense of Western Europe (the outcome of the Second World War). The 1914–44 period ended and the 1944–75 period began with the division of Europe into two parts. Russia, which had played an important part in the first stages of the 1914 war, had then changed its regime and stepped out of it. For these reasons it did not take part in the peace-making of 1919 and 1920 and was thereafter considered by the Allies as outside Europe, an outsideness which was later extended to the other countries of Europe reached by the Russian armies in 1945. The alternative futures for Europe which we have now to consider cannot assume that a division which has lasted a mere thirty years will continue to prevail over centuries of cultural and political affinity.

Not only is the Community only a part of Europe; it also depends upon phenomena outside Europe altogether. The main feature of the last thirty years has been the role of America in Europe, and it is mainly by the position in 1945 of the outposts of the Allied armies, in which America predominated, that Western Europe is now defined. Our tremendous post-war economic development was seeded and made possible by American aid, and the receipt of this aid was the first occasion for European powers to put together their experts in spelling out the needs of Europe and measuring the 'gap' between these countries' capacity to finance their imports and their possible means of payment. These sessions between experts played no mean part in the formation of the concept of Western Europe as an economic unit.

While attention was focused on economic growth, there occurred a capital change in the map of the world, from which the great overseas empires of all Western European states were cancelled, chiefest of them the British Empire. The lands which owed some form of allegiance to the British crown had covered nearly three times the extent of geographical Europe and contained nearly twice its population. Now they have gone their own way. The British Commonwealth and the French-speaking world retain a unity based only on language and on some elements of law and higher education. One may see in the new Lomé Convention a possible embryo of a Community Commonwealth, but the situation is probably a transitory one, since Asia and Latin America are excluded.

If one takes a long backward view, it appears that our small peninsula of Eurasia was for some five centuries the source of changes in other parts of the world, the launching pad of impacts on their societies and civilisations. How brutal these impacts were at first need not be dwelt upon here. The point of present interest is that the peoples whose histories have been changed by the impact of Europe have now acquired a freedom of action allowing them, in turn, to affect the history of Europe. Notwithstanding its great distance from Europe (in terms of seafaring two centuries ago) and notwithstanding the smallness of its population, the nascent American nation was the first to have a return impact upon Europe; indeed, its War of Independence generated a wave of influence which played a great part in the toppling of the French monarchy and in the introduction of bourgeois democracy in all Europe.

The Third World could once be thought of as in some way 'outside'. But in the years to come, we must think of Europe as 'within' a world system where relative weights may change very rapidly. There have been calculations of the decades, or generations, which the poor countries would take to catch up with the American per capita product as it then stood, but this was a narrow view indeed. Political roles do not wait upon the achievement of a standard of living. The very period during which Western Europe became substantially dependent on Third World resources was also that during which Europe lost any form of overt control over them. Soon after the French oil find in the Sahara, Algeria ceased to be 'part of France'. Nigerian oil and independence emerged together. Britain has been steadily reducing its presence in the Middle East since 1945. At the moment when Angola proved a great reserve of oil, Portugal at last had to concede independence.

It seems clear that the next thirty years will be marked by continuing vast changes in the relationships of Europe with the rest of the world, among them those arising from the disappearance of European ownership in other lands, from the increasing external ownership of Europe, and from two-way migrations of workers of different sorts and qualifications.

May we expect a class war to develop on a world scale? Should industrialised societies as a whole, given their consumption of materials and energy, now be regarded as among the world's exploiters, and the poorer societies as a whole be regarded as the world's exploited? Was the recent 'energy crisis', in which some of the whole world's have-nots stood shoulder to shoulder to raise the price of the main thing which the world's haves needed from them, analogous to the first strikes in the industrialised world, when each country's have-nots stood shoulder to shoulder to raise the price of their labour? If there is indeed a world class war, will any international assembly be ready in time to articulate and mitigate it, as the parliaments of the Western world articulated and mitigated our national class wars? Will the UN family of organisations become equal to the task? Or will the world class war follow instead the bloody pattern of the Russian one? These questions are susceptible of rational discussion, and within this field of discourse alternative aims and policies can be formulated, assessed, and compared.

Thus far, we have, in a sense, been discussing the question: 'What is Europe that it should need forecasting?' We must now turn to the question: 'What is forecasting that Europe should need it?'

We all try to interrogate the future, mainly in order to help us decide what to do. The peoples who used to (and those who still do) open animals to see their entrails, or cast pebbles or drops of wine on the ground, or go to the cloudy and euphonious oracle, did so not for curiosity but because they had a decision to make (Shall we give battle? Shall I build a house?). Divination was for action; divination, like judgement and like will, was a component of decision.

Equally, in modern times, forecasting is seldom done for its own sake; it is done to help someone take decisions. Even in the least-planned national economies, economic forecasting is supposed to help manu-facturers, merchants, and entrepreneurs to place themselves in a position of their own choice in the real world of unfolding events; and the more centrally planned a society is, the more will forecasting seek to help a government which, by definition, takes many and weighty decisions, and the less will it be distinguished from the planned enforcement of those decisions themselves.

In recent years a whole academic world of forecasting has grown up, and many sub-worlds within it. We will none of us forget that much of it was initiated in the USA and that some of it contributed to policies of the Kennedy and Johnson administrations which, in Viet-nam and in the strategic relationship with the Soviet Union, almost entirely failed in their purposes. It is also right to remember that this whole structure of techniques is only a concentration in specialist hands of a universal human function, and that although the 'scientific' competence of the American thinktanks was often high, their political, historical, and philosophical competence was sometimes low or even nonexistent.

So far forecasting has mainly been done by people trained in the physical sciences and the more number-based social sciences; the epistemology of forecasting is still in its infancy. For the time being, practitioners from these sciences might agree that the usefulness of long-term forecasting is clearest in certain fields, which fall into two groups. First: if decisions or actions taken now or in the near future can produce important consequences in the long term, then forecasts for a correspondingly long period are useful. Some major infra-structure investments (for instance, in transport and education) are irreversible and inevitably last for a very long time. Again, the development of new technologies may produce permanent changes in people's lives. Second: forecasting in some fields itself demands forecasts of associated factors in other fields which might not in themselves have given rise to a need for long-term forecasting.

What exactly is meant by a long-term forecast? It usually consists of deductions from a set of assumptions and hypotheses, and of propositions or discourses surrounding those deductions. The as-sumptions are usually quite numerous but are not always made explicit. For instance, it is sometimes assumed explicitly that there will be no world war during the forecast period; more commonly, that assumption is left implicit along with a great many others. The art of forecasting lies largely in the development and use of deductive methods, allied with the application of common sense, imagination, and judgement.

The assumptions on which a forecast is founded may arise in various ways. Some may be technical or other assumptions within the sector where the forecast is being made. Others may derive from forecasts already made in other sectors; for instance, forecasts in many sectors need to draw on population and income projections. Forecasts in one sector appear as inputs to others, and the comprehensive and coordinated interchange of sector forecasts is thus a large part of integrated forecasting. Assumptions of a third sort concern policy: they postulate, for the purpose of the forecast, that certain policies shall continue or shall be changed in specified ways.

All these sorts of assumptions can be varied for the purpose of the exercise and thus lead to different forecasts. Some of them may be varied within postulated limits of uncertainty, by taking upper and lower limits. Policy assumptions can be varied in order to forecast the consequences of alternative policy choices. It is possible in this way to examine rather speculative hypotheses and thus to assist a public power (in our case, the European Community) in promoting, if it so wishes, public debate on alternative directions and opportunities.

The prime object of forecasting is to provide estimates relating to the future, based on rigorous analysis of the present and past, as a contribution to the assessment of existing or possible new policies. The forecast, of course, is only one element in such an assessment. A secondary object of forecasting can be to help society at large to appreciate the longer-term prospects facing it and the potentialities for change. It can be a contribution to the self-consciousness of a society, and thus to its self-government.

But forecasting should by no means be confined to the elaboration of that which can be expressed numerically, however wisely that may be done. It must also keep a firm and distinct hold of political and social reality, and any forecasting team must include people who know how to do that. This means people with experience, preferably direct, of politics, since they are the people who know without calculation whether a given calculation leads into the area of impossibility by implying, for instance, that the old may welcome change or the young forgo it, that those 'whose wrongs give edge unto their swords' can be oppressed for ever, or that ignorance, any more than injustice, can be perpetuated. Forecasting for human beings can only be done by the whole human being, and calculation is only one among the human gifts.

To say anything about the future, we must know the past. There is only faint forecasting without the projection of historical trends. In the fields we shall discuss later, historical time series data are to be had to very varying degrees. The extrapolation of single trends enables you to know (supposing you have good data) what would happen if everything went on happening as it had happened before, if nothing ran out, and if the impact of some other trend or trends did not disturb the one you were extrapolating. The provisos are obviously at least as important as the extrapolation, which is why this necessary but humdrum part of forecasting is now recognised, when it is done alone, as being naive. Things do run out; other trends do hit yours, and they are quite often trends no one was measuring at all. (For example, the oil price increase of 1973–4 could not have been foreseen by extrapolating the oil price trend or the oil depletion curve, or from their interaction. But it could have been foreseen by extrapolating two political trends: that of post-colonial politics in general, and that of the reaction of governments everywhere to the occupation of their territories by invading armies. The probable interaction of these trends with that of the oil price was not hard to discern. But since they could not be cast in the form of 'historical time series data', they were invisible to the specialist eye.)

If by systems analysis and modelling we work out the cross-impacts of various current trends upon each other – for instance, energy use, materials use, agricultural productivity, population growth – we very soon hit disaster in all sorts of ways. But disaster has often been foreseen in the past and did not occur because we 'saw it coming' and we took avoiding action. By changing policy we changed the trends and cancelled the foreseen impacts.

Cassandra was always right and always disbelieved. She said: 'The city will be taken and sacked.' The people were already besieged; capture and sack was precisely what they feared, so they put her prophecy down to defeatism and did nothing they had not done before. And the city was taken and sacked.

We must remember why Cassandra was always right and always disbelieved: her ears and eyes had been cleansed by the Serpent of Understanding when she was a child, so that she should read the signs of nature aright. When she grew up Apollo, the god of moderation and harmony, wooed her, but she refused him. Since he could not take away the gift of prophecy, he left her with the curse of incredibility. The Serpent had made her a good statistician, systems analyst, and scenario-writer, but she refused the god of daylight and political reasoning. If she had said: 'The Greeks may be preparing some trick; let us think of all the tricks they might prepare and guard against them', then these propositions could have been debated and have led to action. But no; she refused to explain herself and went straight for the theatrical effect of the unqualified future tense: 'The city will be taken and sacked.' She was an immoderate mystagogue, and her mystagogy allowed the city to be destroyed when her pre-science could have saved it.

A prophecy of woe is only true when disbelieved, and only belief can falsify it. Otherwise put: if people believe their present courses will lead to disaster, they will amend their courses. Otherwise put again: the publication of unfavourable trends allows them to be corrected. But Cassandra must always haunt us; if we do not explain the publications and make sure they are accepted for what they are, the city will again be lost, and it's a bigger city now.

What Cassandra did not do was to put her prophecy in the conditional mood: 'If we did nothing, the city would be taken and sacked. On the other hand, if we did this, that, or the other, it would not – it's up to us.' Setting forth alternative courses of action (of which inaction is one) and measuring their effects on a trend projection is, in the case of a 'bad' trend projection, a way of helping people to bend away from it. It is a way of correcting any naive tendency to 'believe' a projection as if it were a prediction.

There should be no hesitation in admitting that in a field which depends as much on epistemology as forecasting does, we in Western Europe are hampered in any international project by our language differences. In English, there are at least thirty tenses and tense uses

which apply to the future.[1] Every one of these has a different meaning, and probably none of them can be automatically translated, in all
contexts, into any one tense in any other language. The other European languages each have their own wealth of distinctions in the
future use of verbs (though perhaps none has quite the unbridled
fertility of English), and probably from none of them can any of these
uses be translated one-for-one into any of the others. This general fact
constitutes the first difficulty in any attempt at forecasting by an
international team of workers. But it is fortunate that our languages
are so rich in inflections of meaning, and a full and conscious use of
those inflections is one good way of avoiding the misuse of forecasting.
Very many of the common objections to forecasting spring from a
confusion between 'shall', 'will', and 'would'. You can only say, for
instance, that wealth *shall* be more evenly distributed if you yourself
have decided it shall, and if you are in a position to enforce your
decision. You can only say wealth *will* be more evenly distributed if
you believe nothing can stop its becoming more evenly distributed,
whatever happens. And you can only say wealth *would* be more evenly
distributed if you go on to describe the conditions which must be met
if it is to be so. 'Shall' is the language of decision, 'will' is the language
of prediction, and 'would' is the language of forecasting. It was
because she said 'will' that Cassandra was disbelieved and, because
disbelieved, vindicated.

We turn now to the meaning to be assigned to the word 'forecasting'.
One may agree with Bertrand de Jouvenel[2] in disliking not only the
word 'prediction' – all agree that is a mug's game – but also 'projec-

[1] Take the verb 'to go', and consider a person who has not gone somewhere but
whose going is under discussion. We can say:

He will go	He could be going
He would go	He must be going
He can go	He ought to be going
He could go	He may be going
He shall go	He might be going
He should go	He was to be going
He must go	He is bound to be going
He has to go	He is bound to go
He ought to go	He has to be going
He may go	He was going
He might go	He is about to go
He is to go	He will be about to go
He was to go	He was about to go
He is going	He is by way of going
He will be going	He is by way of being about to go
He would be going	He is due to go
He should be going	

Add to this the double negatives, as in 'He can't not go', etc.

[2] *The Art of Conjecture* (London: Weidenfeld and Nicolson, 1968).

tion' and even 'forecasting' itself. We agree with him that 'conjecture' is the safest word. We like the French word he coined, '*futuribles*', a word which can be translated into Italian but not into the other Community languages, even by neologisms. It rests on the oldest sense of the Latin word '*futurus*', which means 'about to be generated'. '*Futurus*' is also the future participle of the verb 'to be', and it has a strongly passive ring to it. Somebody has to do something now if there is to be a *future*; they have, precisely, to beget it on the present. All this meaning inheres in the French neologism '*futuribles*'; it means all those things which we might beget upon the present and which might therefore turn out to constitute the future.[1] Action there must be; it is unavoidable; we can, therefore must, shape our futures (if we don't someone else will). Diversity there is: things will turn out in one of many possible ways, and that is why we have a variety of choice until the last minute. And certainty there is too, but it resides only in the negative. We can never be certain what things will happen, but we can be certain that some things will not. It may be that the greatest service a forecaster can render a decision-maker is in identifying the impossible.

But the word 'forecasting' is used throughout this book. We do not mean by it simply the casting forward of past experience, or projection, though we include that. We use it rather in the way one says 'cast your mind forward', like 'cast your mind back'; 'try to imagine', like 'try to remember'. By 'forecasting' we mean simply casting around ahead of us, by the application of all the mental processes which may rationally be applied to the future, save one alone: decision.

It is clear that there is no point in forecasting except to help decision and that one cannot rationally decide without forecasts. But the two things are different in nature, and they should be, and are, done by different people. Only rulers may take decisions about the future of society, and in democracies only elected politicians may rule. The distinction is obvious, and so is the reason to labour it.

What sort of forecasting, then, is useful to those we elect to rule us? One may deploy in one's mind an image of the future as a cone. The further we look ahead, the wider is the range of possibilities open to us, the more numerous the *futuribles*. Tomorrow will probably be pretty like today, the day after tomorrow less like. Outside our cone lies the impossible (for instance, short-term reduction in world population without war or famine). Inside it lies the range of the possible.

---

[1] This discussion holds good only for English, French, and Italian, which have the words 'future', '*futur*', '*futuro*'. The German and Dutch '*Zukunft*' and '*Toekomst*' simply mean 'that which is *coming towards* us'. The Danish word '*Fremtid*' means 'forward-time'.

Now let us consider the plane which can be thought of as lying across the base of the cone, say thirty years hence. It strikes us as very broad: so many future states of world and European society may rationally be imagined. But what can be presented to the Community decision-makers is a number of conceivable future conditions of European society, including its relations with the rest of the world – states of things which could, without flying in the face of reason, be provisionally adopted as long-term goals; states which do lie on the plane across the base of the cone of possibility thirty years ahead, or at whatever shorter term may be adopted for a particular purpose. Inconceivable states of affairs, which could not for whatever reason be rationally adopted as goals, lie outside the cone altogether.

Let us now suppose that the decision-makers adopt one of the described states of affairs as their goal. The choice of a particular goal thirty years ahead implies the adoption, at the right time or times, of the means or policies to reach it. But there are usually many alternative combinations of means to a given end. If we want to have a tree twelve feet high in thirty years' time, there are many things we can do tomorrow. We can plant an acorn; we can plant a six-foot tree and cut it back so that it grows regularly over the thirty-year period; we can plant a six-foot tree, let it grow uncut to twelve feet, and then prune it so that it keeps to that size; and so on and so on. But if we do nothing for twenty-nine years, so that our will for a twelve-foot tree in thirty years becomes a will for a twelve-foot tree next year, we can do nothing but buy a twelve-foot tree.

There are many things we can do now to get our tree the size we want at the time we want, but as time goes by there are fewer and fewer. The cone running from the small definite now of actuality to the wide plane of possibility x years ahead must be echoed in our imagination by an inverse cone running from the wide *now* of means choice to the small definite *then*, x years hence, of our chosen goal. These two interpenetrating cones, the goal-choice cone with its apex now and its base in the future, and the means-choice cone with its base now and its apex in the future, seem to us a useful image of what really happens in forecasting and planning.

An appropriate number of alternative states of European society and of its relations with the rest of the world could be described, any one of which could, without requiring the impossible, be adopted (provisionally but usefully) as the goal to be reached in, say, thirty years' time. The plane could be placed not at thirty years but at any shorter date, where the cone will be narrower. The incompatibilities between these possible goals could be set out and the costs and benefits of each described. The benefits would be in terms of social goods apparent

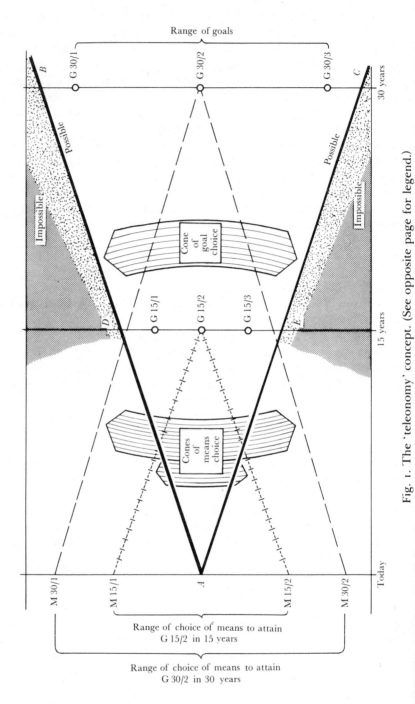

Fig. 1. The 'teleonomy' concept. (See opposite page for legend.)

14

to all at the time, such as (at the present time) justice, harmony, real wealth, 'quality of life', etc. – none of them, it is worth noting, strictly quantifiable. The costs would be opportunity costs. Each alternative goal could be structured to give pre-eminence to one social good, and the cost of choosing it would be the rejection of the other goals, which gave pre-eminence to other goods. This way of setting things out can be given the name 'teleonomy', the arranging of goals (analogous to 'agronomy', the arranging of land). A European forecasting instrument would from time to time present revised teleonomies, as the general perception of what is desirable or possible or unavoidable changes, as forecasting techniques develop, and as time itself unfolds.

This description is highly schematic, not to say ideal. At least until forecasting reaches a stage of development which is now only imaginable, the reality will no doubt be much more muddled. But one thing which we do believe could already be done with some confidence is the separation of the possible from the impossible. The cone itself can be drawn, and probably drawn rather clearly. Inside uncertainty will prevail, but outside will be a 'no-go area', and this awareness in itself could save us and our descendants from a multitude of woes.

All this is general and conceptual. Before proceeding to the particular and practical, this is the place to say something about cost. It cannot be claimed that the European Community has as yet found its true potentiality. It has not been a ringing success from the beginning; nothing ever is. There have been misjudgements and accidents. It may be likened to a car without headlights on a dark night, which from time to time collides with other traffic on the road (America, Japan,

---

Fig. 1. The future is regarded as an ever-widening cone of possible situations (Cone of *Goal Choice*). Everything inside the cone ABC is considered to be possible and everything outside impossible.

The points G30/1, G30/2, and G30/3 lie within the bounds of possibility. The distinction and description of these points constitutes a *teleonomy*, i.e. the arranging of alternative goals. Suppose that the point or situation G30/2 is chosen as a goal for the Community. Then the Cone of *Means Choice* (broken line M30/1–G30/2–M30/2), with its apex at goal G30/2, will widen as it is projected back to the situation today, showing the range of possible means open to our choice now and also the narrowing of the cone as time advances.

If a fifteen-year goal (G15/2) is selected, the range of means to attain it is smaller than in the case of the more distant goal G30/2 (cone M15/1–G15/2–M15/2).

As emphasised in the text, this concept is just that: a *concept*, a way of imagining things. In real life the business of choosing ends and means is, as everyone knows, much less tidy.

the oil producers) and with the street furniture itself (raw-material dependencies, geographical fixed factors of all sorts). The politicians' instinct (and the Community is run by politicians) is to say: 'Here, let me take the wheel.' But in 1974 the Community wisely said: 'Let us try headlights', and they set up the Europe Plus Thirty study. The name 'Europe Plus Thirty' was chosen to convey a general impression of the *far* future, and not because thirty years, rather than (say) ten or sixty, has any special significance.

The work of the Europe Plus Thirty feasibility study group has thus been a work of headlight design; headlights to identify dangers ahead, to see crossroads, to give the drivers time to change gear, brake, accelerate, turn right or left. Meaningful headlights will cost an annual sum which, while negligibly small in the normal scale of research costs, yet runs to a few million Units of Account,[1] and the Institutions of the Community will very properly look critically at the figures. Hard-headed people will think of the economic crisis which began in 1974, of inflation, of 'runaway public expenditure', of the undesirability of allowing new Community instruments to proliferate, of the uncertain economic future. But they should remember that it is precisely to reduce the likelihood of these things continuing or recurring in the future that a permanent instrument for long-term forecasting called 'Europe Plus Thirty' would exist. It would exist (among other things) to foresee crises, to forecast about the underlying cause of inflation, and generally to reduce the uncertainty of the future. Europe Plus Thirty would act directly to remove the very troubles which might prevent its creation. It would be paradoxical, to say the least, if the European Community were to judge itself already too ill to reach for the medicine.

THE SHAPE OF THIS BOOK

Part I deals first with the actual business of forecasting under three headings: the inputs you need, the methods you can use, and the way to put the outputs, or results, to the best use. Chapter I.1 thus looks at forecasting techniques in general, with only passing reference to the particular needs of the European Community. Then chapters I.2 and I.3 describe the forecasting which is at present done by the European Community and in its member countries. These chapters look at the scene and ask: What is done now? Should more be done? If so, does the capacity to do it exist? They suggest that more should be done, and that the capacity to do it exists in large part and can be created as to the rest. Chapter I.4 then suggests purposes and principles in

---

[1] The Unit of Account equals roughly the value of the U.S. dollar in 1970.

the light of which long-term forecasting should be undertaken by and for the European Community itself, through a particular instrument to be created: Europe Plus Thirty.

The whole of Part I insists on the need for integrated 'cross-sectoral' forecasting but says little or nothing about the sectors themselves which must go to make it up. Part II becomes particular. Chapter II.1 introduces the Part as a whole and gives in passing three examples of the way integrated *problem-oriented* forecasting is and could be carried out, as opposed to the teleonomy we have just described. The remainder of Part II (chapters 2 to 17) discusses sixteen separate fields or sectors, and in each of them the possibility and desirability of long-term forecasting being undertaken (a) at all and (b) by Europe Plus Thirty. It concludes that in most of them Europe Plus Thirty should be, to a greater or lesser extent, actively engaged, but that in some it should not, since the necessary work is already done elsewhere. Part I gives the bones; Part II puts the flesh on them.

Part III considers Technology Assessment. It attempts a definition and points out the overlap between this work and forecasting about technology, industry, society, and the environment, which have already been treated in Part II.

Part IV turns finally to the constitution and working of the new Community instrument, Europe Plus Thirty, and to the way it should be related to the Community's existing Institutions. It describes the headlights themselves.

PART I
FORECASTING: CAPACITY AND PROCESS

1. *The forecasting process*

This chapter, on the forecasting process, falls into three parts: inputs, methods, and outputs. Forecasting is a process, and like most processes it requires raw materials: the inputs of forecasting are in the form of information about the past and present. Like all human processes, it uses methods: sometimes alternatively, sometimes sequentially, sometimes in combination. The methods of forecasting are described in the second part of this chapter and are grouped to show what part of the forecasting process they are of most use for. Like all processes, again, forecasting gives rise to an output, a product or result, and if it is to serve its purpose this output has to be brought to the right person in the right form. The relationship between forecasting on the one hand and planning and decision-making on the other is treated in the third part of this chapter.

There is an anology with food. If forecasting is a meal, then the inputs are the raw foodstuffs, and statisticians are the farmers. The methods are the pots and pans in the kitchen. The outputs are the meal itself, and policy-makers are the guests. The forecaster, the central figure in the chain, is the cook. This chapter treats first of farming and harvesting (inputs), second of cooking (methods), and third of laying the table and serving (outputs).

INPUT: THE RAW MATERIALS

If we want to forecast about something, we must know what it is, and to know what it is we must know its history, however slightly. This is true even if a forecast is mainly based on guesswork, since guessing itself can only be based on some kind of knowledge about past developments. The quality of forecasts depends critically but not exclusively on the quality of the input, whether we use conceptual models in our minds or the computer models which reflect them. But knowledge about the past is not sufficient, as the following example will illustrate.

National forecasts of consumption patterns several years ahead are made in many countries, either by government authorities for national economic forecasts, or by private organisations or firms to help plan the future production of goods. The first step in this particular process, as in most forecasting, consists of choosing a 'model' – whether conceptual, mathematical, or other – that can 'explain' past and present consumption trends, in the hope that it will hold true also for future trends. To choose and to test models, you need all kinds of historical inputs, qualitative as well as quantitative. You have to be able to explain slow, systematic changes in the composition of house-hold consumption (e.g. the declining percentage of food in the daily budget) and if possible also more sudden shifts in consumer behaviour (such as those caused by the introduction of the automobile). A good forecasting model is one that displays identifiable and stable relation-ships between the variable you want to forecast and a set of 'explana-tory variables' which can be accepted with confidence or can be controlled (by policy, say, or by sales promotion). Experience in many countries shows that fairly realistic models of consumption patterns can be constructed, provided variables such as income, household composition, and trends in relative prices are to hand.

Careful studies of changes in relative prices have shown some fairly stable long-term trends (e.g. labour-intensive goods and services be-coming more and more expensive). Similarly, studies of demographic and sociological data show that the household composition in Europe has so far changed fairly systematically towards smaller households, the number of children per family decreasing and the span of years without small children in the average family increasing, largely inde-pendently of short-run economic and social changes. All these are useful in assessing the future. As regards the remaining explanatory variable, future trends in income distribution, the forecaster will have to rely on the results of other forecasts, e.g. of the levels of employment and economic activity. Frequently, then, the forecaster will have to use several assumed future income trends, themselves based on historical evidence of past developments.

It is obvious that no foolproof long-term model can be made to explain all the changes in consumption patterns. Even if careful studies of past experience confirm relationships which seem to with-stand short-term disturbances, this stability may not endure. There-fore the forecaster must go on collecting new input to confront his forecasts with developments in the real world. Are new family struc-tures or new life-styles emerging which may radically change con-sumption patterns? Will the consumer behaviour of young families in the late 70s or 80s begin to level off (saturate), in a reaction to the 'economic growth era' of the 50s and 60s? These are questions of great importance in forecasting long-term consumption patterns; but many of the necessary inputs are themselves forecasts and thus are only verifiable with the passage of time.

Different types of forecasting require different types of input. Very often, the main input has to be knowledge of the past as it led up to the present: historical data series, or time series data, to use the statistical terms. Sometimes, knowledge of the present situation may suffice, but only when other 'outside information' is at hand as a substitute for history. That outside information may be in the form of technical 'laws', for instance concerning the energy requirements of alternative patterns of production. (The production of steel and of most fertilisers requires much energy, while textile industries mostly consume relatively little.) Outside information may also come in the form of accepted political plans, for instance plans for the regulation of agricultural production and trade in the Community. In the latter case the forecaster may say: 'Since you are determined things in this field shall be done thus, I assume they will be done thus. Let us now see what effect that might have on things in other fields.' Of course, if things are not 'done thus', or not for long, then the forecaster's work may turn out to be less relevant – unless indeed things were no longer 'done thus' precisely because his forecast showed that that would have been a bad idea.

But in many cases 'outside information', however important, is not a substitute for historical data. The data problems in forecasting are formidable. Most of the historical data which would be most useful to a forecaster do not exist. Those that do exist tend not to be mutually compatible (even when officially predigested), and many of them cover only a few decades with relatively coarse (yearly) time intervals, displaying undesirable traits like collinearity, and not being law-abiding at all (e.g. not converging towards stable probability distributions). And perhaps worst of all are data which are outdated. As the British economic forecaster Professor R. J. Ball pointed out at a recent conference, 'Forecasting...is often like trying to find out where you are going when you don't know where you have been.'

In long-term economic forecasting, for instance, the data available may consist of time series ending three or four years ago. Some of the figures in the model, e.g. the so-called technical coefficients in the input–output tables, may date back even longer, perhaps ten or fifteen years. Luckily these coefficients seem to change fairly slowly, but economic model-building might yield more reliable forecasts if more up-to-date values of, for example, these input–output coefficients were available. According to the present commitments of the statistical bureaux of the member countries, input–output tables, and hence those coefficients, will be updated more frequently in the future. Even so, the existing systems of collecting and handling statistical data in the European countries have been constructed primarily for evaluating past and present developments and policies, and not for forecasting. Changing those systems is a very slow and laborious process in a single country, to say nothing of getting them to converge into full compatibility in nine countries at the same time.

If the general economic development of the Community is to be analysed, compatible national accounts data and input–output tables have to become available. This will involve a further development of the application in the member countries of common definitions and classifications within the field of national accounts data. Only when this is realised can Community-wide data series be constructed and be analysed by such criteria as urban/rural, highly developed/less developed, etc., and by economic and other sectors for the Community as a whole instead of by nations as at present. The pioneering work which has already started at the Community Statistical Office on a common input–output table is very promising.

In some cases data can be obtained by historical reconstruction. In fields without ready-made historical time series, the need for 'hindcasting' is obvious. In many countries the need for macro-economic time series covering several decades has led economic historians to make impressive studies, enabling them to put together comparative time series for key variables from circumstantial evidence.

Few things are more important than the continuous checking of forecasts against what happens. If events seem to be writing a scenario which was not among those considered by the forecasters, the sooner that is detected the better. The data needed for this continuous validation may be different, though not very different, from those needed for the forecasting itself. Most forecasting models will contain a set of exogenous or independent variables, determined outside the model, and a set of endogenous or dependent variables, the values of which it is the task of the model to determine. The values of the exogenous variables in forecasting have to be assumed in advance. In these cases it is very important, as soon as preliminary estimates of the 'true' values of these variables are available, to check the model values.

In the real world – and hence in realistic models of economic, social, and technological developments – there is usually a certain sub-set of variables which is more significant in determining the results than others. Raw-material prices, investment in key industrial sectors, and demand for automobiles are traditional examples of such variables. These variables have great influence in many ways. In fact, quite substantial changes in many other variables have less effect on the total economy than do changes in these 'heavyweights' which are smaller than the margin of error with which they can themselves be measured.

For long-term economic forecasting, one needs inputs of a non-economic nature: information on social developments such as trends in the employment of married women outside the home and the effect of such employment on the birthrate, labour conditions, preferences for different types of work and for leisure time, trends in family patterns, and changes in life-style more generally. Fortunately this non-economic input is increasingly needed for shorter-term purposes as well. Many governments and political parties have started to question the social benefits of certain state activities in their present form (health services, education, etc.) because they are absorbing an ever-increasing part of their countries' resources. Until fairly recently, it was common to judge success in these fields by the resources allocated to them, but this is clearly unsatisfactory, indeed misleading: it is the effects of these allocations that have to be evaluated. If we want to know how healthy the people in a country are, we must look at its health statistics, not its health expenditures. Hence the growing interest in non-economic yardsticks over the past decade, particularly the so-called social indicators, which are now being developed in many countries, in the European Commission, and in the OECD. For if we want to plan expenditures aright, we must find means of establishing the relation between expenditure and the results of expenditure. We must make input–output tables for welfare.

This will not be easy, if only because variations in the 'objective' indicators which seek to represent people's conditions do not always agree with the way people perceive their conditions subjectively. For instance, a recent survey about levels of satisfaction carried out for the European Commission (see *Trente Jours d'Europe*,[1] January 1974) showed that while the average standard of living in the EEC rose by about 20 per cent between 1968 and 1973, 25 per cent of the respondents thought they were worse off than five years ago, and 33 per cent declared that they had noticed no change in their situation. Two alternative interpretations are possible: (1) that the 58 per cent who declared 'worse off' or 'no change' did enjoy an actual increase in their standard of living, which was offset by some hidden deterioration in other components of their welfare; and (2) that at least part of the discrepancy between perception and reality is explainable in terms of the uneven character of the progress of the standard of living – namely that the rich got richer and the poor did not. In either case, this is an important example of the sort of social information which should be available to policy-makers, since it provides an argument against

[1] Published monthly by the Paris Information Office of the European Commission.

taking the 'output' of public policies too literally and neglecting their socio-psychological aspects.

So far there is no generally accepted idea about what social indicators are, and it is interesting that one publication which at present holds international attention, the OECD's 'Social Indicators', is subtitled, more correctly, 'List of Social Concerns Common to Most Member Countries'.[1] But social indicators are conceivable, and their use should be developed.

In the very difficult forecasting that concerns non-economic aspects of society, experimental social innovation deserves special consideration. Controlled social innovation programmes, set up according to the rules of experiment design known from the physical and biological sciences, are rare – some would say impossible. During the sixties a few experimental social programmes, or something very near, were conducted in the U.S.A. on negative income tax, family planning, different types of housing subsidies, etc. In Europe the OECD has started a programme concerning 'Innovation in the Service Sector' which comes close to experimental innovation.

Just as nature often sets up different situations which natural scientists can observe and compare ('de facto experiments'), so political events, or history, often set up different social situations which can be studied in the same way. For instance: in Britain the telephone service is state-owned, the pubs are owned by the brewers, and domestic water is paid for by a fixed local property tax. But there is one town where the telephone system is privately owned, one town where the pubs belonged for decades to the state, and one town where domestic water is metered. If anybody wanted to investigate the social or economic effects of those alternative innovations in that country, historical accident gives him his 'de facto experiment'. And there are hundreds of such situations throughout the Community, waiting to be identified and examined.

The countries of the Community, which have different systems for this or that, themselves constitute a web of de facto social innovation: each has evolved its own pattern of social service, health service, education, and foreign policy. In the 1950s the advantages of early intervention in psychiatry were demonstrated in the Netherlands at the same time as some mental hospitals in Britain were experimenting with 'open' (unlocked) wards. Both experiments yielded results, and the policies have been adopted elsewhere. In the 1960s Denmark made an intensive effort to provide better and more decentralised services (including social and occupational training) for the mentally handicapped. It worked; others watched; lessons were learned. The

[1] OECD pamphlet, Paris, 1973.

Community itself is, after all, one vast and unprecedented social experiment.

Forecasting by and for the European Community will have to be conducted in the greatest possible knowledge of global trends. At present much information is lacking or is too unsystematic and unreliable for forecasting; and yet it is clear that forecasts concerning the Community have to contain assumptions about what will happen, or may happen, or cannot happen, in the rest of the world. These assumptions must be explicit. The question will arise again and again of how they are to be made. Other people's figures and forecasts should be used where possible. Where not, Europe Plus Thirty will have to obtain what figures it can and make its own forecasts for other parts of the world as well. The work of judging what to use will itself be considerable. For most continents it will be a financial and man-year problem, but as regards Eastern Europe a diplomatic problem may exist as well, since the Soviet attitude to the European Community is still uncertain. If that is so, every effort will have to be made to solve the problem; forecasts about our part of Europe have to be related to the best available forecasts about the other part. In many things Western Europe does, it is as strongly conditioned by the giant beyond the rivers as it is by the giant beyond the sea, and in some things more.

METHODOLOGY

If inputs are to forecasting as a farm is to a hot dinner, methods are as kitchen utensils: indispensable, but often interchangeable. Good cooks (and good forecasters) can do great things with simple tools provided the right ingredients are available, whereas even the most sophisticated tools are of little use in the hands of the inexperienced or in the absence of edible materials. In short, it is the way in which the available methods are used that counts. In both cases seemingly minor mistakes are sufficient to make the end results unpalatable, and cooks and forecasters are alike in knowing that their work is never done: hunger for food and hunger for forecasts return at punctual intervals.

However sophisticated forecasting methods may appear, underlying them are certain simple notions: that processes can be explained in terms of simplified structures, that there may be causal mechanisms acting between different parts of the structure, and that all these have a certain continuity of time and space. The use of these notions permits generalisations and theories to be made. Knowing this, one can cut away much of the confusion and mystique surrounding forecasting methods, the more readily to judge their merits and limitations.

Most of the methods described in this chapter have been developed for industrial or commercial short- or medium-term forecasting, and were derived from the methods of the natural and engineering sciences, where the characteristics of the systems under observation naturally make a systematic quantitative approach most likely to be successful. Long-term forecasting, on the other hand, has until recently consisted more of literary images of utopian or catastrophic futures.

The various forecasting techniques can perhaps be most usefully categorised by the following three purposes they serve:

(1) to combine and to carry forward quantitatively or quasi-quantitatively expressed knowledge of the past and the present;

(2) to help to imagine the future, or a future, or futures, by developing hypotheses;

(3) to help determine what might or must be done, now and later, to make things go the way we want.

In what follows we use the portmanteau words (1) 'projection', (2) 'image creation', and (3) 'policy analysis'. All three categories can and should be used in defining both cones described in the Introduction, though projection serves more for the definition of the goal-choice cone, and policy analysis for the definition of the means-choice cone.

The theoretical legitimacy and practical utility of forecasting methods vary greatly. This is one reason why we present these descriptions with considerable hesitation: there is no correlation between the 'value' of any method and the amount of paper we use to describe it. Our second reason for being hesitant is that the very idea of long-term forecasting has met with rather strongly polarised responses: it has been either rejected too flatly or swallowed too whole. Therefore, our description of forecasting methods – like forecasting itself – faces a Scyalla-and-Charybdis situation: on the one hand, it may over-impress people and make them expect too much from forecasting; on the other hand, because of the extreme brevity of our descriptions, it is all too easy to find fault with them. We are not even certain that all can be regarded as forecasting methods; they would be more accurately called 'of use in forecasting and related activities'.

The presentation here roughly corresponds to an increasing level of sophistication, moving from straightford graphical and intuitive methods to those which require more data input and more complex manipulation. The kind of forecasting each serves best (i.e. projection, image creation, or policy analysis, as described above) is mentioned in each case.

SIMPLE METHODS

Single-Variable Extrapolation (Projection)

This consists of the extrapolation into the future of a particular variable from a table of historical data. The data are usually displayed graphically, and the curve formed from the points is extended into the future. This may be done by eye or with the aid of statistical techniques, which allow the best fit to the historical data to be found, given the general shape of the curve (e.g. linear, logistic, exponential).

Extrapolation is widely used in many fields. Its use for prediction must assume that the mechanisms underlying observed historical trends will continue undisturbed (the naiveté of this assumption has been discussed in the Introduction). It is of no direct use for long-term forecasting, where mechanisms are usually expected to change; but it can, and should, provide a preliminary basis for discussion and scenario-building.

Envelope Curves (Projection)

These are used to forecast possible future trends for a given variable (usually technological – e.g. transport speeds), from time series data. The method is based on the observation that a technology is often replaced by a 'superior' technology when the first begins to show diminishing returns for further improvement in some critical parameter, generally money. The data for each successive technology are plotted against time, giving a family of overlapping curves from which the 'envelope curve' – tangential to and connecting the family of curves – is drawn.

Analysis by Precursive Events (Projection)

The idea here is to forecast a particular technological or social trend from time series data of past developments whose behaviour is thought to be analogous. The method has been used to forecast developments in racing cars and aircraft and to forecast the saturation of markets for various goods. The maximum speed of transport aircraft has been found to increase in a way similar to that previously observed for military aircraft. Crime trends, strange as that may seem, have been forecast in a similar way, e.g. Europe following the United States. The assumption that two phenomena will follow parallel paths of development, one following the other after a fixed time, may be justified if there is a causal relationship between them or if their progress has a common cause.

'INTUITIVE' METHODS

Scenarios (Image Creation and Projection)

Scenario-writing describes, in words, possible future events and the forces giving rise to them. It is in universal use wherever forecasting is attempted, and it constitutes the main vehicle for the application of human intelligence to the problem of the future.

Delphi (Image Creation and Projection)

Unhappily named after the Delphic oracle, this is a technique for obtaining from a group of individuals a consensus on some topic or event, usually a forecast of when an event will occur or (to help assess R & D priorities) of when a scientific breakthrough will be realisable. A questionnaire is circulated to experts asking for estimates of, for example, when a given technological development will occur. The replies are analysed, and the experts are informed of the spread of estimated dates and of the arguments put forward by the other participants and are invited to revise their estimates. The process is repeated several times.

Originally developed at the Rand Corporation in America, Delphi has been extensively used by industrial bodies to forecast technical change. It is a popular method in Japan. The advantage claimed over viva voce discussion is that social distortions arising from differences in status and personality are eliminated; that is to say, people are not cowed by a powerful person or talked down by a garrulous one. In practice, it does produce some shift in people's estimates towards the middle; but this would only be valuable if it could be established that the truth commonly lay near the middle, and if that could be established the second and subsequent rounds of a Delphi would be unnecessary in any case. A recent Rand-sponsored survey concludes: 'Conventional Delphi is basically an unreliable and unscientific technique.'[1]

Brainstorming (Image Creation)

This is a way of obtaining new insights into a problem through intensive talking. Participants are asked to contribute ideas, even if they do not seem to be directly relevant; there is some evidence that more 'good' ideas are produced by this means than if only 'good' ideas are sought.[2] No attempt is made to criticise, discuss, or explore the ideas which come up in the brainstorming session, since this might inhibit it, thus negating the purpose. Order can be introduced later.

Brainstorming has been used in industry and, to some extent, in military forecasting (NATO Long-Term Scientific Studies).

Morphology (Image Creation and Policy Analysis)

The word 'morphology' ('study of forms') was first appropriated in 1942 to describe a particular way of exploring alternative strategies for achieving a given end. The issue to be explored is broken down into component elements, all possible states of each are identified, and finally all possible combinations of these states are listed and mapped and their relative performance estimated.

Morphology has been used to study technological choices available in rocket construction. In one such study,[3] eleven factors were identified, and between

[1] M. Sackman, 'Delphi Assessment: Expert Opinion, Forecasting, and Group Opinion', Rand Report R1283 PR (Santa Monica, Calif.: Rand Corporation, April 1974).
[2] E. Jantsch, *Technological Forecasting in Perspective* (Paris: OECD, 1967).
[3] *Ibid.*

two and four alternatives were identified for each (e.g. gas, liquid, or solid propellant; internal or external thrust generation), giving a total of over 25,000 possible combinations.

Morphology is mainly an attempt to structure thinking, rather than a forecasting device. For a system which can be broken down into quasi-independent components, it is a useful way of reducing the risk that viable alternatives will be overlooked.

SEMI-QUANTITATIVE ANALYTICAL METHODS

Relevance Tree (Policy Analysis)

This useful and important technique is best understood through an example. We quote here one devised by Beate Kohler and Renate Nagel[1] (see Figure 2). The tree reads downwards. The purpose in this case is a large one: to find a good way to increase social welfare.

By a quantitative method outlined below, the 'optimum' chain of alternatives from the present to the future goal can be determined. Our figure is incomplete in that (1) not all the possible alternatives are spelled out at each stage and (2) only the final chosen route in this hypothetical situation is indicated, namely the application of tax incentives to savings in order to encourage property formation as a basis for social welfare.

At each stage a quantitative value is worked out for each of the alternatives. This is done by means of a matrix in which the alternatives are matched against criteria. The criteria are given weightings (adding up to 1) and the alternatives 'significance numbers' (also adding up to 1). The criteria weightings relate to the long-term goal (i.e. they are 'vertical' with regard to the tree as a whole seen from a particular stage); the 'significance numbers' assess the contribution of the alternatives to each criterion (i.e. they are 'horizontal' and refer only to one particular stage.) The matrix for the seventh stage in the tree is shown in a table below Figure 2; there is a corresponding matrix (not reproduced here) for each stage. The numbers in brackets are the products obtained by multiplying criteria weightings and significance numbers; the sum of these products gives the 'relevance number' of each alternative. In this example, 'tax-free savings' wins easily.

If all the relevance numbers obtained at each stage in any chain of alternatives are multiplied together, the result is the 'relevance figure' for that chain. Comparison of these figures allows conclusions to be drawn about which chain is best.

Cost–Benefit Analysis (Policy Analysis)

The aim is to judge the desirability of a proposed project or policy. A time horizon is specified, and all the consequences of the proposal that can be foreseen are listed. 'Costs' and 'benefits' are attached to each consequence, usually in monetary units with discounting to present values, and total costs and benefits are compared.[2]

[1] Die Zukunft Europas (Cologne: Bildungswerk Europäische Politik, 1968) as presented in And Now the Future (London: PEP, 1971).

[2] See (e.g.) R. Layard (ed.), Cost–Benefit Analysis (Harmondsworth: Penguin, 1972).

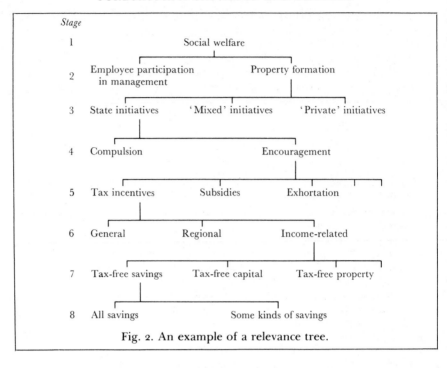

Fig. 2. An example of a relevance tree.

		Alternatives		
	Matrix for stage 7 of Figure 2			
Criteria	Criteria weighting	Tax-free savings	Tax-free capital	Tax-free property
Net property formation	0.4	0.7 (0.28)	0.2 (0.08)	0.1 (0.04)
Social justice	0.3	0.6 (0.18)	0.2 (0.06)	0.2 (0.06)
Minimisation of loss of tax revenue	0.2	0.1 (0.02)	0.3 (0.06)	0.6 (0.12)
Minimisation of administrative costs	0.1	0.2 (0.02)	0.3 (0.03)	0.5 (0.05)
Relevance number		0.50	0.23	0.27

This is of course the basic method used in private and public business to determine investments. It is also used by governments in assessing large-scale technological projects. It permits systematic evaluation, although problems of subjectivity in excluding or including phenomena and in weighting them properly are formidable. In some studies using a simple checklist, no effort is made to weight phenomena. This avoids quantification problems but provides no means of separating important and unimportant factors.

Planning, Programming, and Budgeting System (PPBS)
(Policy Analysis)

This is a large-scale planning system, evolved for the management and control of resource allocation.[1] Like cost–benefit analysis, it is more correctly described as a planning technique than as a forecasting one, but it is closely allied. The planning phase of PPBS involves defining objectives and testing for incompatibilities. Various methods such as trend extrapolation or mathematical modelling may be invoked here. Programming involves the sub-division of objectives and developments of strategies (programmes) for achieving these 'partial' objectives; these alternatives may each be subject to a cost–benefit analysis and may be represented by a relevance tree. Budgeting requires the allocation of resources according to the 'value' of each possible programme.

PPBS was introduced in the U.S.A. in 1961 (and subsequently elsewhere) with a view to tying together all the work of the Department of Defence. The main result was intended to be a flexible five-year plan. Empirical studies[2] on the effects of PPBS on government planning are contradictory but suggest that it may be useful in some areas of planning.

NETWORK METHODS (POLICY ANALYSIS)

Network techniques are used as a management tool for the control of complex projects and provide yet another device for 'structured checking'. They are designed to facilitate the making and management of plans, rather than forecasts as such. A network of possible steps in all branches of a project or strategy is mapped to determine the 'critical path' on the basis of, for example, lowest cost or least time. The critical path method (CPM) involves the construction of 'flow charts' indicating alternative combinations of factors required for the realisation of a project, and estimates are then made of the time required for these factors to be developed to the necessary degree. In this way possible bottlenecks are indicated, and evidence is provided of where the greatest input of effort will be needed to complete the overall project. The programme evaluation and review technique (PERT) is similar to CPM: it involves stochastic inputs and is used to compute probabilities for the time or cost involved in a project. It was first developed for the Polaris missile system.[3] Surveys of thirty-seven government-financed R & D projects in the US suggest that PERT offered no improvement in technical performance but reduced the probability of a cost or time overrun.[4]

Decision Theory (Policy Analysis)

Relevance trees, cost–benefit analysis, PPBS, PERT, and CPM may all be considered as branches of decision theory. Under this heading, however, we

[1] See (e.g.) C. L. Schultze, *The Politics and Economics of Public Spending* (Washington: Brookings, 1968).
[2] Jantsch, *Technological Forecasting in Perspective*, I.3, p. 16.
[3] *Ibid.*
[4] K. Pavitt and C. Maestre, *Analytical Methods in Government Science Policy* (Paris: OECD, 1972).

also consider methods where explicit account is taken of external events. A set of policies is specified, and the future events which are expected to influence the effectiveness of the choices, but over which the decision-maker has no control, are listed and weighted by probability of occurrence. An optimum (e.g. a least-cost) solution is sought which gives an acceptable probability of attaining the overall goal. In risk analysis, probability distributions rather than 'absolute' probabilities are used to give guidelines for an optimum pattern of strategies.

Goal-Setting and Goal-Weighting (Policy Analysis)

Goal-setting is sometimes used as part of a planning process. It makes the distinction between 'desirable' and 'achievable' goals. It may begin with a brainstorming session to collect elements for a 'goal hierarchy' to be constructed with the help of cause–effect relationships. An alternative way of collecting meaningful goal elements is the 'content analysis' of various programmatic documents. A goal hierarchy is evolved. The goals defined do not require information with respect to time or space, or magnitude: they are only 'directional'.

The weighting of the goals with respect to their relative importance within one level of the goal hierarchy can be carried out in a matrix by 'pairwise comparison' or other suitable methods. If a goal system of higher order is available, to which the goal system considered belongs as a sub-system, then the goals of the superior system should be used for the weighting process. The relative importance of the goals is determined by subjective value judgement and is indicated on a cardinal scale. Adding up these numerical values for any one line of the matrix gives relevance figures which then are normalised and as such represent the percentage distribution of the overall weight among the goals at one level of the hierarchy. Methods are available to take into consideration the interdependence between the goals.

A goal system can be made operational by assigning suitable indicators to each goal element located on the highest level of the goal hierarchy. The quality of such indicators as measuring devices for determining the degree of goal achievement produced by alternative courses of action is taken into consideration by a separate weighting factor. (See note on Conflict Analysis, below.)

Value Analysis (Policy Analysis)

Value Analysis has been developed out of decision theory. It is the most general case of a cost–benefit analysis, since it allows various cost criteria to be used during one specific valuation within one goal hierarchy.

It aims to allow one to add up the value of apples, trees, and hospitals, since the measuring scale is 'dimensionless'. The 'value' of the state of a system as judged by an individual is quantitatively weighted on a subjective basis. Full goal achievement is given a value of 1. The contribution of a project or course of action which aims to improve the state of a system is then measured on the value scale, and the sum total of all weighted arguments for or against it is derived. The derived value describes the degree of improvement of the system under consideration after the action has been completed. A goal hierarchy is needed to make a value determination. Indicators in time series are needed for the conversion of objective information to subjective value as seen by the person making the valuation. Utility functions are used to formalise this conversion and make it explicit. These utility functions are selected or constructed by the person undertaking the analysis. In this way the different values of interest groups in judging a certain action or situation may be made 'explicit'.

Value analysis allows one to determine the relative merits of alternative courses of action from the different viewpoints of various interest groups or persons, and to measure the expected effects of a project on a system over time. (See note on Conflict Analysis, below.)

Conflict Analysis (Policy Analysis)

Conflicts existing or to be expected among individuals, interest groups, nations, etc. can be described, measured, and ranked with the help of formal goal analysis. Conflicts arise when there are differences in goal structures and/or goal priorities, especially where the latter are strongly influenced by time. By measuring the degree of disharmony or incompatibility between any two goals (by 'pairwise comparison') and multiplying this factor by the difference of their respective weights, one obtains a 'conflict factor' indicating the magnitude of a potential conflict between the adherents of different goal systems. These conflicts can be ranked for any one point in time, provided that the weights of the goals are given as functions of time.

Conflict analysis can also be extended to the indicator level and will thus produce detailed information on conflicts with respect to the target dates or sizes of individual goals. If such an analysis is carried further, one can investigate the degree to which these conflicts might be reduced or eliminated by suitable courses of action.

Note: the last three methods listed – Goal-Setting and Weighting, Value Analysis, and Conflict Analysis – must obviously be used with extreme caution, since they all rest on assumptions about what other people think. At best this is a risky procedure, and at worst it may lead to damaging delusions.

Markov Chains (Projection)

A matrix is drawn up to represent the probability of transition of individual objects or persons from one class to another, usually on the basis of past data. For example, individual persons are assigned to income groups, and data are used to indicate how the number of individuals in each group has changed over time. This permits the calculation of the 'transition matrix' which shows the proportion of those individuals formerly in each income group who have moved to each of the other income groups. This matrix can then be applied to the latest data set to forecast future distributions, assuming that the forces historically governing changes in income distribution (which need not be specified) remain the same.

Game Theory (Projection and Policy Analysis)

Game theory is concerned with decision-making where alternatives are influenced by the actions of others. A set of possible strategies for the 'players'

33

is devised, and the 'optimum strategy' is calculated for one player, given the alternatives available to the other.

A simple (and well-known) example is the 'prisoners' dilemma'. Two prisoners are separated and told by their captors that they will get a ten-year sentence if they both confess and five if neither confesses; if one confesses and the other does not, the former will get five years and the latter twenty. What should each do?[1]

		No. 2	
		Confess	Not Confess
No. 1	Confess	$-10, \quad -10$	$-5, \quad -20$
	Not Confess	$-20, \quad -5$	$-5, \quad -5$

The first number in each pair refers to prisoner no. 1, the second to prisoner no. 2. According to game theory, each calculates his 'expected' or 'average' return from each strategy. For each prisoner, confession means ten or five years; non-confession means twenty or five. Thus both reduce their 'expected' sentence by confessing, which represents the best strategy for each individually according to the theory, even though this means that each gets ten years instead of the five which would result from neither confessing.

This is in fact a weak example, since trust is not incorporated. Moreover, numbers are often difficult to determine in more realistic examples, particularly where the object is to forecast behaviour rather than to devise a strategy; it is not always clear what people want to maximise.

Game theory has been widely experimented with, notably by the Rand Corporation in America, for military strategy and politics. Some hold that American military failures in the Vietnam War were partly due to excessive reliance on this method, and it was certainly much used in the 1960s in the unsuccessful attempt to devise ways of halting the arms race without seeking agreement with the Soviet Union. It is apparently no longer widely used by sociologists, mainly for the reasons given above, and its limitations are indeed obvious.

Cross-Impact (Projection and Policy Analysis)

Cross-impact methods are designed to illustrate the effects of policies or future events on various related phenomena. A matrix is constructed, with rows and columns labelled with variables related to a particular theme, e.g. transport. The matrix element shows the magnitude of the impact of each one variable on the others. The number will be positive, negative, or zero, according to whether the first variable increases, decreases, or doesn't affect the other. A Delphi survey is often used to obtain values for the matrix elements representing the 'cross-impacts'.

The technique has been adapted to enable mathematical calculations to be carried out on a computer showing possible future developments of the

[1] M. A. Beauchamp, *Elements of Mathematical Sociology* (New York: Random House, 1972).

variables selected. The effects of governmental or corporate policies can be included at the outset or during the computer run.

The technique has been applied to the question of whether the Minuteman missile would be deployed.[1] It suggested a 73 per cent probability of deployment, as opposed to the 20 per cent probability obtained in a Delphi survey of the same experts who provided the cross-impact values. (Minuteman was, of course, deployed.)

'QUANTITATIVE' METHODS

Input–Output (Projection)

This method is used to represent the dependence of different elements in a system on one another and to represent transfers between them. The form of representation is similar to that used in cross-impact: a matrix is set up whose element represents (for example) the value of purchases of each industry or sector from each other, per unit value of output produced. This relates final demand to final output of each industry or sector. The technique was originally static, but several attempts have been made to dynamise it. The matrix elements can be made time-dependent to permit representation of, for example, technical change.

The method is widely used in economics not only as an accounting framework but also to evaluate the consequences of changes in final demand (e.g. disarmament) or of bottlenecks in the economy. Successful attempts have also been made to let an input–output model be part of a more general macroeconomic model.

Regression Analysis (Projection)

This is a statistical technique used to verify hypotheses about relations between variables which may be of any nature (economic, social, etc.) and to estimate the magnitude of the coefficients which appear in the specification of these relations. The statistical data required may be either time series or data referring to a set of persons, firms, etc. at a given moment or during a given period. Such relations often play a very important role in forecasting models.

Multivariate Analysis (Projection)

This is used to determine, from data, the best variables with which to represent a given system. The method involves the identification of mathematical quantities which may not correspond to real features of a system but provide a concise description of it – i.e. 'canonical factors' or 'principal components' from a set of data, enabling a system to be parameterised with the smallest number of 'orthogonal' variables or associations.

Multivariate techniques are used in ecology, sociology (particularly in the analysis of survey questionnaires), and economics.

[1] T. J. Gordon and H. Hayward, 'Initial Experiments with the Cross Impact Method of Forecasting', Futures, 1, no. 2 (December, 1968), pp. 100–16.

ANALYTIC SOLUTIONS
Mathematical Models (Projection)

These aim to represent mathematically the interactions between factors in a system, usually with a view to exploring their future relationships. The essential difference between these methods and those described above is that these have a greater theoretical content.

A mathematical representation of certain relevant features of a system is sought which is simple enough to be tractable algebraically. 'Realism' is often sacrificed to this, in the belief that the manipulation of ideas is more fruitful if they are simplified. The value of this approach is that it permits the dependence of the solution on the different contributing factors to be easily seen, and so also permits concepts and theories to be extracted more easily.

The method enables ideas to be explored quickly, cheaply, and (if one understands the mathematics) clearly.[1]

Computer Solutions (Projection)

Simulation models are usually constructed for exploratory purposes where the theories are rather weak or the calculations are highly complex, so that simple algebraic solutions cannot be obtained. Models may be deterministic, may contain optimising or other control routines, or may be stochastic. Relationships between variables are specified individually, either algebraically or directly into a computer simulation language, and the consequences of their interactions, which may have time delays, are projected.

Stochastic methods (Projection)

Stochastic methods include Monte Carlo simulation, i.e. randomly selecting values for parameters from probability distributions. In this approach, explicit account is taken of uncertainty in the input data; the model may be run for several hundred combinations of values for input variables, a value for each such variable being selected at random within its range of uncertainty for each run. In this way a range of values for the output variables is obtained which provides a measure of their uncertainty.

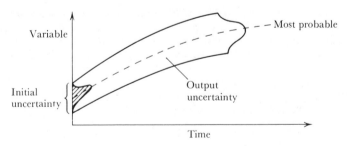

[1] See, e.g., J. Maynard Smith, *Models in Ecology* (Cambridge University Press, 1974).

Gaming Models (Projection, Image-Forming)

These models are computer simulations which contain an explicit recognition of the role of human choice. These models usually include a causal simulation model, in a game theory situation. They attempt to separate out 'intangible' factors which are given values, in the course of the computer run, by an operator (or operators who may have conflicting goals). Thus, 'policy decisions' can be directly inserted to influence the observed evolution of the model. This method is most useful in situations where the separation of subjective and objective features of a system is possible.

'Optimization' Techniques (Projection and Policy Analysis)

These include linear programming, non-linear programming, quadratic programming, calculus of variations, optimal control, and many others. These methods are employed in an effort to determine the best method of reaching an explicitly defined goal; they belong to the second cone described in chapter I.1 – the cone of means choice – with its base now and its apex in the future, at the already-selected goal.

A mathematical 'objective function' whose maximum or minimum value represents a desirable situation is formulated, and, subject to specified constraints, the 'policy' needed to obtain the desired goal is calculated. An example is the Bariloche world model, where human life expectancy is the quantity to be maximised subject to various economic constraints. The model suggests how available resources should be allocated between various sectors of the economy to achieve this goal.

These methods were generally developed for operations research and widely used in an industrial context. They provide a useful method when model, objectives, and constraints can be stated realistically.

A peripheral research proposal

The Introduction touched on the long history of forecasting. We have still available to us thousands of forecasts made in the West over the last two thousand five hundred years, and in the East over the last four thousand years, about events that have long since either happened or failed to happen. That until the last hundred years they were mainly qualitative and not quantitative should not worry us; they were still forecasts. But this wealth of historical material remains virtually unexamined. There have been a few anecdotal anthologies of old forecasts: Yesterday's Tomorrows by W. H. G. Armytage[1] is a notable one. In his Art of Conjecture, Bertrand de Jouvenel[2] analyses a few eighteenth- and nineteenth-century European forecasts, but only as examples and not in the pursuit of general lessons. We think Europe Plus Thirty should do what it can to have these lessons pursued by stimulating certain historical research.

[1] London: Routledge, 1968.
[2] The Art of Conjecture (see p. 11, n. 2).

37

There might be one or more research programmes in which the writings of social philosophers, of statesmen, and of historians were scanned to identify forecasts. They should seek to identify the method used in making each forecast and should classify the forecasts into 'good' and 'bad' – that is, according to whether the assertion identified as a forecast, with whatever qualification it carried, later turned out to be 'the case'. The lessons learned might be useful not only to Europe Plus Thirty, but to forecasters everywhere.

The State of the Art

Over the last two decades, as we have noted, increasing attention has been given to the problem of *how* to probe the future. Initially, this was attempted mainly by devising piecemeal a whole range of techniques, such as those we have described, some quantitative and others non-quantitative and not always strictly scientifically based, for the attack on specific problems. None of these has proved completely satisfactory or generally applicable. More recently, comprehensive but not always sophisticated attempts have been made through dynamic modelling, including methods which react with the 'policy-maker'.[1] It would be wrong to assume, however, that techniques immediately and universally effective are already in existence.

Mathematical modelling has been most successful in the engineering sciences, for obvious reasons; with a man-made system, more often than not the real system obeys the theory underlying the model. Even in the physical sciences, on the other hand, many complex phenomena are only understood in an order of magnitude approximation, even though the underlying elementary mechanisms are known to a high level of precision. For example, the critical temperature of a superconductor or the tensile properties of an alloy are usually determined experimentally, not by calculation. One would therefore expect the more quantitative forecasting methods to be more applicable to the physical or 'ponderable' component of any issue, and this is so; for example, computer simulation models are very useful in meteorological work and in certain aspects of forecasting in economics, resources (including energy), transport, and communications.

Quantitative methods have a lesser use in other areas, though in (for example) agriculture and sociological studies, multivariate techniques (see p. oo) are invaluable for data analysis. Otherwise, the scope of quantitative methods is limited in the social sciences. Fundamental questions such as how to define variables and scales and how to measure – and anticipate – changes in the complicated pattern of

---

[1] One such reaction is described in Appendix 2.

human preferences and relationships have not been solved and may never be. Controlled experimentation is almost impossible. Different (and maybe contradictory) theories of society may be found equally valid, to the extent that they can be tested, and may be equally widely advocated. Moreover, society itself and theories about society evolve together, whereas theories about the physical world are usually taken to be successive approximations to the way it has really been functioning all the time. All this does not mean that the prospects of quantitative methods in social forecasting are hopeless. But it does mean that their scope is limited and that semi-quantitative and qualitative methods still have to be extensively relied on.

The methods sought should provide the right kind of communication across the specialist areas of research within and outside a research team. If they do, that will reinforce two things: interdisciplinary teamwork and 'multi-disciplinary individuals'. The importance of building up these particular skills cannot be exaggerated.

Equally important is communication between forecasters, policy-makers, and the public at large. By presenting an overview of the linkages between complex policy areas, and by making sure that all important aspects are brought out explicitly and clearly by showing the conceivable consequences of different policies, it can help structure thinking about alternative futures among all concerned. Long-term forecasting can be a form of mutual education by public conjecture and hypothesis.

Although a certain method may seem most appropriate to the analysis of a particular issue, its results may not satisfy the policy-making process it is designed to serve. Urgency for information marks democratic government: politicians facing urgent problems cannot wait for comprehensive analyses to emerge. Almost by definition, many important issues are new in some way, and although they could, in principle, be 'best' dealt with by a certain combination of methods, that combination it useless if it takes too long. So the simpler and more straightforward forecasting methods have tended to be used for urgent policy questions, despite their acknowledged inadequacy. By devoting unprecedented attention to the rhythm of the decision cycle (which we consider below), the permanent Europe Plus Thirty could go some way to putting this right. In the meantime, it is worth noting that a 'better' forecast which arrives too late need not be entirely wasted; it can be checked against events, and the lessons can be turned to account next time. So can the lessons learned from the 'successes' and 'failures' of everybody else's forecasts (which is why forecasts, perhaps more than anything else, ought to be published).

Europe Plus Thirty would be well placed to improve on existing methods and combinations of methods in forecasting, because it would be looking at all aspects of the life of 250 million people who are among the most 'developed' in the world, because those people have a new, still rudimentary, form of common government, because it would be closely and directly related to the decision-making processes of that government, and because this collection of attributes does not apply to any other forecasting agency in the world.

USING FORECASTING: THE OUTPUTS

So much for the kitchen. Now for the table.

When discussing the use of forecasting, it is important to have a correct mental image of the subject, which is *not* one of a policy-maker rapidly turning the pages of a booklet containing forecasts. One should on the contrary adopt a systems view and regard a forecasting institute as a unit continuously interchanging information with its 'customers' on a number of different levels.

Let us start with a simplified and schematic picture of the policy-making cycle. This picture does not correspond to any particular part of any particular power structure, and there are parts of particular power structures which do not resemble it at all. But we think most of them do resemble it most of the time.

(1) The cycle has three phases, and we will break into it at a point where the public power concerned *has* a policy: the policy is being applied, is having some effect, and is not too much questioned. (There are moments like that – very brief ones.) Then defects in the policy begin to appear; it is not having the desired effect; or it is, but the effect itself begins to appear pointless or noxious. This ends the first phase.

(2) The organs of power enter the second phase of the cycle: consideration of policy change. This means, first of all, seeking alternative policies which promise to achieve the objectives of the former policy in a better way or to achieve new successor objectives instead. The search will take into account three kinds of evidence: (a) experience gained during the first phase, (b) the experience of others, if any, who have been pursuing different policies (de facto social experiment), and (c) forecasting about the possible effects of various alternative new policies (which will itself, of course, also take (a) and (b) into account). After this, the various policy options have to be evaluated, their costs and benefits have to be compared, and a choice has to be made. This does not mean that the policy-maker will automatically follow the reasoning of his forecasters and policy analysts, because he also has to consider the immediate demands of

the electorate who put him where he is, to say nothing of his own conscience and standards. The outcome of this phase of our idealised policy-making process is the selection (or confirmation) of one or more objectives expressed in dates and figures (Cone 1 of Figure 1 in the Introduction) and the formulation of plans of action to achieve them (Cone 2).

(3) The third and last phase of the policy cycle consists of putting whatever plan is adopted into action, by the exercise of the political power appropriate to the social framework within which it is to operate.

This sketch of a decision-making process laid up in heaven is useful because it enables us to see that forecasting affects the cycle of policy-making in two of the three phases and is affected by it in the third. Near the end of the first phase, when the defects of the current policy are beginning to appear, forecasts must already be at hand to explore the long-term surrounding context in which new policies would take effect, to see if it may not undergo changes that would themselves affect the choice of a new policy.

In the second phase, forecasts have to be made of the costs and benefits of the alternative policies so as to reveal their positive and negative impacts. This aspect of forecasting is all the more important when it is carried out for a social and economic entity the size of the European Community, because the decisions that the EEC takes have multiple consequences, not only within the member countries but also on other countries.

The third phase, that of policy implementation, affects forecasters, for as soon as they know the policy to be applied, they have to set up observations to check the accuracy of what they themselves have been saying about it. Many of the failures of forecasting so far have been due to lack of contact between forecasters and policy-makers *during and concerning* the implementation of a particular policy, which is no doubt due to the correct conviction of both sides that the forecaster has nothing to do with the process of implementation itself: that is for executive government and belongs to elected politicians and, under them, administrators. But this does not mean the forecaster has nothing to *learn* from the implementation phase of the policy cycle. By definition, the implementation problems are the largest where the gap between plans and reality is greatest, and any forecaster who ignored the significance of this gap would be of little use to his fellow men.

Real-life examples of this gap are plentiful on the national level: ambitious building plans that were not realised (sometimes because the responsible administration could not spend the money voted); plans

41

to eliminate regional disparities that turned out to have all kind of consequences – except the expected and desired ones; agricultural and industrial reforms that ran aground because of various deadlocks; even (so far) the Community's own plans for economic and monetary union; and so on (energy) and so forth (transport). The mechanisms that play a part are numerous; they range from intrinsically ill-conceived plans to the influence of particular political leaders and the inertia or incompetence of administrative units. Any forecasting that ignored these difficulties would be '*weltfremd*', and if anything is liable to be more dangerous than a 'wrong' forecast, it is a '*weltfremd*' forecast. Corrupt administration, powerful and eccentric political leaders, a stubborn and apparently 'reactionary' regional public opinion – all these are part of the real world, and the real world is what forecasters are attempting to forecast about.

It is not enough for the policy-maker (whether, for instance, a national minister or a European Commissioner) to have by him people who are executing his current policy; so much is obvious. He must also have – close by him – people whose job it is to help him sort out all the pressures towards change, and all the ways in which change can be considered. (Of the latter, the attempted rationality of forecasting is only one.) These people must have a carefully considered mix of professional and political backgrounds, and they must be organised and placed in the structure in exactly the best way. What this means in practice is bound to depend to some extent on the politics and personality of the decision-maker. 'People of the Left' commonly favour planning, and 'people of the Right' commonly look askance at it; but there is no left/right division in attitudes to forecasting. This is another reason for keeping planning and forecasting separate in our minds.

In the governments of the member states, the central planning arrangements within the bureaucracy and the individuals who take part in them vary widely in their ability to handle the 'future-oriented' approach to social, technological, and political affairs, and in their ability to ensure that its fruits are available to the right minister at the right time. This is so not only from country to country, but also from ministry to ministry within the same country. The best are faultless, the worst might just as well not be there at all; it is indeed a wide spread.

Whether they are European or national, complex administrations owe their very existence at least partly to the need to coordinate and condense an enormous flow of information, ideally so that details are taken care of at the appropriate levels on the way up while the essence is transmitted to the top. Necessary as this process is, it entails the risk that important information may be suppressed or distorted, perhaps because it simply is not recognised as such, because it was nobody's job to do the cross-sectoral scanning which alone could have recognised it. In any case the information is bound to be delayed, but, after all, that is better than if it were to remain unnoticed in a flood of trivia.

Any administration must keep a close watch on *how* it filters information and how long the transmission of information takes. The communication system between a forecasting instrument and the public power it serves should be designed so that:

(1) information is exchanged at all relevant levels;

(2) the links at each level are as short as possible;

(3) the recipients and the producers of forecasts have direct access to each other at all these levels (see Part IV).

National administrations have for centuries had to split up their activities – and hence their communications and planning procedures – by either departmentalisation or decentralisation, or by both. Long-term problems are now so wide-ranging and so interrelated that this traditional slicing of activities is becoming less and less satisfactory. Yet the tendency towards fragmentation still flourishes, paradoxically stimulating the need for forecasting which is integrated or indeed for forecasting which performs a re-integrating function, while making it ever more difficult to convert its results into effective policies and plans.

From a forecasting point of view, countries characterised by strong centralisation appear to be in a favourable position, at least at first sight. The difficulties of collecting timely, consistent, and accurate data, of using forecasting in decision-making and planning, and of effectively implementing plans, seem here less formidable. Conversely, if the different parts of a country have a constitutionally guaranteed autonomy, even the collection of basic data may demand excessive effort and cost. On the other hand, strong centralisation of a country may also mean strong ministries or directorates; in some lights it looks like a choice between horizontal and vertical disgregation.

When the European Community was set up in the 1950s and 1960s there could be no question of its resembling a centralised state; it had of course to be far more regionalised than even its most regionalised member. To horizontal disgregation (which was inevitable) was added vertical disgregation (which was perhaps not so necessary); ministerial compartmentalisation was so well established in the member countries that it was instantly reflected in the structure of the Commission.

This does not imply that the prospects for forecasting at this level are hopeless. On the contrary, the existence and the output of an integrated forecasting agency, provided it is granted enough time and weight, could well bring about a greater sense of direction and a better coordination of planning, not only in long-term decisions but in medium- and short-term ones as well.

The European Community is very different from any individual country, and the long-term integrated forecasting instrument it needs will have to be different from any other forecasting unit in existence. It will have a greater variety of contacts and clients, and its modes of operation will probably be different. It will not do any significant data-collecting itself. It will have several clients. It will have to serve the Commission, to assist its planners in developing and evaluating programmes of action, to serve the Parliament of the Community and its member governments, and to inform the public at large.

2. *Forecasting done by the Community now*

There are really two kinds of long-term forecasting: that done for the general reader, and that done for a particular client who needs it for a particular purpose. Both are abundant at the moment. The former kind speculates for the world in general and about the world in general (or about one aspect of it), partly for general education but often also to point out to anyone who will listen that there are dangers ahead. In so far as man in general is the master of his own fate (and the question of how far that is has been debated for some time), such forecasting can be regarded as a help to man in general in deciding what he wants to see done. But in so far as man in general divides himself into partial groupings like nation-states, ministries, firms, etc., to get things done, those partial groupings need forecasting specifically related to their powers and functions. Forecasting for the European Community must therefore be related to the powers and functions of that particular, and unique, grouping.

The Institutions of the Community – Council of Ministers, Commission, Parliament, and Court of Justice – make up an unprecedented mixture of a public power constituted under national and international law, and a regional, multi-purpose, consultative international organisation. The Community is like a nation-state part of the way: it has power over some things, especially agriculture and commercial and industrial competition, and it also seeks to further the interests of its inhabitants as a whole in a general way. It is also a clearing ground for information, research, and the 'harmonisation' of downstream powers among its member states.

In a very simplified nutshell, it works like this. The Council takes the major decisions, but it can only act on proposals from the Commission. The Commission takes minor decisions, under powers given it by the Community Treaties (European Coal and Steel Community Treaty (ECSC), Euratom Treaty, and Treaty of Rome) or following guidelines laid down by the Council. It also acts as the executive arm in general. In the event of dispute between the Commission and a member state, or between the Commission and a commercial enterprise, the Court of Justice decides. The Parliament discusses everything and forwards opinions to the other institutions. It also has a minor degree of control over Community Finances. When it is directly elected, in 1978, it may be expected to extend its area of control.

The European Community came into being by a gradual process of integration, stretching from the ECSC to Euratom and the European Economic Community (EEC), which may continue into the planned economic and monetary union and more and more other areas. Its development was a response to the changed requirements of the member countries, which agreed to share sovereignty in certain areas. Accordingly, its further development – that is, the strengthening of its competence and the extension of its radius of action – depends upon whether the members believe that, for instance, the problems of environmental protection or external monetary policy can in future be better dealt with on a European than on a national level. This presupposes a forecast not only of future problems but also of the development of national and European policy-making capacities.

The increased interweaving of the economies of the member states of the European Community, and consequently the mutual influence of social and political processes upon each other, means that even short-term policy planning on the national level cannot be done without regard to developments in other countries of the Community. The longer the time horizons for planning, the stronger are these interdependencies. For instance, we cannot make statements about the long-term industrialisation of a certain region without at the same time forecasting developments in prices, demand, and employment. The individual member states of the Community, and the Community as a whole, are therefore dependent to a comparable degree upon long-term forecasts with a European dimension.

There are thus two different tasks for Community-wide research on the future: first, to contribute to goal-seeking for the further development of European integration (if that is desired); and second, to help set out options in various fields of European policy, and to help select the means of realising the options chosen.

In contrast to the nation-states, the centres of political decision in the European Community cannot freely decide upon its goals; they are bound by the limits of the founding Treaties. These limits are much narrower than those of a national constitution; the parties to the Treaties not only limited the competence of the European Community to certain functions of government, but at the same time laid down certain goals. Thus the Treaty of Rome determines the general economic and socio-political goals of the EEC and lays down the manner of their realisation, namely by the construction of a common market according to certain principles. The Treaty itself can be seen as a programme of long-term policy planning, concerned only with achieving the Community goal and not with setting any new goals.

In the late 1960s, after the creation of the customs union and the virtual achievement of the provisions of the Treaty, the European Community was in a state of unstable balance. Every means of stabilising the situation implied political decisions as important as the Treaties themselves.

The Treaty of Rome, in spite of its forward-looking nature, was not based on forecasting in the strict sense of the word. Scientific policy consultation was commissioned by governments only after the basic political decisions had been taken. Equally with economic and monetary union: the decision of the Hague summit conference was a response to past and present problems. The 'phased plan' was not based on any analysis of long-term tendencies but was merely an attempt to describe a static model of monetary union; it is perhaps not surprising that the decision was overtaken by events.

Corresponding tendencies are apparent if we consider the ongoing decision-making process. In decisions on European integration the governments of the member states have regarded it as their prerogative to lay down the common goals of a European economic and monetary union (Hague summit), and have secured for themselves direct participation in the working out of proposals and procedures (Werner Report). The detailed follow-up of these decisions was, to be sure, handed over to the Commission, but it is in fact still carried out in close cooperation between the Commission and senior civil servants of the member states in various committees. When it is a question of *setting* new goals for the Community, the Commission clearly plays a subordinate role; but this fact says nothing about its significance in the European *goal-seeking* process, or teleonomy as we called it earlier.

It is well known that the Commission very early on put forward proposals and preliminary studies for the further development of the

46

Common Market towards an economic and monetary union. But comparable ideas were also developed by independent experts and in various national ministries, and the continuous and close cooperation between the Commission and member states makes it nearly impossible to trace ideas and political initiatives back to their origins. Still, the Commission is the turntable around which the Community network of communications is disposed, and it can make a special contribution to conceiving future developments. It is in a good position to solve problems in a way appropriate not only to the state of affairs at Community level but also to the balancing-out of diverging national interests. It already fulfils this task within the scope of the Treaty: the right of initiative was given to the Commission for these very reasons.

Even if the Commission, from the viewpoint of its critics, has lost its political impetus, it is still the organ of the European Community which is most capable of policy planning. We cannot expect continuous conceptual work either from the Council or from its Committee of Permanent Representatives, sitting between ministerial meetings. Political initiatives by the Council, or rather by individual Council members, are generally the result of domestic perceptions and processes. The Permanent Representatives differ from the Council in that they work continuously, but the structure of their organisation and the tasks they are charged with make them more akin to an international administration, from which one cannot expect planning. Their working programme is determined by the preliminary work of the Commission and by the decisions of the Council itself. It is highly fragmented; many and changing experts, according to the subject area, are brought into consultation.

The European Parliament is even less able than national parliaments to undertake policy planning, because it is not directly elected and has such limited powers. The Economic and Social Committee, made up of the representatives of various interests, not only lacks political legitimacy and continuity in its work but is confined by the Treaties to an advisory capacity. For these reasons the Commission is the appropriate patron for a European forecasting instrument. Nevertheless, it still cannot be the sole addressee of forecasts, because policy decisions are made mainly in the Council of Ministers and are based mainly on opinions formed nationally. The effectiveness of forecasts (that is, whether their results are taken into account in policy decisions) depends in part upon whether they can influence political discussion in the member states.

The European Community, as we noted, has now achieved almost all its original goals, and this naturally leads to a certain lack of impetus and direction. It wishes now to set new ones, and for this reason it stands in need of the long-term integrated forecasting which can help it to do so.

Forecasts have been prepared by the European Communities since their establishment. With few exceptions, they are short- or medium-term forecasts of development in particular sectors: for instance, the trends in demand for and supply of coal, steel, farm produce, etc. They are restricted to single sectors because they are regarded as instruments to help formulate and implement the policies embodied in the Treaties. The European Communities themselves were built up according to the principle of sectoral integration, and the structure of the Commission, as the central administrative body, is geared to the individual tasks laid down in the Treaties. There are thirteen commissioners, two each from the larger member countries (Britain, France, Germany, and Italy) and one each from the smaller (Belgium, Denmark, Ireland, Luxembourg, and the Netherlands). They renounce their allegiance to their own countries and transfer it to the Community. They meet once a week in private, and act according to the rules of collective responsibility familiar to all democracies with cabinet government. Under them are nineteen Directors General (we return to them below), each responsible for a particular policy area; each Directorate General thus has its own need for forecasting and, at least until recently, has had the untrammelled right to commission the studies it wanted.

Forecasts in the strict sense of the word have so far been restricted to rather few fields: energy, industrial affairs (particularly where they are governed by the ECSC Treaty), economic and financial affairs, and agriculture. The use of forecasting became more widespread as new fields of activity opened up for the Community (for example, regional policy and environmental protection) and as the existing Directorates General attempted to use forecasts as an instrument for promoting a European policy in certain areas such as transport.

Here is an account, based on the Commission's present division into Directorates General, of the European Commission's forecasting activities as they were early in 1975.

EXTERNAL RELATIONS

Directorate General I

Only limited forecasts are drawn up, for instance of the trends in world trade in the three years ahead. No quantified forward studies are available to underpin notions such as that of a European Mediterranean Policy. Analysis of current and future problems and possible goals of European foreign policy is, however, undertaken by a planning staff dealing with the basic questions of external trade policies.

Directorate General II

SHORT-TERM. Preliminary economic budgets for the next year are prepared by the member states; the appropriate Commission departments and the Short-Term Economic Policy Group of the Economic Policy Committee (formerly the Short-Term Economic Policy Committee) summarise these preliminary economic budgets, check them for compatibility, and compare them with the Commission's own annual forecasts. The economic budgets are then adopted.

Annual reports are drawn up on the economic situation in the Community and on the outlook for the coming year; these serve as a basis for formulating the economic policy guidelines to be followed by the member states in the following year.

MEDIUM-TERM. The Study Group on Medium-Term Economic Assessments draws up reports on the economic outlook in the European Community, covering a period of five years. The members of the Study Group are appointed by the Commission. The forecasts are used as a basis for medium-term economic policy programmes. Forecasts made before 1975 have been re-examined following the enlargement of the Community and in response to the raw-materials crisis and have been presented, with revised figures, as projections for the period 1974–8 in the form of a report to the Council and the Commission in preparation for the Fourth Medium-Term Economic Policy Programme, which will probably cover the period 1976–80. In accordance with the directive on stability adopted in early 1974, the member states of the Community are also obliged to prepare medium-term forecasts and public investment programmes covering a five-year period. The same directive also laid down new provisions governing the Community's medium-term programmes.

There are also occasional future-oriented studies. Methodological studies have also been undertaken. The Central Planning Bureau of DG II has constructed a model to explain and forecast the relationship between trade cycles in the national economies in Europe, which was to help guide short-term economic policy decisions at European level (the METEOR Project: 'European Model for Economic Transmission Effects and Balancing Operations'). Another model is to be used to forecast economic developments in Europe over the next six or seven years. Its construction was entrusted to the Study Group on Medium-term Economic Assessments (the COMET Project: 'Community Medium-term Model').

INDUSTRIAL AND TECHNOLOGICAL AFFAIRS
Directorate General III

The ECSC and Euratom treaties are the basis on which forecasts are made for steel and the nuclear field. The short-term forecasts have a time horizon of one year, the medium-term ones generally five years, and the long-term forecasts fifteen years. The forecasts are made by the services of the Commission itself, since qualified personnel from the earlier ECSC and Euratom Commissions have been absorbed into DG III.

Studies carried out by DG III on individual industrial sectors (textiles, paper, shipbuilding, aviation, etc.) are based on the short- and medium-term estimates of the trends for each sector. They are the basis on which guidelines for action are proposed for each sector.

Individual medium-term and long-term forward studies (for example, shipbuilding 1971–80) are carried out on behalf of the Commission, sometimes at the suggestion of the industrial associations concerned, by ad hoc committees which largely base their work on existing projections.

The services of DG III are also trying to develop medium- and long-term activities, into which they can feed sectoral information for a forward-looking input–output model. This model is being developed by an outside research institute and is intended to reveal the interdependencies of sectoral industrial development.

SOCIAL AFFAIRS
Directorate General V

Short- and medium-term forecasts of the labour market and the employment situation are drawn up on the basis of national statistics, provided they are available and are comparable, in collaboration with the Community Statistical Office and the Directorate General for Economic and Financial Affairs. Work on common methods of forecasting for a European Social Budget is about to be put in hand. The Social Fund Studies which are carred out in accordance with Article 7 of the Treaty of Rome contain, at the most, incidental forecasts, generally taken from national statistics.

AGRICULTURE
Directorate General VI

Medium-term forecasting for the common market in agricultural products dates back to the early 1960s. The most recent projections of the production and consumption of agricultural products only cover the period until 1977. They concern about fifty agricultural products and were drawn up for what were, when the study was commissioned, the six founder member states and the four candidates for membership. The calculations are based on statistical series produced by the Statistical Office of the Community of Six, and on national statistics for the candidate countries. The national studies were prepared by research institutes in the various member states under the direction of the Commission, and a summary was produced by the latter.

The next forecasts will not only be drawn up according to a somewhat different procedure but will also cover a longer period (the years 1980 and 1985 are envisaged as time horizons); there are also plans to roll them forward each year.

Methodological studies were commissioned by the Community in the early 1960s. They concluded that there was as yet no statistical information adequate for refined methods and that even the methods examined were not suitably tailored to making long-term supply forecasts.

Forecasts for particular sectors of the agriculture market have also been prepared, some of which use models. Examples include a paper on the sensitivity of the parameters of a model for estimating pigmeat production.

There has also been forecasting about the agricultural workforce.

TRANSPORT

Directorate General VII

SHORT- AND MEDIUM-TERM. Indicators for short-term transport forecasts are currently being developed. In addition to general economic trends they are to cover important features of the transport market, and they are to be linked to a medium-term forecasting model. A permanent information service on the situation and trend of the freight transport market, which will have a time horizon of two or three years, is also planned. The necessary statistical material is to be supplied by national authorities and undertakings.

LONG-TERM. Long-term forward studies of passenger and freight transport serve as a guide for infrastructure investment in the Community. The European Community is taking part with OECD in a programme called 'COST 33', forecasting the demand for passenger transport between major conurbations. The time horizons of this study are 1985 and 2000; a report will probably be made in 1976.

A report called 'Preliminary Research with Reference to the Development of a Forecasting Model for Freight Transport in the EEC' was submitted at the end of 1974 by a contractor. It recommended that a freight study should be carried out and closely aligned on the COST 33 passenger study as regards the time horizon involved, the breakdown by geographical region, the socio-economic definition of a region, the comparability of the socio-economic data, and the transport systems to be covered. The project would use a model.

RESEARCH, SCIENCE, AND EDUCATION

Directorate General XII

Two studies in the methodology of forecasting have been commissioned or supported financially: 'A Feasibility Study of Socio-Economic Models of Europe' and 'Le Système matériel d'une région'. The first was carried out by a university research group under contract; the second was a model, also developed under contract, as the basis for a possible major socio-economic simulation model for Europe. Our own study, 'Europe Plus Thirty', which was set up by a decision of the Council of Ministers, is attached to DG XII.

REGIONAL POLICY

Directorate General XVI

SHORT- AND MEDIUM-TERM. As yet no coherent forecasts exist of the regional development of the European Community as a whole. However, within the framework of the FLEUR study (Factors of Location in Europe), which is being carried out under contract to the Commission, forecasts with homogeneous data might become possible. A feasibility study on forecasting the balance between regional labour supply and demand in the Community has also been undertaken on behalf of the Commission.

At the request of a number of member states, the Commission has also sponsored studies on the development of certain particular regions. Any short-term or medium-term forecasts contained in these studies were, however, taken from forecasts for the country in question.

ENERGY

Directorate General XVII

SHORT-TERM. The Commission prepares an annual report on the short-term energy situation in the Community, which contains forecasts for the following year. For the coal sector, a separate one-year market forecast is drawn up.

MEDIUM-TERM. Medium-term forecasts and guidelines for individual sources of energy such as gas, coal, or oil are prepared at irregular intervals.

LONG-TERM. The European Community's long-term energy forecasts cover fifteen-year periods and are rolled forward every five years. In preparing the forecasts, the Commission's departments draw on statistical material available in the member states, bearing in mind the medium-term economic forecasts for the Community. The statistical sources and forecasting methods have been continually improved over the past years, but the energy crisis has meant that much recent work requires revision, and it has also made it doubtful whether it is possible to go on using the existing forecasting methods.

In mid-1974, the Commission submitted to the Council a comprehensive research and development programme for the energy sector, including systems-modelling of alternative options for a common R & D strategy. It considers that the techniques require further improvement.

Systems-modelling is also to be used in the near future for two other studies: one concerns the socio-economic consequences of different energy supply breakdowns, and the other consists of an economic appraisal of different energy supply and demand patterns, mainly in the investment field.

CREDIT AND INVESTMENTS

Directorate General XVIII

Surveys among undertakings and trade associations indicate what the probable supply situation in the coal and steel sectors will be, and on this basis the Directorate General for Credit and Investments prepares annual supply forecasts for the following four years. They serve as a basis for decisions on the granting of industrial and reconversion loans under Articles 54 and 56 of the ECSC Treaty. Forecasts of demand trends are prepared by Directorate General III (Industrial and Technological Affairs). The 'general objectives' are revised every five years.

BUDGETS

Directorate General XIX

In cooperation with national government departments and in the light of the estimates of the Medium-Term Economic Policy Programmes, this Directorate General prepares financial forecasts which cover three years and are rolled forward annually.

Methodological studies are being carried out at the moment to improve the forecasts.

Of the Directorates General not mentioned above, Directorate General IV Competition, Directorate General VIII Development and Cooperation, Directorate General IX Personnel and Administration, Directorate General X Information, Directorate General XI Internal Market, Directorate General XIII Scientific and Technical Information and Information Management, Directorate General XV Financial Institutions and Taxation, and Directorate

General XX Financial Control, do or cause to be done only minor studies. Directorate General XIV has been distributed among other Directorates General and no longer exists.

OTHERS

Some forecasting may also be carried out in or for two new dependent organs of the Community which have been proposed.

The European Foundation for the Improvement of Working and Living Conditions

This Foundation is intended to undertake research into working and living conditions, including the environment, and their improvement. Long-term studies, such as that on water-supply prospects in Europe in the next thirty years, which at present are done under contract for the Commission's Environment and Consumer Protection Service, may then become the responsibility of the Foundation.

European Communities Institute for Economic Analysis and Research

This proposed new Institute springs from the desire to place policy measures for the further economic integration of the European Community on a more scientific footing. The Institute would carry out both economic research and medium-term forecasting and would deal with the methodological problems of economic forecasting.

Only ten of the nineteen Directorates General undertake forecasting, and what they do concentrates on the short and medium term. The Commission is, however, increasingly aware that it must also have at its disposal longer-term forecasts if it is to be in a position to develop a coherent system of goals and strategies into which to fit its short- and medium-term policies. There has been more and more evidence of the limitations of sectoral forecasts, and attempts are at present being made to overcome them through closer cooperation between the Directorates General concerned and at Commission level, and also by contracting out some very limited work on integrated forecasting models.

Under the present arrangements the responsibility for deciding whether or not forward studies are to be carried out lies with the individual Directorates General – unless, that is, such studies are mandatory under one of the Treaties or under a Council decision, or unless their cost exceeds the funds available to the Directorate General concerned. Only recently have attempts been made to achieve inter-departmental coordination: in early 1974, a study group was set up to coordinate research projects internally (it began its work only at the beginning of 1975).

Since it has no lower-tier administrations, the European Community is dependent on statistical material and forecasts provided by the member states; the insufficient comparability of national statistical data and forecasting procedures has already been noted above. The Statistical Office of the European Community makes a major contribution towards achieving standardisation. Once standardisation is achieved, the next problem to arise is the inadequacy of traditional forecasting methods. Accordingly, various Directorates General have commissioned the construction of forecasting models, which have revealed that computer science does indeed offer almost unlimited possibilities but that the present state of economics and social science, and also the existing level of information, impose considerable constraints. Because of their high degree of aggregation and above all their necessarily narrow assumptions, these studies have so far been of only limited use in policy-making. The small size of the Commission's staff means that most forecasting work has to be contracted out. However, preparatory work in the Commission must be carried a certain distance before outside experts can be asked to draw up forecasts.

As the party commissioning forward studies has so far been identical with the party for which they are intended, the forecasts have in a certain sense by definition met the Commission's information needs. But this does not yet mean that they are appropriately assessed or used for the formulation of policy proposals. The inadequacy of many forecasts has given rise to marked reticence, because their statistical base is too narrow, or their theoretical premises are disputed, or the results are too general, or fundamentally interdependent relationships have been disregarded. Other difficulties in exploiting the results for policy-making have been due to a lack of planning at the receiving end.

In some contexts, such as medium-term economic programming, forecasts are or should be an integral part of programme planning, of which Council decisions or Treaty provisions are the basis. Not only is there thus a guarantee that the results of the forward studies are taken into account when programmes are being drawn up, but there is also permanent and close cooperation between outside experts, Commission officials, and officials of the member states, the last two classes in the Economic Policy Committee. On the value of the economic programmes themselves, as they are at present devised and used, the Economic Policy Committee is divided. In other contexts, the decision on whether or not to use forecasts for formulating Community policy in a specific field depends on how relevant the information provided appears to the Directorate General concerned. This raises the problem of interdepartmental coordination. Programme planning within the individual Directorates General is still in its infancy; there is no certainty that forward studies are always commissioned in consultation with other departments or in accordance with criteria previously agreed. This problem exists regardless of the formal allocation of responsibilities for studies, which varies from one Directorate General to another.

Nevertheless, as a general rule, the Directorates General have been provided – to the extent that this has been financially, statistically, and methodologically possible – with the short- and medium-term forward information necessary for the limited policy sectors covered. But wider-ranging forecasts, as a prerequisite for and adjunct to forecasts in individual sectors, are lacking. The Commission's internal organisation makes in any case for a rigid division between the sectors covered, so that it is difficult to identify and successfully pursue any interest that extends beyond a single department. And each Director General has 'his' Commissioner, to whom he often has easier access than to his brother Directors General.

The European Community needs long-term integrated forecasts of economic, political, and social trends in order to steer its own course. This requires political planning at Community level; it requires the coordination of the proposals and programmes of the individual Directorates General so that they form a true Community policy. Only through such a planning process can the feasibility of, and possible alternatives to, specific policy choices be considered. The European Commission finds it just as difficult as other big administrations to plan its tasks and programmes coherently. As an international organisation, it has to cope with additional problems. And as the first international, multilingual administration in all history to have some direct power over the lives of actual people, it also has to cope with completely unprecedented ones as well.

The ability to achieve coordination depends on whether the body directing policy is capable of arriving at a consensus and of taking political action. The thirteen Commissioners, acting together, constitute the Commission's controlling body. Their unity is in practice impaired by the way they are appointed (which makes them look over their shoulders at their home governments) and by the lack of direct political legitimacy. The Commission is, it is true, designed as a collegiate body, but it functions de facto on strict departmental principles. Toleration of an excessive workload, the continued existence of separate Treaties, and the working methods of the Committee of Permanent Representatives are further reasons for this state of affairs.

But the responsibility for coordination cannot be taken over by the Commission's departments. They possess neither the political legitimacy nor the necessary power; the result is that they can play only an auxiliary role by helping either to cut down the surfeit of information or to coordinate implementation of the various departments' separate tasks. The scope for 'autonomous self-coordination' at the level of the Directorates General is limited: it is largely restricted to an exchange of information and the formal delimitation of spheres of work. It is still to early to judge more recent tentative coordinating efforts, for instance in the contracting-out of research by the Commission. These and other attempts are an indication that a shortcoming has been recognised.

Much useful work is being done, but it is clearly not free from waste and overlap. More: the work is sectoral, and most of it (except in DG II and DG VII) is rather short-term. A new instrument of integrated long-term forecasting is clearly needed, and it will clearly have to be carefully coordinated with the short- and medium-term sectoral forecasting which already exists. If it is to have any purpose, it must be a truly integrated project, which means that it must work in all fields where long-term forecasting makes sense and must integrate them. (These fields are identified in Part II below.) If long-term forecasting is being done in an integrated project, it must be decided whether it is also a good idea to do it in a series of separate sectoral projects. Obviously it is not, and certain changes should be envisaged.

3. *Forecasting in member countries of the Community*

What sort of forecasting is already being done in the Community countries? In the last ten years several investigations have been carried out in Europe and elsewhere;[1] they suggest that forecasting as a formal activity is increasing. The range of techniques employed has also increased, and so has sophistication in general.

[1] For example, N. Sombart, 'Long-Term Planning and Forecasting in Europe', *Long Range Planning*, vol. 5, no. 2 (June 1972), pp. 47–52.

There is much variety in the pattern of forecasting in different countries, and in the methods used. It depends on the issue under consideration, cultural outlook, personalities, organisation (including the organisation of government), and previous experience. To know why forecasts began to be made and why particular methods are used today would involve a historical study, which could be of the highest interest.

European forecasting lies between two polar stereotypes: the Soviet Union (highly centralised, rigid five-year plans based on estimates of economic, social, and technological possibilities at a national, sectoral, and regional level) and the United States (largely decentralised forecasts, with an emphasis on short-term issues, by departments and agencies at all levels of government and by industries and universities, with minimum coordination between groups of workers).

In the Netherlands, the Federal Republic of Germany, the United Kingdom, and Belgium, government has a strong regional element, and much planning is decentralised. In France the reverse is the case. In the United Kingdom, power lies largely with individual ministers, and long-range planning tends to be departmental or sectoral. France and the Eastern European countries have for some time produced comprehensive medium-term plans. In the Federal Republic of Germany, as in the United States, there has been no planning of this kind. The Netherlands, Italy, and Sweden have produced long-term, macro-economic projections on a less comprehensive basis and have tended to focus on a particular issue such as regional sectoral disparities in Italy or industrial production in the Netherlands. In the main, planning has been undertaken to help tackle a particular problem, or even to generate a sense of purpose. Plans usually cover a five-year period and are either regular, as in France, or occasional, like the ill-fated British National Plan of 1965.

All European nations, within their ministries of finance, have for many years carried out annual budgetary forecasts, usually based on econometric models. Most engage in mid-term forecasting up to five to ten years. In industry and government budgetary planning, much shorter planning horizons operate: they are dictated largely by the prevailing discount rate and (it is commonly believed) by the lifetime of democratically elected parliaments; nevertheless, the amount of long-term thinking has increased. The annual budget is what affects people's lives immediately, and the very great difficulty of translating long-term strategies into short-term tactics has meant that national plans, even where they have been coordinated by the finance ministry, have tended to have less effect.

As well as finance ministries, most government departments carry out forward planning and have at least a nominal forecasting capability. At this level studies are intended to provide background information for policy formation (beforehand) and assessment (afterwards). Sometimes it is done for specific policies but often, for example with demographic forecasts, for a wide range of policies.

Overall plans sometimes originate within the finance ministry, but more often in departments set up for the purpose. The aims of overall plans vary. Often they have been initiated (as in France, the United Kingdom, and Ireland) to relieve economic troubles. But they are also intended to provide strategic guidelines within which sectoral and regional policies may be devised. The need for such guidelines has become accepted for many reasons, particularly perhaps because of the increase of state involvement in industry.

Where the preparation of an overall plan is not the intention, the need to coordinate plans and forecasts between ministries is increasingly recognised. In Eastern Europe, and to a lesser degree in France, formal coordination has existed for several decades. In the United Kingdom and the Netherlands it is more recent, and inter-ministerial activity is obtained more often through committees than through joint analyses. Most countries suffer from lack of interdepartmental communication. Traditionally powerful finance ministries are loath to concede power to national planning agencies. In the United Kingdom, coordination was significantly improved when a number of spending departments were grouped into new and larger 'super-departments' (e.g. Department of the Environment).

Typically the time scale for ministerial forecasts is five to ten years, but 1985 and the end of the century have been common horizons for about a decade. There is at least some recognition of the physical, technological, social, or economic time scales characteristic of each policy area. Land-use planning, for example, is normally recognised as having physical implications up to and beyond sixty years (the theoretical physical lifetime of dwellings). Energy requirements are normally considered on a scale of several decades, corresponding to the lead time for new technologies, the economic life of power stations, and physical limitations (fossil-fuel reserves, environment). Some aspects of social policy (for example, planning for retirement pensions) also require forecasts of at least thirty years.

Although the time horizon and the scope of forecasting do seem to be extending, several countries which have experimented with forecasts and plans of long time span or great detail are now redirecting their efforts towards less ambitious projects. The attempts during the 1960s to produce long-term, very detailed forecasts of wide scope were not entirely successful. In Hungary, in France, and in Ireland,

59

for example, the time horizons of government forecasts have short-ened, and the level of detail in long-term forecasts has been reduced significantly.

Social factors are becoming increasingly prominent in governmental and other forecasts: in some cases this means attempting to display social and environmental costs in economic terms, in others it involves merely indicating the social implications of economic and other poli-cies. Problems arising from increasing urbanisation and industrialisa-tion, the ecological aspects of environment, and most recently the energy crisis have all contributed to this widening of perspectives. In several countries new government departments have been established which focus on these issues. A need for 'social indicators' with which to monitor the effects of social policies is recognised (we discussed this subject earlier). The Netherlands and Sweden have set up agencies to examine the assumptions and goals implicit in govern-ment policy.

But the purpose of forecasting is seen differently in different Euro-pean countries, and in each country the perception and emphasis has changed continuously. In Eastern Europe, France, and Norway, fore-casting has been closely intermeshed with planning and has thus been more 'political'. Such forecasting as has been attempted in Belgium and Italy has also been of this nature. In the Netherlands, the United Kingdom, and West Germany, it has been rather more removed from the hurly-burly.

There are also differences in the overall approach to forecasting. Some countries, such as the United Kingdom and Norway, emphasise the formulation of alternative hypotheses concerning future trends. By contrast, in France the approach to medium-term planning has been to specify by systematic (iterative) trial and error the policies which – taken together with estimates of social and technological changes – will lead as close as possible to a specified set of objectives. In some countries (e.g. Hungary) attempts have been made to arrive at such 'solutions' by using programmed optimisation methods. In no European country is anything approaching the teleonomy we outlined above attempted, though it is by the Economic Council of Japan.

An important factor determining governmental planning activity is the level of public ownership in a country – whether, for example, forecasts are oriented toward revenue or production. Even in Eastern European countries, as experience in Hungary shows, there is a conflict between perceived industrial and governmental forecasting needs, with industry in general preferring a shorter planning horizon. In the West, different perceptions with regard to, say, the question of taxes, make full cooperation between companies and governments quite difficult. Nevertheless, the expectations of businessmen concerning levels of investment and of technologists concerning the lead time for new technologies are relied upon by most government agencies in making detailed sectoral forecasts. Although most industrial forecasts are narrowly product-oriented, some industries (e.g. oil and transport) find it essential to consider a wide range of social and environmental issues.

This applies particularly to large firms and public ventures (including nationalised industries) many of which have their own long-term forecasting groups. The size of a firm and the character of its products naturally have a greater impact on its own planning effort than does the pattern of national economic planning. Where interests do not clash directly, several companies cooperate to sponsor research associations or conferences. There are, in fact, several forums, both governmental and non-governmental (such as the ECE seminars for senior economic advisors, or the Institute of Administrative Science Congress), for exchanging ideas about forecasting methods and applications.

It is difficult to make generalisations about forecasting research in universities, private organisations, and consultancies. If anything, interest in forecasting among them exceeds that in government departments or industry. Some universities conduct programmes of research into forecasting in general and in relation to specific topics. Attitudes to work by universities and consultants vary between countries; in Europe (compared with the United States) university research tends to be viewed as 'too academic' or irrelevant. But non-governmental research often contributes to a widening of perspective which is lacking in narrowly defined governmental forecasts, and it points to neglected issues which are often not viewed as central problems by the governments of advanced nations. In some countries (for example, the United Kingdom), it has been stated as a deliberate policy that speculative long-term issues should be publicly aired by non-governmental agencies. There is considerable variation in the level of interdependence and cooperation between government and non-government research teams. This also includes groups not engaged specifically in forecasting, such as government statistical offices and many university departments which collect and monitor data.

The work of inter-governmental agencies, such as the United Nations and OECD (especially the latter), is often well thought out and executed. OECD is one of the main sources of comparative data, not only in the field of conjunctural economics but across a wide span of sectoral activities such as agriculture, energy, science and technology, environment, education, social policy, and development aid; and its work is, in general, rather more concerned with the longer-term trends than that of other international organisations. But it has so far made little attempt at an integrated forecasting approach of the type which we advocate in our report; its work is essentially on a sector-by-sector basis and is not policy-oriented. Its work cannot be regarded as an alternative to the creation of a sound and integrated forecasting capacity within the Community, where such forecasts, to be effective, must necessarily be close to the points of analysis and decision. The European Community is to some extent an executive, having powers of its own, and forecasting done by it or for it should therefore be more policy-oriented than can, or need, be the case in OECD.

The range of techniques used in forecasting has increased in the last twenty years, and greater sophistication is evident. There are several reasons for this. First, techniques, technology, and expertise have been carried over from military, engineering, and scientific endeavours – from the operations research and 'systems' approaches which had their origins in the Second World War. Second, there has been a tendency since the War, in government economic planning particularly, to define a relatively small set of objectives (economic growth, full employment, etc.) and to adopt a managerial approach to achieving these objectives, which in turn helped to promote the use of more formal techniques. Finally, there has been a demand for methods which can cope with issues which are realised to be increasingly complex.

For the resolution of issues which have recently become political eye-catchers (energy, ecological aspects of the environment), systems analysis and sophisticated modelling methods are often used. International agencies and international non-governmental projects are sometimes front-runners in experimenting with and supporting studies based on new techniques such as dynamic modelling. In long-term economic studies, both formal mathematical methods and informal discursive methods are generally used. All countries carrying out long-term exercises make use of non-formal methods such as qualitative analysis (including scenario-writing), international comparisons, and of course the simple extrapolation of past trends. The degree of emphasis depends on the overall approach used. In general, the more detailed an analysis, the more expert judgement as opposed to econometric or other models is relied upon. Even with short-term forecasts there are considerable variations in approach and in the assumptions underlying the models constructed in different countries.

In France, Italy, the Netherlands, and the United Kingdom, experience with the use of aggregated economic models is generally considered to have been satisfactory. Although the Czechs, Italians, and Dutch have all experimented with non-linear versions of their aggregate macro-economic models, there is a tendency for models actually employed in the management of economies, and particularly trade models, to be mathematically relatively simple. They consist for the most part of linear relationships. Optimisation methods and dynamic programming are used less often. One reason for this is the low quality of data, which makes estimation of relationships difficult and the use of more sophisticated methods dubious. This situation is improving, although Europe as a whole still lags behind the United States.

There have been failures, from all of which we must learn. It has proved difficult to produce consistent long-term demographic forecasts as, for example, the experience of both the Netherlands and the United Kingdom show. Attempts are being made to extend the extrapolative methods based on fertility rates and cohort analysis to include other non-demographic variables. Similarly, models of technological change have tended to be too primitive. In an industry such as electronics, a new generation of components may appear in commercial application less than five years after the discovery of the basic physical phenomenon. In other industries, such as nuclear power, forecasts of lead times are hazardous. For this reason estimates of expected technical changes and costs tend to be based upon the opinions of large numbers of industrial and scientific researchers. This seems to be especially true of Japan and the Soviet Union. PPBS (Planning, Programme, Budgeting System) has had mixed fortunes in several of the countries in which it has been introduced, particularly the Federal Republic of Germany and the United States, and has largely been replaced by the less complicated 'management by objectives' approach. One of the more commonly advanced and more charitable reasons for this failure in the United States is that its introduction in several government departments at once overstrained the supply of policy analysts.

But teething troubles are to be distinguished from inherent limitations. Leontief's input–output methods, for example, were strongly criticised by many other economists when they were first introduced. So were heliocentrism, railways, anaesthetics, aeroplanes, contraception, etc. by the orthodox in their day.

4. *Integrating Community forecasting*

The European Community is made up of member states that are doing forecasting and connected studies for public policy purposes (although mainly for the short and medium term), and it appears that the first step towards integrating Community-wide forecasting could be the process depicted in Figure 3, which provides two routes from national sectoral forecasts to Community comprehensive forecasts: via Community sectoral forecasts and via national comprehensive forecasts.

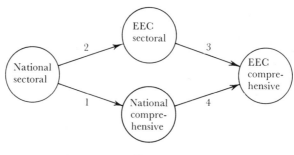

Fig. 3.

Since the Community has its own sectoral policies, is already a common market, and intends in due course to become an economic union, the upper route – via Community sectoral forecasts – is clearly the more useful for its purposes. But the lower route – via national comprehensive forecasts – might also be followed, if manpower is available, for two reasons. Firstly, it should provide a check on the upper route; and secondly, it would parallel the main route by which, for the time being, a permanent or continuing Europe Plus Thirty will have to obtain comprehensive forecasts about the world outside the Community, namely by the integration of national aggregates.

The four integration processes displayed in the figure are considered in turn below.

1. NATIONAL LEVEL: FROM SECTORAL TO COMPREHENSIVE FORECASTS

Every national comprehensive forecast represents a convergence of three partial forecasts, each deriving from a particular 'resource' of group of 'resources' – people, goods and services, and geographical space – and each setting out, for a nearer or further time horizon, what might be the future situation on:

(1) the demographic aspect: the number of total inhabitants and of the active population, broken down by multiple criteria (age, sex, education level, employment sector, socio-professional class, etc.);

(2) the socio-economic aspect: production, imports, internal and external use of national production, and social parameters, calculated on the basis of the demographic data and on hypotheses about the behaviour of economic and social agents, and distinguishing between different industrial sectors, public versus private enterprises, etc.;

(3) the geographical aspect: the distribution of the above variables according to regional and type-of-settlement criteria (rural versus urban, metropolitan versus small and medium cities, city centre versus suburb, etc.).

The techniques of this integration of sectoral forecasts into a national framework are not uniformly advanced. Aspects (1) and (2) are adequately articulated, and so are aspects (1) and (3), but we have to admit that we do not know very well how to integrate aspects (2) and (3) – that is, to foresee either the socio-economic implications of different spatial alternatives or the spatial implications of socio-economic alternatives. Nevertheless, the two aspects have strong mutual influences which it would be good to unravel in advance, rather than contenting oneself with ex post facto perceptions. Most of the necessary work will have to be done at national level.

2. FROM NATIONAL TO EEC LEVEL: SECTORAL FORECASTS

To make this step, Community-wide standardisation of data is urgently needed. This sectoral integration to Community level would present no further difficulty if all the resources concerned stayed put inside each member country; in that case it would be enough to add up all the national figures to arrive at a European total. Unfortunately for forecasters, the stay-put case is not the general one.

As we shall see in chapter II.3, forecasting migration is the most fragile part of demographic forecasting. This difficulty is accentuated by the principle of free movement of persons inside the EEC, and by the possibility that heavily labour-exporting countries, like Turkey, may sooner or later become members of the Community. That is one important source of incompatibility among national forecasts, and it consequently furnishes an argument in favour of trying to construct a Community-scale forecast which would, in effect, apply a coherence test to the national forecasts.

The geographical aspects seem at first sight simpler, since land does not move (though the juridical ownership of it does), and since the internal frontiers of the Community are, in the absence of territorial claims, stable. So one might conclude that totting up national forecasts of land use (particularly for urbanisation) would necessarily lead to a coherent total at the European level. But there are two exceptions to this rule. The first follows from the existence of migratory move-ments – among the active population, like workers in frontier zones, and among the inactive, like retired people – for which the sum of national forecasts might come to a non-zero result. The second excep-tion concerns the resources one might call common or not appro-priated, like stocks of fish beyond national zones, the atmosphere, and international waterways. These resources present a problem in that they could give rise to mutually incompatible claims or uses by two or more member states. Since they are not yet generally the object of explicit forecasting, this difficulty has not yet been clearly felt, but there is no doubt that here too the sum of national forecasts need not necessarily lead to a correct Community forecast. That is the second field in which the application of a coherence test would be justified.

As regards goods and services, it could be that the sum of the exports to its Community partners foreseen by each member differs from the sum of the foreseen imports over all member states. This risk has been increased by the oil crisis, which would lead the Western European nations to 'export their deficits' by reducing purchases and boosting sales. Now it is clear that the sum of these courses of action would lead to results which are incompatible with the expectations of the separate countries. The problem has certainly not gone unob-served, but its solution is hindered by the fact that the national foreign trade forecasts of the member countries do not always dis-tinguish between the EEC and the rest of the world. This obstacle has been surmounted by the European Commission's Study Group on Medium-Term Economic Assessments, which has devised a coherence test taking as its point of departure the total volume of *imports* foreseen by the member countries for 1978, and inferring from it the proportion which, according to past trends, should go to swell intra-EEC export flows. The result represents the fraction of total imports which is assumed to be covered by exports out of the EEC. The relation between this future result and the total of exports going out of the EEC allows us to see whether the expected growth of the latter is implausible.

It is clear therefore that the compilation of Community sectoral forecasts does not pose especially arduous problems and the risks of incoherence are fairly limited. As for what sectors should be tackled first, this must depend on an assessment of urgency which can most usefully be made when the work is about to start. No doubt at the moment energy and agriculture would be high on the list, but that is only at the moment. Five years ago it would have been environment, and two years hence there may have been another 'crisis', perhaps in other raw-material dependencies or in labour mobility. Owing to the crisis-oriented way in which affairs have been managed until now, accents tend to shift rapidly. As for the most serious methodological difficulty – the interrelation of economic and geographical aspects – this stems not from the Community-wide character of the forecasts but from the present state of our knowledge.

3. EEC LEVEL: FROM SECTORAL TO COMPREHENSIVE FORECASTS

Technically, the work at this stage would be the same as that at (1), namely the integration of national sectoral forecasts into national comprehensive forecasts. This is the stage which would provide some of the teleonomies suggested in the Introduction; it would define the first cone, and it should be conducted so as to provide the sharpest separation of the range of the 'impossible' from the range of the 'possible'.

4. FROM NATIONAL TO EEC LEVEL: COMPREHENSIVE FORECASTS

This work should be done as a check on stage (3) above and as a frame of reference for whatever integration of extra-Community forecasting has to be attempted. Since the national comprehensive forecasts do not yet really exist, it could not be started as soon as (3).

Our era is characterised by two great groups of changes now in progress. One is the new insistence in Western Europe on greater social relevance in government policies, and on reduced human inequality. The other comprises the increasingly 'systemic' nature or interconnectedness of society's problems and the emergence of a 'world system' in which no country can ever again be an island unto itself, and in which a new volatility of social structures is bound to create more and more discontinuities in the fabric of human history. These two clusters constitute a strikingly new environment for collective action. They make some older concepts obsolete and call for fresh approaches.

'Social relevance' means that the members of a polity increasingly expect public policy to make a real difference in their condition in a direct, tangible way. This expectation is at variance with conventional styles of policy in which outcomes are expressed and measured by the amount of resources used. By contrast, its fulfilment requires *result-oriented* policy making. This implies that consciously collected information about past or current results is taken into account while making decisions, which is in itself a kind of Copernican revolution in the world of politics. Among other things, it would imply that the goals (instead of the means) would have to be specified in meaningful terms, and that policy evaluation would be done on a regular basis.

The drive for greater equality is bound to affect public policy, because policy has so far usually been assessed by looking at its *average* outcomes. There is now a greater concern for its distribution among various nations, age groups, sexes, socio-economic classes, residential areas, and so on.

The 'systemic' character of social issues means the well-known, though often ignored, interrelations typical of advanced societies where developments in one sector both influence and are influenced by many other sectors. The traditional picture of a direct relationship between means and goals has to give place to a more complex vision, in which any policy or programme may be helped or hampered by what happens in others, on which it may in turn have a number of positive and negative effects. Hence the current interest in impact assessments comparing alternative systems (in production, transportation, service delivery, etc.) in terms of their comparative advantages and disadvantages.

The world is now at last perceived to be a single system, an international configuration in which the effects of trends or events in one region are disseminated very fast into the others. The more one sees things this way, the less can one ignore extra-national and extra-EEC forces, or the external impacts of domestic and EEC policies, and the less can one believe, whether implicitly or explicitly, in uniquely national or EEC solutions. More and more, the existence of 'only one earth' requires that policy-makers, including the Community policy-makers, take factors and impacts outside Europe into consideration.

We have seen that the first consequence of the need for social relevance is that policy-design variables should reflect the effects on the 'target population' as closely as possible. At present this is not the case. To repeat an example used earlier: in health matters, the most widely used information is the amount of public and private expenditure allocated to medical care, which – although pleasantly precise, readily obtained, and easily compared to other expenditure – gives an indirect and distorted picture of the real health of the people. Expenditure on education is an equally bad way to measure the 'educatedness' of a generation.

One way of putting the few currently available social indicators to practical use would be to undertake social forecasting to obtain qualitative answers to such basic questions as: in which direction are the constituent factors of the welfare of the Europeans likely to develop in the future? Are they likely to progress, stagnate, or regress? Before launching a series of forecasts intended to delineate the range of possible futures in various areas of social concern (the goal-choice cone) it might be worthwhile to undertake a thorough assessment of the present situation and recent history.

There is no meaningful break between future and past, but rather a continuum which unites what has existed until now and a plurality of imaginable futures. Yet, though the fabric may be continuous, certain threads may be broken, and texture and colours may change abruptly. We cannot predict where and how such changes will occur in the future, but the least we can do is to draw upon the lessons derived from the route travelled so far, and then to speculate.

Two key problems of orienting social policy towards results are perhaps best tackled by looking at the past first, identifying the components of European welfare (using, e.g., the OECD List),[1] and gauging the extent to which what we see indicates 'progress'. The first problem is that of the difference between intermediate consumption (allocations) and end product (result).

If we want to know how the health of Europeans has changed (improved or deteriorated) since, say, 1955, we must first 'operationalise' the concept of health. Unfortunately, most of the available data relate to the technical, financial, and human *means* allocated to the health care delivery system, representing what the economists would call 'intermediate consumption', while – as discussed earlier – the variable of concern is of course the effect or 'end product' called health.

The second problem is that of choosing a method of non-monetary weighting for the things measured. When dealing with market goods and services, it is possible to synthesise the diversity of upward and downward movements in different sectors into a single aggregate, by

[1] 'List of Social Concerns Common to Most OECD Countries' (Paris: OECD, 1973).

weighting the contribution of each sector through the market price of its output. This enables us to calculate the GNP and, for instance, the way it changes owing to increased industrial and tertiary output on the one hand and a decline in agricultural employment on the other. It is hard to transpose this approach to an area like that of health, even though one is faced with the same kind of problem, i.e. that of measuring changes in opposite directions by a single aggregate figure: it can happen that death rates drop at the same time that disability among the elderly increases. Certainly the utilisation of 'shadow prices' makes it possible to make certain comparisons, but their use is strictly limited. For example, if the 'value' of the supplementary years of a working person is represented by the wage he or she earns, people outside the labour force would be misrepresented seriously. The difficulties become even more formidable when one tries to compare changes in dissimilar social concerns (like crime, communications, transportation, and pollution). This is why it makes no sense to synthesise these divergent developments arbitrarily into some kind of social GNP by assigning 'market values' to non-market outputs (see II.15 below). The only reasonable course is to translate the developments as well as one can into (non-monetary) social indicators, leaving everyone to make his own weighting in view of the diversity of past and future developments. (We will meet exactly the same problem in connection with effect or impact assessment.)

The result-oriented approach makes sense only if the studies are conducted not once and for all but steadily or at regular intervals. The accumulation of social knowledge thus obtained would be not only of scientific interest but also of the highest political value, because it would provide the Community with a collective feeling of its 'present' state, and thus of a shared future. One possible form for these enquiries into European welfare might be the gradual development of a social report, published at regular intervals (for instance every two years) as part of and backing for the forecasting or teleonomies, which would not aim immediately at extensive coverage but would proceed step by step, dealing first with the more tractable aspects of the matter.

For policy *evaluation*, social monitoring is not sufficient. To stick to the same example: states of health in a country depend on many factors apart from health care delivery (for instance, environmental variables and life-styles). There is a separate case to be made for evaluative studies. Their aim would be to assess, about some condition of society, the amount which is due to a specific policy or programme, and the residual explainable in terms of other factors (including the effects, whether intended or not, of other policies). Policy evaluation could follow this pattern:

(1) Specification of the goals: that is to say, the desired future shape of a system, e.g. exploitation of technology, education, transport, agriculture (goal-choice cone – see Introduction).

(2) Translation of this desired shape into a certain number of indicators. These will often have to be tailor-made (location of 'goal' on the plane across the base of goal-choice cone).

(3) Rough estimation of the desired values of these indicators. (This is optional, for it may be sufficient to establish an ordinal ranking and to show the direction and sequence in which the indicators should move if the relevant policy is to be considered successful.)

(4) Determination of the real and the desired rates of approach to the goals (relevant to the means-choice cone).

(5) Measurement of the changes owing to the policies assessed. This is a difficult task, but it should be done whenever it is possible to compare the 'treated' with an 'untreated' sample (i.e. one not affected by the policy in question).

An insistent demand for social equality is indisputably part of the current *Zeitgeist* in Western Europe, and policy-making has increasingly to allow for it. Even policies explicitly focused on redistribution of income are still largely unconcerned about the real effects of the huge amounts of money they recycle every year as social cash benefits. Of great importance are also those sectoral policies that do not have clear egalitarian goals but that nevertheless strongly affect distribution. For instance, the discussion about revising the Common Agricultural Policy would be much improved if it could be based on adequate studies assessing its social and international distributive effects. Major new policies at EEC level, before being introduced, should therefore be assessed as to the way their various benefits and disbenefits are likely to be distributed among different social groups, different member nations, and different parts of the world outside the European Community.

One big advantage of the approach advocated here is that it aims to reveal the interactions among policies, and their expected and unexpected effects on any group of people. There are many ways of comparing alternative policies in terms of costs and effects, monetary and otherwise; we must emphasise again the importance of not forcing individual effects into the straitjacket of cash valuation or utility-weighted units. There are several reasons for this. Among them are that a single measure of effectiveness would conceal areas of strength or weakness in each solution and would rule out cross-impact comparisons between systems; that unquantifiable impacts would have to be excluded from the analysis, so they would have to be displayed in a different, 'softer', and possibly less convincing form; and that translating qualitatively different impacts into commensurate units implies value judgements by the analysts, which may or may not be visible and may or may not agree with those of the decision-makers. This last is especially troublesome in a political environment such as the European Community where one has to consider a diversity of decision-makers at different levels, and where development of agreement on the desired weighting or importance of various impacts is a significant part of the decision process itself. Therefore the procedure used for comparing the impacts should probably seek to show how the alternative policies would be ranked for each particular effect, rather than evaluating them by some common yardstick.

The increasing interdependence between the various parts of the world means that the approaches outlined above should be applied to the external policies of the Community as well as the internal ones. This implies, firstly, the identification of the constellation of policy goals (among which some trade-offs will have to be struck); secondly, a comparison among alternative policies; and thirdly, sensitivity analysis of the rankings thus obtained, to see whether they are substantially changed by taking into account different future world developments. This is a counsel of perfection, but without counsels of perfection even the moderate cannot be attained.

It is generally accepted that sound policy-making must take due consideration of the future under two aspects: as a potential outcome of current processes, and as the intended goal of deliberate actions. As explained at the end of the preceding chapter, it is very difficult to ensure that the results of forecasting are effectively used in the policy-making and planning process, and forecasting therefore runs a perpetual danger of degenerating into a substitute for action rather than contributing to it. No ready recipe exists to avoid this, but the more forecasting is rooted in the past, and the more securely it keeps hold of the distinction between the future results of our own actions (which we can control) and the future results of others' actions (which we cannot), the less likely is it to degenerate into an academic pastime.

In considering the priorities which should govern the inception of a programme of long-term forecasting for the European Community, we can use three pairs of complentary variables: First: past versus future. To look into the future is a basic requirement for effective collective action; an awareness of the past is indispensable. Second: process versus policy. Social reality is a mix (in varying proportions) of processes and policies – or, to use different language, of conditions and will. Third: EEC versus outer world. The European Community is, like every living entity, divided between the conflicting loyalties of what it owes to itself and what it owes to the outer world, and this tension is present everywhere, including the choices that can be made about how forecasting should be done.

By combining these three pairs of variables we obtain eight cells, each of which represents a field of activity for a future Europe Plus Thirty instrument.

	Past		Future	
	Intra-EEC	Outer world	Intra-EEC	Outer world
Processes	(1)	(2)	(3)	(4)
EEC policies	(5)	(6)	(7)	(8)

Cell 1: Social and other monitoring, in welfare terms where possible, within the Community.

Cell 2: Worldwide monitoring.

Cell 3: Exploratory facet of forecasting. ⎫ (Mainly Cone

⎬ of

Cell 4: Contextual exploratory forecasting. ⎭ goal choice)

Cell 5: Ex post facto evaluation of EEC internal policies.

Cell 6: Ex post facto evaluation of EEC external policies.

Cells 7 and 8: Policy analysis proper, combining goal definition, impact-assessment, and means choice (teleonomy as a whole).

This scheme is of course extremely simplified. A future Europe Plus Thirty cannot theoretically neglect any of the cells. But in practice cell 2 will have to be eliminated for systematic study; it is simply too vast. It must just be held present in the mind and interrogated when necessary. Cell 6 can also be eliminated, since Community policies towards the outer world really only began with the Yaoundé Convention of 1971 and are too recent to be assessed for the moment. The greatest attention must clearly be given to cells 7 and 8, and to the other four – that is, 1, 3, 4, and 5 – as backing and context for 7 and 8.

The question of the time horizon to be adopted by a continuing Europe Plus Thirty is a difficult one. The name 'Europe Plus Thirty' was never intended to suggest an exclusive concentration on the year which happens to be thirty years from now, a focussing of the beam precisely on thirty years ahead and never less or more. Figure 1 (at p. 14 of the Introduction) made this plain. In some fields it is extremely difficult to forecast (even in the general sense of the word used here) as much as thirty years on; in others it is both possible and necessary to look a century ahead. The real long-termers in forecasting are climate, population, education, environment, and transport (our railway systems are over a hundred years old, and in Rome there are two bridges, not only the location but the masonry of which has not changed in two thousand years, which still determine the flow of traffic in that city).

Long-term forecasting for the European Community should therefore start where short- and medium-term sectoral forecasting must leave off because of the increasing interdependence between sectors: at four or five years. It should leave off wherever it becomes impossible to say anything interesting about the matter in hand, which will be less than thirty years for some things and much more for others.

A more prolix but more correct title for Europe Plus Thirty would thus be: Parts of Western Europe, Seen in Context, Plus Anything-over-Four.

PART II
FIELDS FOR FORECASTING

1. *Introductory*

Integrated forecasting means two things: first, forecasting integrated well enough with the Community policy-making process to be of real help to those developing, implementing, and evaluating policy; and second, forecasting not limited to a single sector, like technology or economics, but encompassing all sectors relevant to the particular problem area in question and to the teleonomies described in the Introduction.

During the remaining sixteen chapters of this Part, the reader is invited to remember the overriding necessity of integration, in both these senses. By including so much material on these sixteen separate sectors, we risk his forgetting it; but that risk we have to take. Western Europe is not such a light or simple phenomenon that one can throw up an airy arch and say: 'Look, that will take the strain.' It is on the contrary old, heavy, hurtling, and complex; and a very great deal is known about it and all its parts. A proposal for forecasting which took little or no account of this weight and complexity of knowledge would not correspond with the scale of the problem.

Therefore, detail about the different sectors cannot be omitted. But before coming to that detail, we pause here and give (to use the jargon) a cross-impact matrix of the sectors, and three examples of problem-oriented intersectoral forecasting. The cross-impact matrix is the square in Figure 4 below. The sectors ('Climate', 'Population', etc.) are numbered to follow the order of the succeeding chapters. The influence of the sector at the head of each column on each of the sectors down the left-hand side is shown thus:

Large

o Smaller but real

Negligible

By 'influence' is meant two things: (1) Would a change in the top sector entail a change in the left-hand sector? (2) Does the top sector make demands on the left-hand sector?

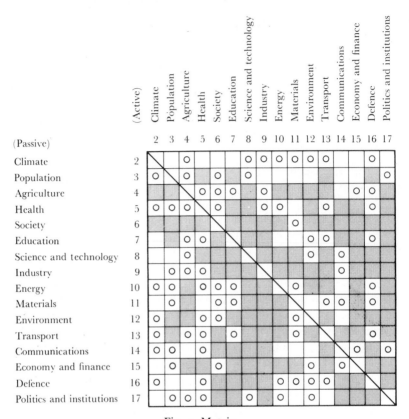

Fig. 4. Matrix

All such schematic formulations have to be matters of opinion, and the reader will no doubt find things to quarrel with in this one. For instance, the statement that a change in climate would have a negligible effect on industry is debatable. It is to be read as meaning that a change in climate of the kind one might plausibly expect within the next thirty years is unlikely to have a much more than negligible effect on the kind of industry we might plausibly expect to have over the same period. And so on. This is to return to the language of the Introduction, the language of conditionality and probability.

One might attempt to set out in words what this matrix says in signs, but it would be a long job. Somewhere about the middle of a verbal account, you might find such a statement as:

A change in energy-consumption patterns would probably have some effect on the climate (through thermal and particulate pollution), but not much effect on population trends; a change in energy prices would have a big effect on agriculture (through fertiliser and mechanisation), but only a smaller one on health (hypothermia among the old if there's a price increase). Energy patterns certainly greatly affect the shape of society, since our sort of society depends on using energy to turn one thing into another. Though education as such demands virtually no energy, the intelligent planning of energy production and consumption requires that science and technology respond quickly to urgent needs, and of course industry (as we have just remarked) depends entirely on energy. Energy conditions the demand for raw-material imports in Western Europe to a very large degree, as no one needs reminding; the main event of the last three years in the relations between Europe and the Third World was when the latter insisted on talking about all their raw-material exports, not just oil. Energy production and transmission strongly affect the environment through water and air pollution, and through pipelines and grids. Energy directly affects transport policy via tankers, ports, railways, and roads; and through the price mechanism it affects the 'modal split' – that is, whether people go by car or by bus. It doesn't affect communications much; they use amazingly little energy. The economies of our countries, and our financial institutions, are still reeling and look like going on reeling for some time under the energy price changes of 1973–4. Defence, both in industry and in operation, is a noticeable but not very considerable energy-consumer, and, though it is probable that our political institutions and customs would survive even quite major changes in the consumption, price, and technology of energy, yet if we ever have to go back to firewood and horses, political and institutional changes would become desirable.

The same sort of verbal statement can be made about each of the vertical columns in the matrix. Equally, a converse sort of statement can be made about each of the horizontal lines, the lines about things affected as opposed to the columns about things affecting.

To make a sectoral forecast about either a single vertical column or a single horizontal line, one would have to take all the others into account, deriving values from data and playing around with alternative values, relations, and probabilities, as discussed in Part I above. Integrated forecasting is doing that not with one column or one line but with all of them at once, and though it would not be impossible to talk about that in words (it is not impossible to talk about anything in words) it would be so colossally time-consuming that the effort would be absurd. Mathematics is the only language capable of handling such a wealth of relationships in a comprehensible way, and only later can language take over again.

We turn now (and still in words) to three examples of the way in which partially integrated forecasting might be carried out to meet particular demands, or to solve particular problems, as opposed to fully integrated forecasting for the teleonomies described in the Introduction.

Our three examples are (1) a high-speed railway system, (2) a low-energy-use scenario, and (3) the effects of different education patterns, especially on labour. The first, on transport, is in fact already being carried out; it is the so-called COST 33 programme undertaken jointly by the Community and OECD, already mentioned in chapter I.3 above. It is a well-thought-out job. The other two, on energy and education, are not being done anywhere, but they well might be. They are thus naturally described more tentatively than the first, which has already had the benefit of much skilled definition and refinement.

A TRANSPORT EXAMPLE

This example is very much technology-oriented and is in fact close to a technology assessment. A proposal has been made for the construction of a very-high-speed railway network for passenger movement between major European cities. This proposal would require co-operation between governments and probably major government assistance in several ways. It is therefore relevant to ask what long-term effects such a development would have on the volume and pattern of passenger traffic by road, rail, and air; on transport costs (including man-hours spent travelling), energy consumption, accidents, air pollution, land use, and regional distribution of population and of employment; and on the cities served by the system. In order to answer these questions, one needs to forecast events both with and without the proposed railway system. (Of course, there may be more than one possible 'without' situation.)

In this example the *endogenous variables* consist of the railway system and other transport and planning factors that could be controlled and specified as part of the policy on which the forecast is based. They are primarily technological.

The *Exogenous variables* include:

(1) size of population by country;
(2) distribution of population by region;
(3) distribution of population between urban and rural areas;
(4) distribution of population by household size;
(5) gross regional product by region;
(6) average household income by region;
(7) distribution of household income by income group;
(8) proportion of car-owning households by region;
(9) unit operating costs (in real terms) of cars, aircraft, and railways.

The *fixed factors* include those parts of the transport system not subject to change: geographical features, climate, social habits and conventions, political conditions, and economic policies.

The *dependent factors* are then those effects which the forecaster is asked to forecast, i.e. traffic volume, costs, energy consumption, etc.

It is clear that the endogenous variables must be carefully defined and specified as forecasting assumptions. The exogenous variables must be forecast for the target year. The fixed factors must be identified. Then, given these three sets of factors, functional relationships must be found between them and the dependent variables. It is these relationships which constitute the technical part of the forecasting procedure.

Now, in the example cited, the transport system provides most of the endogenous variables and the fixed factors; these parts of the work lie within the normal competence of a transport specialist. But the exogenous variables, on which the results of the forecast depend, consist mainly of matters outside his expertise. He is not the best person to make forecasts of population and income, nor of the prices of materials and labour upon which future vehicle operating costs will depend.

Again, while some of the dependent variables are transport variables, others are not and lie outside the transport specialist's field, e.g. environmental effects and regional policy issues. Transport studies often raise social and political issues which are all too easily ignored in a straight technological approach.

The planner making an integrated transport forecast of the type described should be able to draw on other forecasters for the demographic and economic forecasts he requires; and in the development of functional relationships between the dependent variables and other factors, assistance should be obtainable from specialists in the various fields involved. These relationships are of value to both sides: the environmentalist is as interested in the effect of transport on the environment as is the transport planner. In other studies it will be the environmentalist who comes to the transport specialist for a forecast; for him, transport may be an exogenous variable.

A high-speed passenger transport system is only one among many transport systems and inevitably has repercussions on the development of the others, so that fixed factors might have to be treated as variables in a second round of the study.

Thus, for this particular example of a high-speed railway project, one sees the need for close collaboration between forecasters working separately in the demographic, macro-economic, energy, regional planning, and environmental fields as well as in the transport sector itself.

AN ENERGY EXAMPLE

Suppose that the European Commission decided to examine deliberate policies to reduce energy growth rates substantially. Studies of this kind have already been made in the U.S.A. and have been started in many European countries. A question might be put as follows: given a specified (low) rate of energy growth, what effects would be expected on certain energy-using sectors?

Within the Commission and its affiliated institutions there is much expertise on how to design lower growth rates for energy *supply*. These questions fall within the energy sector. What the Commission now lacks is the expertise to consider the multitude of impacts that low energy growth would make on energy-*using* sectors – that is, on the demand side of the energy equation. These impacts are certain to be complex, with effects that reverberate throughout many different sectors. They demand integrated forecasting.

This example is one in which scenario-writing would play an important part, although systems-modelling would no doubt come into the picture as well.

To illustrate, we give here just some of the questions that would have to be considered by forecasters working within and across various subject areas.

Agriculture is a fairly energy-intensive industry. Would the use of machinery and fertilisers decrease and the use of labour increase? What effects would the latter change have on land-use planning, transport policies, and the like? Since animal products are the most energy-intensive, would countries like the Netherlands be more affected than others which are predominantly cereal-producers? Since more intensive production of any kind increases energy use, what are the implications for broad policies of food self-sufficiency and of food imports? Could agriculture itself become a substantial supplier of energy, through the conversion of animal and vegetable wastes into fuels, or even by growing crops intended solely for fuel production? In the European Middle Ages, brushwood was cultivated for fuel, and cow-dung is still the main household fuel of India. Again, what are the regional implications?

Industry uses energy-intensive materials and has increasingly replaced labour by energy-intensive machinery. Would there be a partial return to more labour-intensive methods, and if so, with what implications for employment rates, settlement patterns, the siting of industry, transport, and so forth? Would there be significant shifts in material use, and with what effects on trade (e.g. natural rubber and textiles in place of synthetics)? Which sectors of industry would be most

affected? Might some industries (e.g. aluminium) respond by trans-
ferring out of Europe? What changes would there be in the relative
prices of different products and services? And how might these affect
consumer choices? Would they create new patterns of 'selective
growth'?

Transport would certainly experience major impacts. These in turn
could affect regional planning, urban forms, the siting of services such
as 'out-of-town' shopping centres, and (not least) tourism. Forecasts
would need to ask searching questions about the degree to which
transport industries can adapt – e.g. by producing more energy-
efficient vehicles – and the degree to which public policies could be
influential – e.g. the promotion of public as opposed to private transport. One would also need to examine the possible role of communications in reducing the need for personal travel.

Environment and pollution impacts might be considerable. Lower
energy growth would alleviate many pollution problems which arise
directly from the burning of fuels, but it might create new ones.
Pollution abatement itself consumes energy: would industries be able
to 'afford' it? New products designed to help save energy might impose health risks on workers: the use of the highly toxic weed-killer
paraquat to raise yields on the farm is a notable example. Many
similar effects would need to be forecast.

To what extent could technological innovation be directed towards
more energy-efficient production, such as enzyme technology, integrated 'total energy' systems, more durable 'long-life' products,
recycling techniques, and so forth? What would be the effects of any
of these changes on other sectors – employment, industry, materials,
etc. – and on energy demand itself?

In these and other ways the forecaster in the energy sector needs
the close collaboration of forecasters working in other sectors, just as
they in turn need his particular expertise.

AN EDUCATION–EMPLOYMENT EXAMPLE

This third example is the most challenging of all since it has to deal
with many unknowns. It would require a highly 'creative' and informed group of professionals to come up with results.

Suppose that the Commission wished to explore the implications of
certain proposed educational programmes. A question might be put
to Europe Plus Thirty as follows: what are the implications for the
active population of a raised level of formal education and a system
of recurrent education?

This question would first have to be set in an analytical framework, which would require refinement of the question itself. Secondary education is now universal in most Western European countries, and higher education is fast becoming an activity for the general public. Schemes providing for educational leaves of absence and for family support during these leaves are being explored or legislated for in several countries. In short, given our current knowledge of the numbers of people that will most probably fill each cohort, and the likelihood of their attaining given educational levels, we may expect a labour force with a higher level of formal education at the end of the century, and one that continually updates its skills and knowledge through recurrent, job-oriented training (see II.7 below).

The implications of these dependent variables are complicated and extensive, and they reveal connections with several other sectors. Here is an illustrative list of these implications and connections, many of which are dealt with in greater detail in the following chapters.

Would women continue increasingly to work outside the home? What changes could be expected in work patterns (especially if women choose part-time work), in family life, and in the demand for day-care centres, pre-school programmes, etc.? What would be the effect of less maternal care for infants, and more institutional care, on their characters when they grow up?

How would a raised level of education affect the ability of the individual to cope with modern society? In what ways would improved education increase awareness of the functioning of society and social relationships, and therefore of how better to make one's way in the world? Examples might be the use of contraception, access to official 'channels' and programmes, and to some degree the reduction of accident rates and improved health. Would a generally raised level lead to increased competition for the good things of life or to an increased acceptance that they must be shared equally?

To what extent would access to more education for all lead to increased pursuit of education for its own sake? If education becomes less important in securing individual financial security (see below), would it then be thought of by many students less as a means to more money and more as an end in itself?

To what extent would a shift of emphasis on the intrinsic value of education mean decreased educational equality? If education loses its force as a means to financial security, would it become less attractive to those in 'underprivileged' positions? Would the economically disadvantaged therefore tend not to take advantage of educational opportunities?

What would be the economic impact of recurrent education in terms of GNP, public expenditure, etc.? How would it affect the cost of teachers and the cost of physical facilities and their modification?

What effects would raised levels of education have on work organisation? Would better-educated workers demand changes in job design and organisation, greater participation, etc.? To what extent would these changes include rotation and different mixes of tasks?

Would there be an increased imbalance between the number of graduates and the number of traditionally appropriate openings for them? If people with advanced education begin to take 'lower' positions, what effect would this have on pay differentials between, for example, manual and non-manual work? What repercussions would this have on the aspirations of the less-educated worker and on job design?

How would raised formal education affect the doing of unpleasant work? How would 'dirty' or unattractive work be redesigned or upgraded to be more attractive? Alternatively, to what extent could or should it be moved to other parts of the world? How would this affect foreign worker arrangements and the balance of trade, and what would be the political considerations?

What kind of provision for mid-career education could be expected, and how would such provision increase? How would the job training programmes and paid leaves of absence for recurrent education bring about increased flexibility in terms of substitution for the worker, re-entry into his trade, etc.?

These three examples illustrate the sort of issues, and their relationship with neighbouring expertise, that Europe Plus Thirty could and should tackle.

The following series of short chapters now considers the sixteen different fields of human activity or knowledge, and asks in each case whether forecasting in that field is a necessary part of integrated forecasting; if so, whether it is being sufficiently done elsewhere or needs to be done by Europe Plus Thirty; and, if the latter, what should be done about it.

2. *Climate*

We start this series with a discussion of the possibility of climatic forecasting, for obvious reasons: the climate is the final and absolute arbiter of human destinies. If it changes, there is no fighting against it; we just have to change our way of life or, in extreme cases, go somewhere else (but where?). To know the signs and the causes of changes in the climate and to be able to anticipate them would be helpful indeed.

But first a word about terminology. In meteorology, a long-term weather forecast means a week, or at most a month. In climatology, it means at least thirty years and probably more. For the time scale of Europe Plus Thirty, which we have defined as four years and over, we must obviously adopt climatological language.

From time to time rather abrupt shifts of climatic patterns are observed. The last one happened between 1959 and 1963 and was made sharper by the eruption of the Agung volcano in Bali in 1963. In this shift there was a drop of 0.56 °C in the average temperature of the lower troposphere (0–5,500 metres) over the whole zone between latitudes 65° N and 90° N.

Between 1920 and 1960 climatic conditions had been unusually favourable, and this tends to make us forget that in the last 500–600 years considerably worse conditions prevailed. What has happened may happen again; we have to understand why it happens, and that means looking at the historical data to see if patterns and causes can be established. Instrumental observations exist from about 1680 onwards. Those aside, there are enough reliable indirect sources to allow us to evaluate the climatic development during the last millennium; for instance weather diaries, tree rings, pollen in peat-bogs, cereal prices. With the help of this 'proxy' data, Lamb[1] has estimated the following values for middle England, compared with the period 1901–50, in °C.

	Temperature			Precipitation	
Time period	Winter	Summer	Year	Summer	Year
4000 B.C.	+1.0	+2.0	+1.6	+15%	+10%
A.D. 1150–1300	−0.1	+0.9	+0.7	−15%	+3%
A.D. 1600–1700	−1.1	−0.5	−0.7	0	+2%

The Middle Ages (c. 900–1300) were clearly warmer and drier than today in the warm season (vegetation period): wine was produced in England, and Vikings briefly colonised the east coast of America. After several discontinuities, with anomalies that even by today's standards were extreme (especially 1310–50 and 1428–60), there was a transformation which began in about 1560. This cold and snowy period,

[1] H. H. Lamb, 'The early medieval warm epoch and its sequel', *Palaeogeography, Palaeoclimatology, Palaeoecology*, 1 (1965), pp. 13–37.

exaggeratedly referred to as a 'little ice age', lasted with a few small breaks until 1850; it was marked by strong precipitation and a high water level of the lakes in the Mediterranean area, in the Near East, and in Southern Russia; drift ice blocked the coast of Iceland for five to six months a year and even advanced to the Faeroes. The warm period in the Middle Ages, with noticeably less storms on the Atlantic and the disappearance of drift ice along the East Greenland coast south of *c.* 70° N, brought about good conditions for cultivation in most European countries, but the period of anomalies at the end of the Middle Ages and especially in the 'little ice age' brought many crop failures, especially in marginal lands such as Iceland, Scotland, and Norway. The average growing season was shortened by several weeks. The appearance of worldwide stratospheric turbidity after volcanic eruptions (e.g. 1601, 1783, 1815, 1883, and 1912) led to much adverse summer weather.

The development of the climate in the northern hemisphere in the past fifteen years has shown that the forty-year period 1920–60, usually thought of as a 'normal' period (people's youth is always normal), was in fact abnormal, especially if related to the last 500–600 years. The latest changes correspond more to the climate of the latter half of the nineteenth century than to the decades before 1960. They have had a strong economic impact upon some areas (India, the Sahel belt). The recent cooling of the Arctic (by about 1–2 °C on a yearly basis, by 3–6 °C for the winter months) has led over several years to a shift of climatic regimes, at least in Africa and large parts of South Asia, affecting the water balance.

The sensitivity of agricultural production to anomalies of climate – such as drought or shortening of the growing season – is hardly less today than it was two centuries ago. Recent developments give good examples of the political consequences of food shortages: the revolutions in Ethiopia and Mali, and the crisis caused by surreptitious Soviet grain purchases in America in 1973 and 1974. An earlier climatically induced political event was the great emigration to America. The potato famine of 1846 in Ireland was caused by a period of extreme humidity during the weather-sensitive phase of the potato blight. Today, the possibility cannot be excluded that the world's grain harvest might be reduced, after simultaneous climatic anomalies, by about 10 per cent in one year or by 15 per cent or even more in two consecutive years. Taken with the continuing population growth rate, this might eventually lead to widespread social unrest, to increased international tensions, and to their expression in, for instance, increased terrorism.

The last Ice Age itself was only 17,000 years ago. The ice disappeared 8,500 years ago in Scandinavia and 6,500 years ago in Canada. 6,000

4-2

years ago there was a worldwide warm period which lasted for several centuries. In this period the Arctic drift ice retreated to the north coasts of Spitsbergen and Greenland. The transition between the Ice Age and the post-glacial warm period between 12,000 and 10,500 years ago was characterised by very abrupt climatic changes, and the decisive upheavals may have taken place within a single lifetime. Later climatic changes, too, apparently did not occur slowly, but rather rapidly in the form of often-repeated large-scale weather patterns. This situation leads one naturally to consider whether anomalous atmospheric conditions could be forecast for a whole year and, more to our purpose, whether assertions can be made about the longer-term development of the climate.

In contrast to the weather of a day or a week, the word 'climate' is used for the average atmospheric conditions of a decade or a 'normal' thirty-year period. By climatic forecasting we understand periods of one year and beyond. Whether a realistic forecast on a physico-mathematical basis is possible, and if so how, is being actively discussed in learned circles. Monthly forecasts are being made by different meteorological offices, in the U.S.A., the U.K., West Germany, and the U.S.S.R., with empirical and semi-empirical methods; they are not coordinated. The results are only partially satisfactory: temperature forecasts are slightly better than random guesses, whereas it is difficult to maintain that rainfall forecasts are an improvement on chance. Most long-term forecasts are published only in learned and official circles, and are of only limited use for economic planning. The position today is that short-term weather forecasts (24–48 hours) drawn up by numerical (physico-mathematical) methods can be extended with some skill to forecasts up to about five days. Some experiments have indicated that by including yet more physical processes in the models eight- to ten-day forecasts can be achieved. This work is being carried forward at a new institute for medium-range weather forecasting at Reading, in the U.K., financed by the governments of the European Community countries plus Austria, Greece, Portugal, Spain, Sweden, Switzerland, and Yugoslavia.

In many countries, man's ability intentionally to modify the weather has been extensively investigated during the last decades. It is possible to dissipate supercooled fogs (which, however, are only 5 per cent of all fogs); but many other programmes – artificial rainfall, hail prevention, mitigation of tropical hurricanes – have led to controversial results.[1] This is all the more so if one takes into account the large and

---

[1] Commission on Atmospheric Sciences, National Research Council, *Weather and Climate Modification: Problems and Progress* (Washington: National Academy of Sciences, 1973). W. N. Hess (ed.), *Weather and Climate Modification* (New York: Wiley, 1974).

sometimes unexpected side-effects. Some types of clouds along the upwind slopes of mountains can be stimulated to increased rainfall; but this means only a redistribution of rainfall, at the expense of downwind areas. In the absence of cloud-forming processes – e.g. during droughts or in arid countries, where it is most wanted – artificial stimulation of effective rainfall is (and will remain) unsuccessful.

At any rate, more research is needed before reliable results for the operational use of weather modification can be obtained. Because of the dimensions of decisive experiments in an unlimited atmosphere, the social and legal aspects at national and international levels should receive increasing attention. There is already a proposal at the UN to ban the military use of weather modification; its 'peaceful' use may be just as much in need of regulation.

Two of the most urgent purposes of mathematical models are to describe the possible effects of unpredictable natural events and to foresee the inadvertent and intentional impacts of man on the climatic system. Unpredictable natural events include volcanic eruptions, fluctuations in the sun's radiation in different bands of the spectrum, and, possibly, partial surges of the Antarctic ice. Human impacts include the influx of energy and carbon dioxide; air pollution, including the effect of supersonic transport on the stratosphere; transformation of vegetation, e.g. in the equatorial rain forests; and large reservoirs, river-turning, and irrigation projects.

These 'sensitivity studies'[1] – i.e., mathematical experiments on the response of the model to such events – are an indispensable step towards long-term climatic forecasts. They may be useful for some socio-economic decisions, especially for projects dealing with climate and weather modification, and for estimates of the climatic effects of particles in the air, of the carbon dioxide content, and of thermal pollution. To test these models we need meteorological and oceanographic observations in largely predigested form.

For the development of climate forecasting models, we need at present a series of 'sensitivity studies' to which the results of model calculations and forecasting in the socio-economic field can be subjected. Or, again, one can feed the results of climatological models into an agricultural production model. An empirical model with regional dependencies is in development in the U.S.A., at the Department of Environmental Sciences of the University of Wisconsin at Madison. Further investigations of the social consequences of

---

[1] We are speaking here not of the sensitivity with which the model represents reality but of the degree to which one group of variables as represented in the model shows itself sensitive to changes in others.

climatically conditioned famines are being mounted in international cooperation. A climatic forecast can be prepared with a loose connection to other sectors, and the results can then be put into multisectoral models, and the other way round. The results of the various alternative inputs can then serve as a basis for politico-economic discussion.

Climatic forecasting is not simply extended weather forecasting. It needs to include data on physical processes at the interfaces between atmosphere, ocean, ice, and the upper layers of the solid earth. Research on this – empirical as well as on a model basis – is progressing. The comprehensive models which have been developed so far are capable of taking the interaction between atmosphere and ocean into consideration; they enable us to outline a fairly realistic simulation of the existing climate, even if the mesh of the grid is still too coarse. But a satisfactory climatic forecast cannot be expected from them; we still need improved simulations of the physical processes, but the tremendous amount of calculations required is prohibitive. Undigested data reach the meteorological offices in the range of hundreds of millions a day. So we need to reach simultaneous solutions in a system of at least seven non-linear differential equations at several hundred thousand grid points. The world is represented by some ten thousand grid points, each representing about 400 km of the world's surface horizontally and 2 km vertically. There are six to twelve levels in the atmosphere alone, going up to 30 km, and the interaction between the different levels must be taken into account. All small and medium-sized processes have to be parameterised, i.e. expressed as functions of larger processes. Even for the most efficient computers the time needed for a result is about 10 per cent of the forecast time, which for our thirty-year purposes would mean that a computer would need several years just to work out the calculations. Meteorology's demands on computers are far greater than those of other sciences, but many experts hope that the development of new model types on a statistical–dynamical base will bring improvements.

Given all this, we cannot say whether or to what degree climatic forecasting for a year or a decade will become possible. At least two important climatogenic processes cannot reasonably be forecast: large volcanic eruptions (e.g. Krakatoa 1883, Agung 1963) and possible fluctuations in the sun's radiation. But progress in other fields has been so remarkable and so encouraging that the majority of experts have recently reached a conditionally positive attitude to the possibility of climatic forecasts.[1]

[1] World Meteorological Organization – Global Atmospheric Research Programme, *Conference on Physical Basis of Climate and Climate Modelling*, Stockholm 1974 (GARP Publication Series no. 16, 1975).

Understanding the way man himself inadvertently modifies weather and climate has become one of the most challenging tasks of meteorology. Since the local climate depends to a large extent on the physical properties of the underlying surface and of its vegetation and soil, any substantial modification of these can alter it. A good example is an irrigated oasis: here the maximum temperature is 3–5 °C lower than in the surrounding desert, while the relative humidity increases by 20–30 per cent. Deforestation, overgrazing of natural grasslands (after the destruction of the great predator animals and the domestication of goats, cattle, etc.), and irrigation have caused considerable climatic changes during the last four to eight thousand years in Europe, the Mediterranean, the Near and Middle East, India, and China, over many millions of square kilometres.

Since the beginning of the industrial era, the emission of carbon dioxide from fossil fuels and of air pollution of various sorts, and the direct input of energy into the atmosphere (e.g. waste heat from power stations), have added substantially to the hitherto almost imperceptibly slow processes described above. The carbon dioxide content has increased from 290 to about 325 parts per million (ppm) and will (on present trends) reach the 400 ppm mark soon after the turn of the century.

In spite of the oil crisis, man-made changes in the climate[1] are expected to go on increasing, though perhaps more slowly. The exponential growth of population together with the industrialisation of the Third World and the raising of its living standards will be responsible for that, even if energy conservation and a near-zero (or even zero or negative) growth rate in the developed countries were to replace the recent trends.

The carbon dioxide storage capacity of the oceans, which at present absorb about half of the CO_2 produced by fossil combustion, is limited. Leading specialists expect that after a mixing period of about sixty years the stored CO_2 will be released into the air and that a fivefold increase of the air's CO_2 content or more might be expected in the second half of the next century.[2] These inadvertent man-made effects might then lead to a general warming, and to the retreat of the Arctic sea-ice into a position like that of the early Middle Ages. The diversion of fresh water for irrigation from the Siberian and Canadian rivers, if that were to occur on a large scale (and there are gigantic Soviet plans), would accelerate the retreat and thinning of the Arctic sea-ice. With a drastic increase of CO_2, even its central part, which has probably

[1] *Inadvertent Climate Modification: Report of the Study of Man's Impact on Climate* (SMIC) (Cambridge, Mass.: MIT Press, 1971).
[2] WMO–GARP Conference (see p. 88, n. 1).

remained constant during the last million years, could eventually disappear.[1] In this case a northward shift of all large-scale climatic belts by several hundred kilometres might be expected, together with a disappearance of the winter rains in the Mediterranean, the Near and Middle East, Soviet Central Asia, and California and Utah. Since at present about 8 per cent of the runoff waters from all continents is used by man, such a shift would necessitate, in many densely populated areas, a drastic adaptation to a new and unprecedented pattern of agriculture and water supply. (A major retreat or even the disappearance of the floating Arctic sea-ice would not cause a rise of the sea level, any more than would an ice-cube melting in a glass of whisky. The melting of the continental ice-sheet of Greenland, on the other hand, would; but this should be a very slow process lasting probably more than a thousand years.)

Now this catastrophic chain of events is something which *might* happen; nobody can say it *will*, and nobody can say how likely it is to happen. It is taken seriously in learned circles; that is all we can say at the moment, and that is good enough reason for the nations to press ahead with the construction of the models we have mentioned above, since only by their use can the probabilities of these events be made amenable to discussion. Until this is done, there can be no basis on which to consider whether we ought (because of this scenario) to start burning less fossil fuel now, or indeed to start planning for a new sort of economy in fifty years' time.

Of the other sectors in which Europe Plus Thirty will be forecasting, the one most obviously sensitive to climatic change is that of agriculture, forestry, and fisheries. The implications are of their nature even more critical for food storage than for food production. Health and energy consumption are also directly dependent on climate. Through these three – food, health, and energy – most of the other sectors considered in this section of our report depend indirectly on climate.

All this, of course, is a world job, not a specifically European one: it is mentioned here because it will (or should) provide the general framework within which, in climatology, Europe Plus Thirty must operate and draw its own local conclusions.

Climatology is therefore not a subject where Europe Plus Thirty, as the long-term forecasting agency of the European Community, will need to do its own forecasts. It will be enough if it knows what is going on elsewhere and encourages studies which are useful to it. It should from time to time call conferences or seminars on the subject, but it

[1] M. I. Budyko, *Izmeniya Klimata* (Leningrad: Gidrometeoroizdat, 1974). H. Flohn, 'Globale Energiebilanz und Klimaschwankungen', *Rhein.–Westfäl. Akad. Wiss. Vorträge* no. 234 (1973), pp. 75–117.

should not normally devote resources to research contracts or other down-line work.

3. *Population*

All planning for people, and thus all forecasting for people, must start (after considering climate) from some thoughts about how many people one is planning or forecasting for, and what age and sex balance there is or may be. Demographic forecasting is a twentieth-century phenomenon. Before that, some authors had concerned themselves with demographic development, but they were trying to discover a general 'law', like Malthus in his famous work, which explained population tendencies by means of a law presented generically and in a form hard to quantify. It was the product more of doctrines and theories of population than of a scientific approach to population forecasts. Towards the middle of the nineteenth century, an attempt at the mathematical formulation of a 'law' of population was made by the Belgians Quételet and Verhulst.[1] Verhulst applied a function which was known as *logistic*, and which was much used. Despite other attempts such as the recent recourse to the methods devised by Box and Jenkins,[2] for several decades demographers have more or less given up attempting to project the total size of a population by means of any more or less complex mathematical function. First of all, the rigidity of the function makes it impossible to take into account the fairly rapid changes to be encountered today in fertility and in spatial mobility in the industrialised countries. Secondly, the users of statistics are no longer satisfied by mere knowledge of the projected absolute size of the population. Increasingly, they need information about the development of other characteristics of the population: numbers of births and deaths, number of migrants, structure of the population by age and sex, etc. This is because demographic forecasts are needed today to work out *secondary* or *derived* forecasts (school attendance, working population, households, housing, etc.) which require at the very least a knowledge of the future population by sex and age.

During the two decades before the Second World War, demographers began to concentrate on working out forecasts by the 'component method'. Here the population was projected by age and sex,

---

[1] A. Quételet, *Sur l'homme et le développement de ses facultés, ou Essai de physique sociale*, 2 vols. (Paris: 1835). P. F. Verhulst, 'Notice sur la loi que la population suit dans son accroissement', in A. Quételet (ed.), *Correspondance mathématique et physique*, vol. 10 (Brussels: 1838).

[2] G. E. P. Box and G. M. Jenkins, *Time Series Analysis: Forecasting and Control* (San Francisco: Holden–Day, 1970).

differentiating the separate development of fertility, mortality, and, if relevant, of spatial mobility. Briefly, this method would start with a population broken down by age and sex according to a census taken at moment t (the 'vector' at moment t). A so-called 'projection matrix' is then applied to it, summarising the fertility, mortality, and possible spatial mobility within the span of a period of n years, and one thus obtains the population (projected) at the moment $t+n$. The 'population vector' can also take into account the structure of the population according to marital status, or any other demographic feature. The 'projection matrix' will take into account these added structures by incorporating probabilities of transition from one status to another. But in the absence of data such characteristics are in practice usually limited to structure by age and sex, sometimes taking marital status into account.

At present all industrialised countries use this component method for their demographic forecasts. It also gives information about demographic events (births, deaths, possibly marriages and migrations) that are likely to occur during each stage of projection. Lastly, it makes it possible to take into account the separate development of the components of the trend (fertility, mortality, spatial mobility), and it may incorporate the relations between them. In what follows, we shall restrict ourselves to this type of forecast.

Demographic forecasts are always worked out on the assumption that the population in question will never be struck by a catastrophe. Moreover, demographers frequently accentuate the uncertainty of their forecasts by basing them on multiple assumptions. In an extreme case, that of the Royal Commission on Population in Britain in 1950, no fewer than sixteen different forecasts were presented to the prospective users, based on different assumptions of probable development of the components of the demographic trend. The advice of the United Nations in this context is more modest; it consists of a medium forecast described as 'the most probable', flanked by two other forecasts described as 'high' and 'low'. International practice does not always follow the advice of the United Nations; in the forecasts coordinated by the OECD for example (see below) the UN's advice was at first heeded, then temporarily abandoned, and returned to in the two forecasts more recently published, in a slightly different form – that is, by applying 'correctives' to the forecasts based on the 'most reasonable' assumptions.

If one opts for several forecasts, it is necessary to stipulate clearly the assumptions used for each one, so as to allow the user to choose from among them the assumption which he regards as best suited to his purpose.

As we have seen, the component method is based on the knowledge, at a given moment, of the population (of a country, region etc.) broken down according to certain characteristics – generally age and sex, sometimes marital status. These data are provided by the census, the date of which usually determines the forecasts' point of departure. A 'projection matrix' is applied to this original population, made up of indices expressing the 'likelihood' of bearing a live child, of surviving, of migrating, etc., during the stage of projection selected. The projection is generally made stage by stage: the original population is usually projected over one or five years, then a projection matrix, identical to or different from the first one, is applied to this population (depending on whether the components are constant or not), and the operation is begun all over again. In extrapolating past trends, care is taken to make a retrospective analysis of the demographic situation by means of the appropriate demographic indices: these are usually obtained by combining the data provided by the records of registry offices with those provided by the census. These indices will then be projected into the future and will go to make up the projection matrix at each stage of the forecast.

The basic data are provided by official sources, as far as both the original population and the initial projection matrix are concerned, because only the state has the right to take a census or to record the basic facts of a person's existence (birth, marriage, change of residence, death).

Forecasts of *mortality* are based on an assessment of the trends of probability of survival, according to the age and sex group. This assessment can be made by keeping the probabilities constant, by extrapolating the indices observed in the past through graphic or mathematical graduation, by fixing a target level for future mortality, and by interpolation between the current level and the target level during each stage of the projection. Contrary to expectations, there has been a growth in the probability of death for men in certain age groups during the last two decades in industrialised countries. This novel situation has led some countries (such as the Netherlands) to draw up their mortality forecasts not only according to age and sex but also according to the causes of death. Despite the difficulties of this approach (determination of the main cause of death, modifications in the taxonomy of mortal illness) it is probably better than simple forecasting of mortality by age and sex. The question is not very important, since a mistaken assessment of mortality usually does not have such serious consequences for the validity of the overall forecasts as mistaken assessments of fertility and of migration trends.

Correct prediction of *fertility* remains a critical factor in demographic forecasts. In the past, forecasting was based essentially on the extra-polation of the fertility trends by calendar years according to the age of the women. The failure of these forecasts led demographers to question this approach. The fertility indices had been too much influenced during and after the war by postponements and catching-up of marriages and births; they therefore provided an inaccurate expression of the basic tendencies of procreative behaviour. To remedy this fault, two new approaches were introduced: firstly, the indices were made more specific, so as to take into account not only age but also the duration of the marriage and the number of children already born (Bourgeois-Pichat, Henry, Grabill);[1] secondly, separate forecasts were made for groups (cohorts) who were born or married within the course of the same year (Whelpton).[2] The two methods can be combined and their respective advantages considered. There is some diversity in the approaches adopted by the member countries of OECD. In the last series of forecasts it published, fertility was projected, according to the country, in terms of the age of women (sometimes by cohorts and sometimes not), in terms of age and marital status, and in terms of age at marriage and duration of marriage.

The problem is to forecast correctly not only the final number of children of each woman or couple, but also the changes in the spacing of the births. It was thought that this problem could be solved by questioning married women, using a special survey to discover their expectations about the size of their own families; but this proved vain. The family size expected does not remain constant, and furthermore the future birth rate will be largely the responsibility of women not yet married (and even not yet born). Again, couples' expectations about the spacing of births are somewhat vague, and statements about the expected size of a family seem to be a matter of fashion. The recent fall in fertility was not reflected in the level of expectations, which puts the latter's usefulness, as far as forecasting is concerned, seriously in doubt.

It is unlikely that forecasting would be improved by further increasing the specificity of the relevant indices; in any case, it is hard to imagine how the official statistics of the industrial countries could collect more information on the characteristics of births and parents

[1] J. Bourgeois-Pichat, *Mesure de la fécondité des populations*, Cahier INED no. 12 (Paris: Presses Universitaires de France, 1950). L. Henry, *Fécondité des mariages: nouvelle méthode de mesure*, Cahier INED no. 16 (Paris: Presses Universitaires de France, 1953). W. H. Grabill, 'Derivation of age-specific first marriage rates and of birth rates specific for order of birth and interval since first marriage or since birthdate of the first child' (unpublished white paper, U.S. Bureau of the Census; cited in D. S. Akers, 'Cohort fertility versus parity progression as methods of projecting births', *Demography*, vol. 2 (1965), p. 416).
[2] P. K. Whelpton, 'Cohort analysis and fertility projections', in *Emerging Techniques in Population Research* (New York: Milbank Memorial Fund, 1963), pp. 39–64.

without wearying the public and thus endangering the quality of the replies. There are two possible new approaches. One would be further to elucidate theoretical relations between measurements by calendar year and measurements by cohorts. The other, more important, would be to find out more about what determines procreative behaviour, and to go beyond the somewhat naive approach of simply asking women about the kind of family they desire and expect; different methods of research can be used to measure individual aspirations and expectations about fertility which have recourse mainly to projective tests, utility functions of the family size, variable schemes of family size formation incorporating the differential use of contraceptive methods, etc. Here forecasting merges into basic research into fertility and social values.

Migration forecasting remains the most delicate sector of demographic forecasting, for several reasons. First, data on migration, both internal and external, are far from satisfactory; indeed, few countries even require a declaration of residence. Second, clandestine immigration is common; and again, emigrants' departures often escape the statistical net. Lastly, migrations (particularly external ones) are influenced more than other demographic phenomena by economic and political considerations, so that simple extrapolation of past trends may be more misleading than usual. So predictions about this factor are bound to be unreliable; many countries project only the migratory balance (immigration minus emigration or vice versa) which is then broken down by age and added to the forecast. Others use a model estimate (a somewhat arbitrary round figure) of the migratory balance. Others again attempt to forecast the flow of immigration and emigration on the basis of more or less plausible assumptions. But all distinguish two types of forecast, one with migration and one without. The characteristics of emigrants being generally different from those of immigrants, we feel it is preferable to assess the two flows separately; the migratory balance also has the disadvantage of representing a difference between two quantities and may therefore fluctuate quite erratically. But the main problem is to learn more about the causes of migration, the better to be able to forecast it; these causes are complex, depending not only on economic conditions but also upon the individual characters of the migrants. Various econometric works have attempted to pinpoint them, but their usual defect is that they are based on aggregate variables which do not really explain individual behaviour. A more hopeful approach might be to incorporate into a single model the individual variables, and some contextual variables as indicators of socio-economic conditions. One would also have to include political factors, since one may expect the political powers (national or supranational) to intervene more. Once again, it would be difficult to separate demographic forecasting from basic research, this time into the causes of population movement.

When the forecast is a projection, there is no need to assess it (except in the sense of checking the calculations). When the forecast is a prediction, one may and most certainly must compare it with reality when the time comes. One can also compare an older prediction with a more recent one. Experience shows that long-term demographic predictions have not on the whole been very accurate: estimates of the course of fertility and of spatial mobility have often been very faulty. But demographic forecasts remain indispensable. Firstly, one can quite easily forecast the future size of the population now alive, if migration is not too important, which at once makes it possible to forecast, for example, the development of the school-age or working-age population in the short and medium terms. At the national level the external migration balance is usually fairly limited; thus in this case one can make forecasts based essentially on the natural trend of the population, which is less subject to the hazards of the economic and political situation than is migration. Lastly, although the future is as obscure to him as to everyone else, the demographer is probably better than others at avoiding obvious mistakes, such as neglecting the effect of the age structure on the trend, or forecasting fertility on the basis of transitory behaviour. And population forecasts may certainly serve as a basis for action, even if they only draw the attention of the politician to the consequences that the realisation of the basic assumptions of the forecast would have.

Various programmes for the coordination of and research in demographic forecasting have been set up, particularly by OECD and the United Nations. About every five years since 1957, the OECD has published a report on the population forecasts of its member countries. The OECD does not make these forecasts itself but coordinates those produced by the statistical agencies of the member governments. The member governments have all agreed in OECD to take a single starting point (1 January 1970, for the last forecasts published) and to produce the results according to a common pattern, with the same stages of projections, the same terms of projection, and the same presentation. They have not agreed on any particular methodology, but they have agreed that two projections – with and without migration – should be drawn up, that the 'most reasonable' assumptions should be adopted for fertility, mortality, and migration, and that possible variants should be clarified. The OECD also coordinates projections of households and working population made by the members on the basis of population forecasts. The material is collected on a questionnaire devised by the OECD for the member countries.

The United Nations programme is very similar. Forecasts on a worldwide, regional, and national scale were published in 1952, 1955, 1958, 1966, and 1973. Here too the member countries, or at least the industrial ones, were asked to provide forecasts about their respective populations. As far as Europe was concerned, the project was answerable to the 'Conference of European Statisticians' convened by the UN Statistical Commission and the UN Economic Commission for Europe. Like OECD, the United Nations did not standardise any methodology but aimed at unifying the starting dates and results of the forecasts.

Besides these two general programmes, there are several international undertakings more specifically concerned with international migration. The OECD recently set up a 'Permanent System of Migration Observation' (SOPEMI), whose aim is to note the movement of workers from one European country to another: the system is based on the reports of correspondents chosen personally. The United Nations has just set up a new project for the exchange of data on international migration, which should enable a country to know more about the size of its emigration indirectly through the immigration statistics of other countries. Lastly, the Council of Europe has passed a resolution inviting the Intergovernmental Council for European Migration (CIME) to consider implementing a joint project for the elaboration of medium- and long-term forecasts of migration within Europe, also taking into account the countries of emigration of the non-European Mediterranean. The CIME has expressed the wish to work together with the other organisations active in this field.

At present, the European Community has no programme drawing up or coordinating population forecasts, though it does collect available forecasts made by the member countries. Its only currently existing programmes aim at coordinating the censuses of the member countries and at drawing up migration statistics on a common basis, the latter being still under discussion. The Statistical Office of the European Community has recently drawn up a plan in the population field, in which it is proposed to approach member states for information about current work and future plans regarding population projections at the national and regional levels, and to discuss within a Working Group the implementation of a system of projections on a uniform basis for member countries. As the plan is very recent, no steps implementing it have yet been taken. It is obvious that in its policy-making the Community cannot ignore demographic forecasts, since its own policies may influence the demographic variables (for instance, labour policy will influence spatial mobility); and conversely, changes in demographic variables could affect the Community's policies (for example, very low fertility would make for yet older populations and would influence labour and health policies among others). In particular, methods of fertility control have changed radically in the last ten years, and it is to be expected that they will become even safer and more certain in the next ten years. A method of preventing conception after intercourse or of terminating pregnancy very early may become available. Women may then be able freely to determine for themselves how many children they will bear. Fertility could be reduced to a level which would halt population growth or even lead to an eventual decline of population in developed countries.

The Community could also monitor the effects of possible national population policies (no such policies actually exist at present in the Community), and in the case of migration it could establish its own policy. The Community might also in time be led to make its own forecasts, its own estimates and projections, particularly since in Europe many natural socio-economic regions straddle national frontiers and are commonly neglected in national forecasting. It might well also encourage more basic research into what determines mortality, fertility, and spatial mobility, largely by following the main lines of research outlined above. But above all, of course, it must include demographic inputs in any general work of social, economic, and technological forecasting it may undertake. Demography is a necessary condition of all forecasting; whatever Community forecasting unit is set up, it should ensure these inputs. It should obtain from the central Community Statistical Office, from the member governments' statistical departments, and from OECD and the United Nations whatever material it needs, some of which would of course be published in any case. Its next task would be to forecast future interrelations between Community population and Community policy, particularly when the repercussions transcend national frontiers or when the Community is involved as such: for example, spatial mobility within the Community following the freedom of movement, or the demographic and economic effects of a Community policy on immigration from outside the Common Market. Its third, and most important, task would be to provide the demographic data needed by the specialists in economic and social affairs to work out general forecasts and assessments. It is precisely in the interrelations between human activities that demographic forecasting should increasingly be active.

Europe Plus Thirty should be able to call on the part-time services of one or two highly skilled demographers. The main work is already done elsewhere, and it will be enough if Europe Plus Thirty is assured of access to it and of the best possible specialist help in selecting and handling the data necessary for its own work. As with climatology and with education (see below), it should from time to time call conferences or seminars on the subject and commission special studies.

4. *Agriculture, fisheries, and forestry*

GENERAL

The rapid technical development in agriculture in the Western countries in the last hundred years has been largely stimulated by government research which has made it possible not only for production to keep pace with the growing population but also for a steadily shrinking fraction of the working population to be engaged in it. Because of the low price elasticity of both supply and demand, the largely uncontrollable yield fluctuations, and the related instability of agricultural markets, in practically all the industrialised countries the prices of agricultural raw materials on the domestic market are subject to government intervention, to protect either the consumer or the producer against the uncertainties of free market forces.

With fisheries, the situation is different. Outside certain narrow national limits (which are likely to be changed by the third UN Conference on the Law of the Sea), fish are a common resource, to which access is open. The industry increasingly uses techniques of industrialised hunting, and governments subsidise fishing fleets not only to protect consumer and producer against market forces and natural fluctuations in the stock of fish, but also to protect the national 'take' of the common resource against other, competitively subsidised, national efforts. Fisheries are now heavily over-capitalised; the same catch could often be obtained for half the effort. Until recently it was widely believed that the world catch could be doubled or trebled without more than local damage to stocks from overfishing, but this view no longer prevails. The world fish catch, measured by weight, nearly doubled between 1958 and 1968; but since 1968, despite a continued increase in fishing effort, it has failed to increase and in some seas has fallen. Only costs have continued to rise. Effective fishery management, including the regulation of access, could still improve prospects for another increase in the availability of fish protein and a reduction in the cost of obtaining it.

In agriculture, major structural changes have occurred both in consumption and in the production, processing, and distribution of vegetable and animal products. The calorific value of food consumption per head in the countries of the West is very high (c. 3,000 kilocalories per annum); it is now at a standstill or barely increasing, but the volume of agricultural production is still going up. This is due to the replacement of vegetable by animal products, which requires an increasing conversion of vegetable material into meat, with a substantial loss of calories; for instance, in order to produce 100 calories in the form of pork an intake of approximately 400 calories in the form of fodder is needed. Some of the feed intake is waste as regards human consumption; some is not. Take, for instance, fish used for feed (and sometimes for fertiliser). There are three distinct cases, namely: (1) fish which cannot be used directly as food (e.g. anchoveta, fish waste); (2) fish which, though originally suitable for human food, is processed as meal (or fertiliser) because it is damaged or stale; and (3) fish which, though suitable for human food, is processed into meal or fertiliser for economic reasons (e.g. North Sea herring). Obviously the intrinsic soundness of the operation is different in the three cases.

Urbanisation and regional specialisation within agriculture, fishing, and food processing have (within Europe) widened the average distance between production and final consumption. Thus the supply and distribution of food has become increasingly dependent upon the trade and transport system.

In agriculture, the trendwise increase in yield per hectare[1] (c. 2 per cent annually) is accompanied by an increasing use of fertilisers and crop protection agents. In the member countries of the EEC the use of fertilisers has increased fourfold since 1950. The general increase in prosperity has led to the large-scale replacement of farm workers by machinery, which is a way of replacing solar energy by fossil energy. In the last twenty years the number of agricultural workers fell by about half in the EEC countries, and the decrease in animal power was even greater; the use of tractors and other engines and the use of energy (oil, gas, electricity) increased four times.

Mechanisation and automation require larger farms and fewer farmers. Despite the decrease in the number of farms – 2½ per cent per annum in the EEC since 1960 – the small family farm is still characteristic of Western European agriculture. Within the Community, about 80 per cent of farms are smaller than 20 ha. (45 per cent in the U.K., but 95 per cent in Italy). Since 1960 the average size of farms bigger than 1 ha. has only increased from 11 to 13½ ha.

Parallel processes have operated in fishing. Recent increases in the total catch of the nine EEC countries have been modest (1948: c. 3m tonnes;[2] 1958: c. 3.6m tonnes; 1968: c. 4.8m tonnes; 1973: 4.76m tonnes), but there has been a parallel reduction in manpower and a parallel increase in the average size and capacity of vessels and equipment and

---

[1] 1 hectare (ha.) = 2.471 acres.　　　　[2] 1 tonne = 1,000 kg.

in the average consumption of energy expended per unit of food obtained. Equally, there are communities of small inshore fishermen, using traditional small-scale, low-energy methods, whose way of life has changed as little as that of some small farmers.

In the growing sector of food processing, on the other hand, pronounced tendencies are afoot towards concentration. The food-processing industry is expanding its influence on the raw-materials market (contract farming) and on the distribution of the end product. The advent of supermarkets etc. has also caused change in the distribution pattern of foodstuffs, which increases the need for food processing (standardisation, packaging, etc.). All this has been made possible by cheap fossil fuels.

For the most part, the Community eats home-grown food. The following table shows the relation between home supply and home consumption (break-even point = 100) of important food items (1972).

	Grains	Sugar	Po-tatoes	Meat	Butter	Cheese	Veg-etables	Fruit
▪ole EEC	91	89	100	94	92	100	97	81
▪nce	164	150	104	96	111	114	96	101
▪st Germany	83	94	94	85	101	86	45	53
▪y	69	74	97	71	68	85	112	121
▪K.	65	35	96	68	17	52	82	42
▪therlands	36	113	123	175	373	230	183	82
▪gium	45	173	96	122	107	50	118	66
▪nmark	101	118	102	358	297	244	88	68
▪land	80	108	105	271	196	485	103	23

The United Kingdom, West Germany, and Italy are predominantly importers of agricultural products; France, the Netherlands, Ireland, and Denmark have for many products an export surplus. These differences are compensated for by intra-EEC trade (as the first row indicates). Trade with third countries is increasing. In 1972 the values (in thousands of millions of Units of Account) of imports and exports of agricultural raw materials and food from third countries were as follows:

Imports   13.1
Exports   3.8
Balance of trade   −9.3

The balance of trade with four main blocs of partners was as follows:

USA   −1.6
Other developed countries   −2.2
Developing countries   −4.5
Communist countries   −1.0
Total   −9.3

For the most part, the imports of the Community are tropical agricultural products and raw material for fodder.

Among the member countries there are considerable differences in food-consumption habits, partly traditional and partly as a consequence of different prosperity levels. The following table shows the average individual consumption (in kg per head) of important food items in the member countries (1972):

	Wheat flour	Potatoes	Sugar	Meat	Fish	Butter	Margarir
France	73	96	37	69	16.9	8.3	3.4
West Germany	61	101	34	74	7.3	8.3	9.0
Italy	125	40	27	49	9.7	2.0	0.5
United Kingdom	65	101	44	60	8.3	8.3	5.8
Netherlands	61	85	46	45	11.6	2.3	17.8
Belgium/Lux.	78	114	37	60	11.9	8.8	13.0
Denmark	63	77	48	54	4.7	8.7	18.1
Ireland	84	122	52	61	—	—	—

The consumption of meat, vegetables, and fruit has grown regularly during recent decades, whilst the consumption of bread and potatoes has decreased. Denmark, which is the richest country in the Community, has the lowest consumption of wheat and potatoes; and Ireland, which is the poorest, has the highest.

As regards agriculture, the European Community already possesses wide powers in the Common Agricultural Policy (CAP); it is in fact the only field in which the Community has real supranational authority. As regards fisheries, its authority and functions have been comparatively slow to develop. This will change in the likely event of UNCLOS III (UN Conference on the Law of the Sea) permitting coastal states to establish, either individually or grouped in regional bodies, an Exclusive Economic Zone (EEZ) of up to 200 nautical miles, within which exclusively to exploit the natural resources (and perhaps also to control pollution and scientific research).

AGRICULTURE

The establishment of a common market for agricultural produce required a supranational agricultural policy to take over the function of the former national policies for price stabilisation and income support. The goal of the CAP is to guarantee a reasonable income for the farming population, and its main instrument is a price policy. Within the EEC a price level is laid down for a number of important agricultural products which offers a reasonable remuneration for the producers. Via a complicated system of market regulation, the domestic market is therefore detached from erratic price movements on the international markets. Variable levies and subsidies on imports and exports are an essential part of the CAP, and so are intervention measures (support buying, stock financing, encouragement of consumption). In so far as internal production differs from internal demand, equilibrium on the internal market is pursued by influencing foreign trade. Disequilibria on the internal market are thus passed on to the international markets.

The manner in which the CAP supports the incomes of agricultural producers means that consumers of foodstuffs have to pay a price regarded as reasonable reimbursement for agricultural production within the Community. When production differs from domestic consumption, the costs of import or export subsidies (dependent on the price level outside the Common Market) and of possible interventions on the internal market are borne by the European Guidance and Guarantee Fund. The yield of levies on imports or exports constitutes the revenues of this balancing fund. In past years it has become clear how sensitive the Fund's budget is to disequilibria on the home market and to price movements on the international markets. Butter and meat 'mountains' have caused the outgoings from the Fund to reach alarming proportions, and have led to politically highly damaging sales of meat and butter to the Soviet Union at prices much lower than those paid by the consumer within the Community. If charitable subsidies are to be paid by Western to Eastern Europe, the Community would presumably wish as soon as possible to obtain forecasting good enough to ensure that that is done by political decision and not by economic accident. The meat and butter mountains, and the 'wine lake', have been the most conspicuous (though not perhaps the gravest) of the road accidents which could have been averted by proper headlights.

It is also an object of the CAP to encourage structural adjustments in production. In this field responsibility is still vested primarily in the member states. The EEC is trying to coordinate these activities and to key them to common interests. The structural changes in agriculture (increase in farm size, retrenchment of labour, forms of cooperation, contractual ties with trade and industry) have been caused by rapid overall economic growth and technical development, and the present structural policy aims further to reduce the number of farmers and farm workers (alternative employment, retraining, schemes for farm amalgamation), to improve the infrastructure (opening up of remote areas, re-allocation of holdings, water control), and to modernise farm equipment (interest subsidies for certain investments). In this connection 'efficiency' has so far been interpreted above all as lower costs per unit of product for the individual agricultural entrepreneur.

Even within the limited objectives of the present CAP there is a great need for research into the long-term development of supply and demand. Forecasting in this field has confined itself too much to an extrapolation of historical trends, and – as was argued in the Introduction – this alone is never of much use. On the basis of its permanent supranational responsibility for food and agriculture, the EEC will have to widen and deepen its policy. It will not be able to confine itself simply to reacting to more or less autonomous developments in production and consumption. The increasing interweaving of these developments with other social interests (both inside and outside the Community) will make it necessary to formulate explicit longer-term objectives with respect to the volume, the composition, and the technical and economic organisation of food production. The need for policy-oriented forecasting will become more urgent.

The great world food shortage since 1972, which most harms those least able to help themselves, spotlights the role that the agricultural policy of the rich countries (and therefore of the EEC) should play in improving the world food situation. In the short term the wealthy countries, with their agricultural technology, may be called upon to face acute emergency situations by increasing food aid and by building up and financing strategic food stocks. But in the longer term a solution to the world problem can be attained only by stepping up agricultural production in the poor countries themselves, for which financial and technical assistance will have to be increased. Moreover, the agricultural policy by which the rich countries protect their own farmers will have to be amended, in order to achieve stable prices in world markets. The wealthy countries will be able to achieve these conditions by controlling their own production (and if necessary their own consumption too) so as to avoid disrupting the international markets both by price-cutting and by price-raising. This would call for policies capable of influencing the development of agricultural production and food consumption much more effectively than the present market-regulating measures, and devising and comparing alternative policies would call for substantial forecasting. In this, EEC policy will need the backing of research into long-term developments in food on a worldwide scale. This research should be carried out in close cooperation with FAO and OECD. It requires a multidisciplinary approach in agriculture, economics, demography, sociology, oceanography, climatology, etc.

The energy and raw-materials shortage has made us aware of the vulnerability of our food supplies. Recent studies of the consumption of fossil energy will have to extend to the whole chain of the food supply, the transportation and processing of foodstuffs, and their physical location. The merits of alternative production systems must also be evaluated with reference to our long-term expectation about the price of energy and raw materials for food production (more or less regional specialisation in agricultural production and food processing; alternative degrees of mechanisation and of fertiliser use). The agricultural sector is not only a consumer of fossil energy; it can also bring forth products which are useful as fuel (straw, wood, alcohol).

There is increasing concern about the environmental impacts of modern agriculture, particularly in pollution, in ecological disturbance, and in the spoiling of beautiful landscapes by asbestos barns, by the grubbing-up of orchards and hedges, and by the destruction of fine old farm buildings. Forecasting could help assess alternative ways of meeting this concern.

Whether or not battery-reared and fish-fed veal, bacon, or chicken is as good for you as the natural variety, it is certainly not as nice, and everywhere people are ready to pay more for the natural taste. In an industry which stood more or less on its own feet, that would not be a reason for forecasting. But agriculture is, in the Community, highly dependent on public power, and that means that the forecasting done for the public power should include this matter.

Indeed, present agricultural policy bears obvious traces of the 'growth philosophy' of the 50s and 60s. Price support as the principal instrument of income policy perpetuates the prevailing income differentials due to differences in farm size. The resulting economic situation led to an increase in farm size and socially undesirable side-effects, such as depopulation of the countryside, turning rural areas into business centres, demand for more jobs in non-agricultural sectors, etc. Now that increase in productivity has become a conditional objective in our society, there is every reason fundamentally to rethink the part that the agricultural sector should play. This rethinking makes forward-looking research desirable into the effects that alternative forms of production might have on income distribution, population density in rural regions, competition within the EEC and with non-member countries, burdens on the Fund, etc., and above all on employment outside agriculture.

FISHERIES

The period during which exclusive economic zones (EEZs) are likely to be established in the UN coincides with that during which the

Council of Ministers of the Community, according to the 1973 Act of Accession, 'shall examine the provisions which could follow the derogation, in force until December 31st 1982', from normal Community rules concerning non-discrimination towards the citizens and enterprises of other member states. At present this derogation merely allows protection to local inshore fishermen in certain specified waters off Britain, Denmark, and Ireland. But because the establishment of EEZs will permit the regulation of access to what are now high-seas fisheries, the examination could well embrace the whole subject of the Community's functions and policy relating to offshore development and sea-use planning within the new zones. Productive European fisheries are only one aspect of this.

Sea-use planning as a concept, which we discuss in II.12 below, is scarcely beyond the embryonic stage; and fishery management, which must now be developed as a function of government, is still in its infancy. Under international law, access to all fisheries beyond twelve nautical miles from the shore has up to now been open, and state membership of International Fishery Commissions and observance of the restrictions which the Commissions propose have been, in effect, voluntary.

Fast-moving and powerfully equipped distant-water fishing fleets are now ubiquitous; they are able to engage in 'pulse-fishing', to clear one area and swiftly move on to the next. The Russian and the Japanese fleets are by far the largest. Between them, according to FAO figures, the Soviet Union and Japan in 1973 landed nearly 30 per cent of the world catch; in 1968 it had been 23 per cent, and in 1958 21 per cent. Flag-of-convenience fishing vessels are also now operating – vessels, that is, registered in states which do not observe or enforce international norms of crewing, safety, pollution control, etc. These developments will face the EEC with quite unfamiliar problems of physical enforcement. Indeed, the establishment of EEZs will for the first time enable coastal governments, singly or preferably in regional groupings, effectively to manage the fisheries off their shores. Fisheries in the Northeast Atlantic, and particularly in the North Sea, are some of the most prolific in the world, while those in the Mediterranean, though less prolific, are in money terms particularly valuable. In each area there are non-EEC countries conducting important fisheries, and Community fishery management policies will need from the beginning to be coordinated with the governments, fishing industries, and research organisations of these neighbour countries.

Although fishery statistics are notoriously uncertain and the dynamics of individual fish stocks still obscure, considerable information is available from national, regional, and international sources. OECD,

FAO, the International Council for the Exploration of the Seas (ICES) at Copenhagen, and certain other bodies all conduct research and collect and publish information. None of it is policy-oriented, in the way that will be required when the regulation and management of all offshore resources falls, by international agreement, to the coastal state and thereby in turn to the European Community.

FORESTRY

Demand for timber is strongly dependent on technical development. In the U.S. the annual consumption comes to about 2,000 cubic metres per thousand inhabitants, of which nearly 50 per cent is in the form of pulpwood (raw material for the paper industry); the level in the Community is about 800 cubic metres per thousand inhabitants, with the same percentage for pulpwood. In developing countries the volume of accessible forests is the determining factor; wood is mainly used as fuel. FAO projections show a rapid increase in world demand for timber, especially for the paper industry. The average annual growth of timber in existing forests limits production if reserves are to be maintained. In many areas this limit has not yet been reached. Nevertheless, large areas of natural forests in tropical regions are being lost by injudicious unplanned felling, or by turning forests into farm land. On continuation of present trends it must be feared that eventually a structural world deficiency of timber will arise. There are also climatogenic implications: trees take up the carbon dioxide we make and give us back the oxygen we breathe. The threatening scarcity might be countered by enlarging the forest areas. Because of the long time of maturing (fifteen to fifty years, according to the sort of tree), early planning is imperative. Forestry, therefore, is a subject that urgently requires long-term forecasting, and especially forecasting capable of helping decision-makers to correct the present highly dangerous trends.

The EEC is not rich in forests. For each thousand inhabitants there are 110 ha. of forests, as against 1,450 ha. in the U.S. and 3,100 ha. in the Soviet Union. The Community has to import about 50 per cent of its timber (for Britain and for the Netherlands this percentage is still higher), and the annual value of these imports is more than five thousand million Units of Account. Most of the imports are pulpwood; the paper industry in the EEC is 80 per cent dependent on imports from third countries. But the export surplus of the traditional suppliers (Canada, Northern and Eastern Europe) is diminishing fast as home demand increases, and there is a tendency there to manufacture paper for export rather than to export the raw material. This adds to the vulnerability of the EEC timber supply.

The European Commission encourages afforestation in areas less suited for farm production. The Commission's main purpose is to improve the farm land structure, e.g. by protection against storms, and better equilibrium between soil and water. But the production of timber is also promoted because of the growing demand and because of the favourable labour aspects for the agricultural population. Forestry does not need daily attention; it can be conveniently scheduled in the yearly pattern of farm work; it provides a welcome supplementary employment, especially in mountainous and remote areas, and many people from outside agriculture like to lend a hand. It is enjoyable work for the healthy.

All this will require a thorough analysis of the future supply of and demand for timber, both in the Community and in third countries, in cooperation with FAO and OECD. The necessary research should cover all the possibilities which might contribute to a less vulnerable position for the Community. This involves the replacement of wood by man-made materials, particularly in the packaging industry, economising on wood consumption by cutting down waste (e.g. sawing, production of cellulose), and the effect on paper use of introducing modern telecommunications systems. It should evaluate the possibilities of a larger timber production within the Community, observing all the consequences in other fields, e.g. food production. Higher yields from the existing forests through better exploitation and the introduction of fast-growing varieties may be attainable. In the long run, however, a reduced dependence on imports – if that is desirable – can only be realised by an enlargement of the forest area.

Forests do not only provide wood; they also stabilise and enrich the environment, afford space for recreation, and provide differentiation of the inland scenery. A consistent long-term foresty policy should take into account all the manifold aspects involved. The same goes, of course, for policy-oriented forecasting in forestry.

SUMMARY

The many interests mentioned in the preceding sections are closely interwoven and often competitive. Forecasting will have to try to indicate the influence of alternative future developments on all relevant sub-fields (e.g. the internal food supply, the world food situation, environment, the call on raw materials, the uses made of the seas, income and employment distribution, etc.). This overall forecasting must therefore be of a multidisciplinary nature. It will have to be geared to the problems facing policy-making agencies, which means that policy variables should be explicitly introduced into a forecasting model so that the policy-maker can weigh the effect of alternative measures.

If forecasting is to meet this requirement, research should try to identify the causal relations in the socio-economic process. For the food-supply system, for instance, in addition to quantitative information on the technical input–output relations in the various links in the production chain, insight is needed into the conduct of the 'actors' – i.e. the producers and consumers of food – in order to assist the policy-maker in the formulation of objectives which can often be pursued only by influencing behaviour (via prices, taxes, restrictions, etc.).

Policy-oriented research will have the best chance of success if it can take place within a central instrument at Community level which also does forecasting in other fields. Via close contacts with experts in research institutes at national level, technical and economic know-how in subfields and regional statistical information will have to be obtained; but the main emphasis of the research will have to fall on the central team. This set-up is also the best guarantee of close interaction between research workers and those who hope to make use of the results, in order to formulate policy. As far as fisheries is concerned, no relevant research has yet been done.

5. *Health*

The countries of the Community have health patterns which are broadly similar. The differences derive at least in part from differences in the environment and in the national services for the protection or promotion of health. Professional health services are available in all countries at approximately the same level of sophistication, though there are wide differences in their organisation and accessibility to the public. These factors affect the practicability of long-term forecasting for the Community as a whole.

It is possible to define in general terms the factors which influence health and, from recent trends, to suggest what kind of development may be expected in the future. But the likely progress in science relevant to medicine cannot be projected from present knowledge, beyond some cautious estimates for the next decade. Scientific advances could make possible major changes in our ability to prevent or delay the onset of chronic disease, including cancer, or to arrest or control its course. Social and environmental factors could affect the incidence and severity of accidents, which are a principal cause of disability and death. The great advances in control of acute and curable diseases, apart from mental illness, have mostly been achieved already.

Progress in developing the health services has been by a series of short steps with occasional longer strides at times propitious for change, such as the combination of circumstances – social, material, and political – in Britain at the end of the Second World War. Rising costs and the pressures for orderly development are causing a general drift in all countries towards greater centralisation, using regional and local planning within national policies. The method of financing services differs considerably within the nine countries: the use of insurance and of payment by fee per service on the one hand, or central taxation and salary or capitation on the other, has an effect on the form of the service to patients. It does not seem likely that the pressures for change will lead all countries to an almost identical pattern, as has happened in Eastern Europe, but there may well be far greater similarities in the future than exist now. Certainly there are opportunities within the Community for other members to make substantial improvements by applying methods proven by individual countries in an idiom suitable to themselves.

All member countries spend between 5 and 7 per cent of GNP on health. All have broadly similar statistical indices of health, with marginal differences in favour of the Netherlands and Denmark. These indices do not suggest that the amount spent on health correlates closely with the result achieved, but rather that some systems may operate more economically than others for much the same result. This phenomenon has already been discussed in chapter I.4 above.

The cost of health care has been escalating rapidly during the last fifteen years – more in some countries than in others – so that it has become clear that selection of priorities will be necessary in future. No country will be able to provide all the services that would be technically practicable, given the resources. The total demand that such services would make on trained manpower and on money would become prohibitive. Such selection as is practised now is intuitive rather than rational, and all our countries urgently need to devise improved methods of choice and of application of choices.

Life expectancy has greatly increased in all our countries during this century, but that process began in the eighteenth century when the rapid increase in population began, first in France and later in Britain. Similar increases occurred in other countries, though not on exactly the same time scale. They were probably mainly attributable to better nutrition, to improved sanitation and housing, and to better public understanding of the contribution these general factors make to health. The direct contribution of medicine through therapy was limited until the last forty years or so.

Mortality in infancy is now little more than one-tenth of that of a century ago. The present low infant mortality rate of 12 to 20 per thousand may be expected to fall further in all the nine countries, perhaps to a figure as low as 10; but even this cannot produce a large effect on overall life expectancy. Drugs effective against a wide range of infections and vaccines which give specific protection against many common epidemic diseases mainly affecting children have been developed and made widely available in the last forty years and have produced further improvement.

There is now a radical change of emphasis in health care from preoccupation with acute, potentially lethal, but often completely curable disease to simple specific preventive programmes and supportive and ameliorative treatment of chronic illness with the object of retardation rather than cure. The chief problems of the developing countries are still those of controlling infection; and the Community – if it is really to help the developing world – has still to mount a major research effort to reduce diseases that are now rare in Western Europe but still common in developing countries.

It is the experience of all the countries of the Community that the number of people in the population over the age of sixty-five has increased rapidly in the last twenty-five years, and it is certain that this increase will continue during the next decade. Moreover, during that time and in the following decade the number aged over seventy-five will increase proportionately even more. Since the very old make disproportionately large calls upon health services and institutions, the total load on the social budget, including the health budget, must increase.

All those who are born must eventually die; the great change during this century has been that most of us grow old on the way to our deaths. Disease processes of various kinds develop more or less insidiously as ageing proceeds. One or more of these morbid processes will finally be determined as the cause of death, and one or more of them is likely to produce disability before – often long before – death. The great health problem of the future is thus the prevention or postponement of the clinical emergence of chronic degenerative disease and the disability which accompanies it. In all our countries by far the largest component is cardiovascular disease, especially of the coronary arteries. Accidents, poisoning, and violence, the various forms of cancer, and chronic respiratory disease are the other main causes of death. In all the countries the age-specific rates for women are less than for men, excluding cancer. Some relevant figures are given in Table 1; they show that an important factor in future health and social organisation will be the predominance of women in the older age groups.

Table 1

	Life expectancy at age 1		Perinatal mortality per thousand live births	Mortality per million			
				Men		Women	
	Boys	Girls		35–44	45–54	35–44	45–5
Belgium	68.3	74.3	25.1	2,757	7,722	1,616	4,24
Denmark	71.1	75.7	18.9	2,311	5,994	1,886	4,24
France	68.5	75.9	25.4	3,650	8,050	1,773	4,13
Irish Republic	69.3[a]	72.7[a]	26.1	2,612	7,393	1,818	5,18
Italy	69.9[b]	75.2[b]	32.4	2,802	7,046	1,587	3,79
Luxembourg	67.4	73.8	24.7[c]	3,468	8,901	1,784	5,00
Netherlands	71.1	76.5	19.6	2,086	6,100	1,473	3,41
West Germany	68.5[b]	74.4[b]	25.2	3,051	7,372	1,919	4,36
United Kingdom							
England and Wales	69.1	75.1	23.7	2,298	7,242	1,737	4,37
Northern Ireland	69.3	74.0	29.2	2,801	8,263	1,882	4,72
Scotland	67.5	73.4	25.6	3,195	8,757	2,098	5,64

NOTE: Life expectancy figures for 1968 except
  [a] Irish Republic 1960–2
  [b] Italy and West Germany 1967
  Mortality figures for 1969 except
  [c] Luxembourg, perinatal mortality 1968
SOURCE: WHO, UN, and national statistics, quoted by R. Maxwell, *Health Care: The Growing Dilemma* (New York: McKinsey, 1974).

Forecasting in various fields will be affected by changes in morbidity and mortality. We are in much the same position as our forebears a hundred years ago who, without knowing the scientific rationale of what they did, were able to initiate changes in the sanitary conditions of the population which were highly successful in the long run. Once the nature of infective agents was known, the measures were made far more effective. The nature of the underlying degenerative processes may not be known, but some empirical measures undoubtedly would be successful now if the public could be persuaded to apply them. It is probable that identifiable external factors are responsible for the incidence of at least half of the cases of cancer, and cancer of some sites is almost wholly due to a known external cause. In Britain over a quarter of all deaths from cancer are due to cigarette-smoking, and over one-third of those in men; in the other countries the proportion, though not yet as high, is rising in both men and women. Some

– probably most – changes which would have a beneficial effect on health require changes of habit or life-style by systematic individual effort, and those changes would be more likely if, for one thing, the commercial promotion and public facilitation of cigarette-smoking were forbidden.

It is certain that some of the causative factors in degenerative and malignant disease will be more clearly understood within the next thirty years. It is to be expected that some of these factors will be chemical or physical and will be present in circumstances which make it possible to remove or reduce them without calling upon a change in human behaviour. Exposure to various chemical or physical agents in the work situation can be reduced or removed by statutory requirement. Some methods of working which produce damaging trauma over a long period can be modified. Other exposures which affect the unborn foetus will also be identified and modified in ways which will reduce the occurrence of prematurity and congenital defect, e.g. maternal smoking. Atmospheric pollution in general, and exposure to dust and fume in the work situation, will be modifiable. Some factors naturally present in food or added to it in processing may be incriminated. Abuse of alcohol and some psychotropic drugs are common socio-medical problems. Some potent therapeutic drugs may be shown to be toxic to some patients through idiosyncrasy or prolonged exposure, and some may even be effective in the short term but associated with increase in malignant disease after prolonged use.

An association between softness in drinking water and raised mortality from cardiovascular disease has been shown in some countries, and a causal relationship, if demonstrated, would require substantial changes in the water and in the means of its distribution. It is probable also that the possibility of improving health by the addition of some factors to generally used food or water will be established. If so, better means of obtaining public and professional understanding will be needed if their use is not to be frustrated by uninformed opposition, like that to the fluoridation of drinking water.

It is probable that better understanding of diet and nutrition will be used to promote changes in dietary habits, which will affect agriculture. It is to be expected that the use of tobacco in the world will decline – perhaps to a large extent – as understanding spreads. The land used to grow it can then be used for food production (but a reduction in tobacco consumption would also increase the population). The consumption of sucrose may decline as a measure to reduce obesity and indirectly the occurrence of diabetes and perhaps heart disease. The use of animal fats may be reduced, and the choice of alternative vegetable fats may require changes in the type of rape seed used. If human wastes come to be used as fertiliser in Western agriculture, as they commonly are in some Eastern countries, new precautions against the transmission of enteric infections will be needed.

Mental illness and handicap have been making increasing demands on health services for the last twenty years, but during that time methods used in those services have greatly improved (the Danish and Dutch services provide good examples). This has been mainly due to better medico-social management, assisted by the new drugs that have become available. The formerly high mortality from intercurrent infections in hospital populations of the mentally ill or handicapped has been reduced, and those populations therefore now include many older and more dependent persons. It is to be expected that improved pharmacological treatment of the mentally ill will become available, but more social support will then be needed for the larger population of older mentally enfeebled persons in the community or in hostels. For these, and for the mentally robust elderly, energy policies will need to take account of the necessity of adequate space heating in homes.

The study of human genetics has advanced rapidly in recent years, but it is still at a fairly primitive stage. Popular fears about the possibility of 'genetic engineering' probably go much too far, but genetic mechanisms will certainly have been elucidated and more precise prognoses will be available to intending parents, and in some societies artificial insemination by donor as well. Early prenatal diagnosis of some congenital handicaps will probably be possible so that such pregnancies can be terminated where the law permits. As was mentioned in Chapter II.3, methods of controlling pregnancy and parturition may become so safe and precise that they will largely be in the hands of women themselves.

Accidents are the cause of a large proportion of deaths of younger men, and therefore contribute largely to the total years of life lost before the age of sixty-five. If a substantial proportion of these years of productive life could be saved, the contribution to society would be greater than from a small average extension of the life span.

The problem of the increase in venereal disease is closely related to changes in sexual mores. Vaccines could become available should their use be acceptable.

Modification of life-style could make far greater contribution to the improvement of health and the prolongation of active life than more technical medical activities are likely to do within the next thirty years. If such results are to be achieved, governments and the health professions will have to devise more effective measures of health education than they have yet deployed. No serious attempt has yet been made to persuade the individual that his enjoyment and expectation of life would be enhanced if he abstained from smoking cigarettes, driving too fast, drinking immoderate amounts of alcohol, over-eating, and lapsing into physical idleness at an early age. Intrusion into the social choices of the public and the profitability of certain industries would be necessary if governments were to take these possibilities seriously. The gain would be measured in years added to healthier lives – more than might be expected from intervention of any other kind. Since no country has been successful in any of this, the results of such meagre steps as have been taken should be exchanged amongst them. The work of Europe Plus Thirty could not but show the benefits to be achieved.

Much highly sophisticated medical work is already undertaken for gains which may be problematical for the individual and even less certain for society. The pressure of financial constraints on the one hand and of the emergence of new scientific possibilities on the other will certainly ensure that a deliberate selection of priorities within health services becomes normal practice. A forecasting unit can project the trends of such studies and examine interactions with other trends.

The changing pattern of illness, the ageing of the population, and the increasing potency of the drugs available for medical use will make the provision of satisfactory primary and continuing health care even more important. The means used to secure this vary somewhat, and in some countries it has become increasingly difficult to maintain a satisfactory health-care team to work outside hospital. Changes in medical education and the organisation of medical practice are likely to be required as best fits the organisation of health and social security services in each country, but each can learn from the others. Hospitals may become more expensive concentrations of scientific facilities on one side but may also have increasing long-stay components on the other. They will only be economically feasible and medically effective in so far as they are oriented towards the support of community care.

The main need of the countries of the Community is a fuller exchange of information rather than adjustment to a single pattern. This can be developed from existing liaison arrangements. Long-range forecasting on health prospects or bio-medical advance is hazardous and must be imprecise. The application of new bio-medical progress to organised health care could be greatly improved, but by national rather than international effort.

Europe Plus Thirty will need continuing medical input because health is affected by climate, environment, and energy, and it both affects and is affected by the shape of our populations, institutions, economy, industry, food supply, education, and society in general. In all these Europe Plus Thirty should be doing forecasting, and medical inputs based on wide medical and allied scientific contacts are necessary. 'Medical' is taken here to comprehend the health professions and related science.

The simplest way for Europe Plus Thirty to make some general prognostication about potential development in the bio-medical field will be to look at progress already being made but not yet generally applied, and we have given some examples of this above. It will therefore need continuing medical participation and a source of medical advice. On the other hand, it will not require a substantial 'in-house' medical section. The best solution would be the part-time involvement of a senior medical member of an active university department or special institute such as might be found in several countries in the Community. Such a base department or institute might need strengthening so that the senior member would in effect lead a part-time team of other members of the staff. This would give a wider range of expertise and outside information sources. The leader of this group would need to work in close liaison with the Chief Medical Officers or equivalents in all nine countries, with the heads of national medical research agencies, and with the World Health Organisation. The effect would be to give Europe Plus Thirty the equivalent of more than one whole-time medical staff member.

6. *Social structures and values*

The vastness and variety of society, which makes forecasting about it so important, also makes it hard to forecast about. Unlike other sectoral forecasting (technological, demographic, economic, etc.), social forecasting is concerned with the system – society – that controls and contains the behaviour of all the others. At the outset, therefore, we have to stress the difference between forecasting in this area and forecasting in all others. Society is the fabric itself within which all the other 'sectors' are threads. All other variables and systems assume a context, and it is society.

In this chapter we shall not discuss the possibility of forecasting about this whole fabric, only forecasting about certain threads in it which we commonly call 'social' and which are not included in other chapters. We have in mind such threads as religious belief and organisation, the administration of justice and order, the family, trade unions, consumer associations, social work and public welfare, racial and other minorities, the arts and culture in general, and recreation and leisure.

But first, a general caution of the very greatest importance. All the other chapters of Part II concern forecasting about matters which may, and indeed should, be planned in a democracy: technology, the economy, energy, etc. And the same is true of much of this chapter; the administration of justice, public welfare, etc. may and should be planned. But there is an exception: it is contained in the word 'values' at the head of the chapter. By values we mean simply what people think about things, what they think important, what they want. One may legitimately forecast about value changes, about the 'transvaluation of values'; indeed, it is most useful to do so. But one may on no account plan them, in the sense of seeking to bring them about or prevent them. To do so would be to manipulate the very identity of people, and our experience and abhorrence of that is one of the reasons why we have been able to form a Western European Community at all. It is not so everywhere, but our states exist to serve the values and wishes of individuals, and the European Community is an emanation of our states. This chapter therefore treats, in part, of things which must never be planned, and forecasting about which must therefore never tend towards the choice of goals.

There is no such thing as a social expert; nobody can know society as, for instance, the technologist knows technology. There is no body of social theory which allows us to define the structure and properties of the social system as such. One has to approach the subject pragmatically, i.e. to choose the best method for the procurement of the set of facts required. It might be repeated public-opinion surveys; it might be the identification of opinion-forming groups, who we assume think today as others will think tomorrow; it might be official surveys and public records; it might be 'participant observation' (a technique in anthropology whereby a specialist actually lives and works with a group under study); it might be 'analysis by precursive events' as we described in chapter I.1. A vast amount of all of these already exists at national level.

Our expectations and forecasts of social change, as in other fields, must depend on our knowledge of past changes. This knowledge alone gives us some concept of general, systematic change, as opposed to random and contingent changes. As we noted in I.1 above, you need either historical data series or theories, and a theory not based on the former is not much use.

Theories abound in this field. Perhaps society is mainly changed by economic factors, as Marx said, or by changing values and beliefs, as de Tocqueville and Weber said. De Tocqueville's analysis of the transforming force of the 'passion for equality', in *Democracy in America*, remains one of the finest exercises in 'social forecasting'. So also Max Weber and Tawney on the role of the 'protestant ethic' in bringing about capitalist development in Western Europe, and – at the other end, as it were – the force of scientific and technical rationality (or bureaucracy) as the overriding impulse in the future development of industrial society.

Or perhaps it is mainly changed by technology, and all other social changes should be seen as the effects of adjustment to technological change. New technologies, such as railways, force society to adapt. Thus technology shapes our mental map of society. This model is particularly popular with certain contemporary futurologists, e.g. Alvin Toffler: 'Technology, the great growling engine of change.' Or perhaps there is an ineluctable cycle about everything, as Spengler and Toynbee in their different ways maintained.

All these theories have their consequences for social forecasting, but, since they are mostly contradictory, Europe Plus Thirty should not allow its work to be too much influenced by any one of them. It would be better to seek to apply each or any of them – or others – to various situations as hypotheses which may, or may not, suggest useful tools for social analysis, and thus for forecasting.

Putting various theories and preconceptions together with the empirical data which will come its way, Europe Plus Thirty can ask of each: What sort of politics does this model imply? To what extent under this hypothesis do technical possibilities limit the political options? What range of life-styles is possible if society really works as this theory says it does? Can this theory be used to foreshadow demands which may in future be made by society on technology and on the economy? And so on.

For instance, Daniel Bell's contention about the increasing 'technification' of institutions in decision-making is endorsed by many others of more radical disposition like Alain Touraine and Jürgen Habermas. Bell's model – like Marcuse's and many radical ones – comes out of a period of economic growth; it would therefore be instructive for the forecasting team as a whole to compare it with models that accept slow or zero growth, such as Robert Heilbroner's *Inquiry into the Human Prospect* and Schumacher's *Small is Beautiful*. The latter is particularly instructive in emphasising the importance of local control and a human scale with an appropriate technology to match. (These tracts were both written before the energy crisis.)

The values, structures, and life-styles, the rise or fall of which would be fit subjects of speculation for Europe Plus Thirty, could be extremely numerous. What follows is to be taken as illustration, not precept.

The increasing average age of our populations is one certain demographic trend which will certainly affect predominant social values and attitudes; it will promote those which are commoner among older people than among younger, and it may well increase yet further the tension between old and young. It is harder to determine what the older people of tomorrow will actually want – probably stability and order, but to say that is not to imply right-wing politics. The demand could well be for stability and order within a more, not less, collectivist frame. Such questions deserve speculation.

The rational management of production implied in most projections of modern industrial society depends for its working on a strong commitment on the part of the workforce, especially the technical, professional, and white-collar workers. What if – as some evidence suggests – this commitment declines? There has recently been some reaction amongst younger professionals against involvement in conventional professional practices; some lawyers, architects, social workers, teachers, have not wanted to push the familiar career pattern. Status has become less important. Some have simply withdrawn, as casual 'freelances' or social security clients. Others, more interestingly, have gone into or set up new agencies and practices, using their skills and experience in a manner which they consider more truly in accordance with the principles of their vocation. Examples are neighbourhood law centres, community centres, local action groups, environmental groups, etc. These trends point to a weakening of commitment to the existing social structure, and a commitment to something else, more local, more grassroots, more capillary. The shift has been made easier by the dispersal of skills and knowledge which were hitherto concentrated in large cities into small towns and suburbs, as the metropolitan population declines.

The trend implies a disillusionment with the nation-state and its centralising tendencies. But another reaction is also noticeable, and is of more interest to the Community: the one which looks beyond the nation-state to the international level. For some time now it has mainly been the economic and scientific elites which have tried to push international aggregation – and this is very much the knowledge class.

Is there an upvaluation of service, loyalty, and responsibility, because people at the local, smaller level hope to have more control over what happens? If so, it might apply also to industry, where perhaps a radical change within industries – especially the secondary ones – might resolve the problems of boredom, voluntary absenteeism, strikes, and industrial sabotage. Some managements are redesigning the organisation of work to make it more 'involving'. Already some firms have started to break up the assembly-line organisation, in the direction of more autonomous working units responsible for a diversity of tasks and more complete components.

These trends and the problems associated with them are so far rather new, and they deserve close study in so far as they have implications for the future of European societies. It is, perhaps, worth considering whether these trends among European youth may be a product of the last two decades of full employment and economic growth. Recent changes in study and career preferences observed among university students in several European countries (and in the U.S.A.) suggest that doubts as to economic stability and employment possibilities may now be tending to re-establish a more traditional relationship to work, and to reawaken interest in a stable and orderly society. What is the dividing line between a trend and a fad?

What are the limits of tolerance in a society with highly articulated, if not always rational, political and organisational structures? Is it possible to say anything about the 'value stretch' that can coexist with basic efficiency and coordination? Expectations of the future of industrial society mostly assume the scientific view of the world. It was commonly expected that industrial society would bring in the secular society; it would be a society in which people thought more and more of nature and reality as science dispelled the force of the supernatural, the unobservable, the undemonstrable. But these expectations have not been fulfilled. Even if institutional religion has declined, there has been no lack of secular ideologies and 'scientific' faiths for industrial man to espouse. To add to this, in latter years in the West we have seen a great burgeoning of cults and sects of a quasi- or explicitly religious character, which are now reaching back into the established churches. Society still needs emotional bonds which are not found in the realm of politics and economics. Difficult as it must be, we need to get some inkling of the likely character of thought and feeling in the late twentieth century, of the everyday assumptions, beliefs, and working hypotheses by which people will wish to guide their lives, of the aspirations they will have for themselves and their children. How likely, for instance, is a revival of mass religion within the established churches? What of the 'therapeutic communities', of sects, cults, and other expressions of exclusiveness and retreat? What is the future of deliberate unreason?

In thinking about the future Europe Plus Thirty should speculate about the compatibility of a pluralism of values with the functioning of a science-based economy and society. Forecasting about values – difficult as it may be – has to be done, since values are the inner bloodstream of any social system. And this forecasting, as we argued above, must be of a different kind from most that we recommend, since freedom itself is at stake.

The family is worthy of separate investigation. How are its day-to-day and intimate structures likely to develop? What might be the effect on family structure of the determined movement by women to get a uniform equality with men? What might be required to offset the problems of household management and child-rearing, and what would be the effect on the children, if the mothers of young children increasingly seek fulfilment outside the home? For instance, can one envisage that old people could be 'brought back' to play a major role in the upbringing of their grandchildren, or conversely that women would come to demand a basic right to part-time work? Can one assume that the nuclear family will for ever remain untrammelled and free-floating, as the sole relevant family unit – relevant, that is, both for its members and in the eyes of the social institutions outside it?

Significant changes in the family's size and structure and in its life-cycle are already under way in most European countries. The number of children in average families has fallen sharply, with the consequence that the child-rearing period in a typical family is now much shorter than it was a generation ago. Because of higher living standards and improvements in the housing situation, families and even single young people live alone. The time needed for cooking and cleaning has fallen thanks to better technical equipment and changes in consumption patterns (more ready-made food etc.). All in all, family structures have changed, the activities in the family have changed too, and the length and content of the different stages of the typical life-cycle of European families have changed accordingly.

The commune and even the extended family are here and there superseding the nuclear family as the closest framework for the individual, though usually in a transient way. If the trend solidifies, it would have implications for new housing. Even the nuclear family itself has become surrounded by a host of other institutions, advising, giving, cajoling, remedying, threatening. Far from taking the pressure off families, these many points of contact make life more complicated. Families have had to become small archives of information and expertise to cope successfully with the welter of institutional demands made on them, instead of the other way round. These demands appear together with a parallel process which has been making it more difficult for family members to live near each other, to help and support each other, and at the same time has been abolishing or diminishing the informal sources of support and advice once available in neighbourhood communities. All these changes interact.

We care pretty well for the minorities we can see: most member countries devote ever-increasing resources of money and skills to making life decent for the immigrant workers in our industrial cities, and the same applies to the old and the disabled, one-parent families, and so on. But it would be worth forecasting about what may happen to the minorities that 'we' hardly ever see, the very poorest citizens of the Community, the islanders of Italy and Scotland, the Eskimo tribesmen of Greenland. Here the argument shades off into regional policy of the familiar sort, but it behoves democratic and would-be compassionate societies to pay special attention to the poorest of all. The same applies to gypsies, who are suffering more and more from the erosion of their traditional territory, the verges.

What are people supposed to do all day? For a century now it has been taken for granted by all but the arts-and-crafts movements that the pride of science and the duty of technology is to allow people to work less. If three small farms are united and their hedges and walls are erased so that bigger tractors can be used, that is progress and productivity, and the peasant can go to the city and earn more. If an industrial process can be automated, that is progress and productivity too; and if the former peasant is thrown out of work again, that is a short-term structural shake-out, and he will soon be 're-absorbed' elsewhere. If he learns to be a bus conductor, he is caught by 'over-manning' and the one-man bus crew. And if he has a natural gift for juggling or acrobatics, who wants that when they can see the Russians on TV?

Moreover, a certain taint of unmanliness still, in some Community countries, hangs over the whole service sector: it used to be punished by selective taxes in order to get people into the production sector, which seemed much more virile. And so the vicious circle begins again.

It is largely recognised now that the best technology we can export to Asia and Africa is labour-intensive, or 'intermediate' or 'alternative' technology. May the day be coming when our values shift so that we begin to think the same about ourselves? Will the present deep ambiguity in our values about leisure (good) and unemployment (bad) be resolved? And if so, which way?

The whole subject has deep and so far unexplored interdependencies not only with social values but also with politics, resource use and depletion, technology, demography, education, and economics (including for this purpose industry and agriculture).

The countries of the Community are at very different stages on the road to the establishment of worker participation in the control of productive and other enterprises. Germany was the pioneer; indeed the German word 'Mitbestimmungsrecht' is now used quite normally in some other Community languages. Denmark is also well ahead. The acceptability of the pattern depends on the general history and psychology of industrial relations in the countries concerned, and is closely linked (though which is chicken and which is egg is hard to determine) with the degree of material prosperity. Italy and Britain, the poorest of the industrial member countries, still tend to pursue untrammelled confrontation between management and labour.

The possibility of a Community policy in this matter has been under discussion for some time. Such a policy might be linked with the articles of constitution which could be declared necessary if a company were to qualify as a 'European company', or it might be devised some other way. Forecasting about the possible long-term social, industrial, and economic results, and the educational requirements, of different ways of doing it could be a part of Europe Plus Thirty's work.

As we said, there are as yet no experts in social forecasting in the sense that there are experts in technological, economic, or demographic forecasting. Therefore Europe Plus Thirty should include a number of social scientists whose function would be threefold. First, they would ensure, with and through the Community Statistical Office and the national statistical offices, a supply of social data to Europe Plus Thirty which is relevant to its needs, remembering that it will exist to speculate and forecast about the future of the European Community as a whole and to do technology assessment for it. Secondly, they would take part in the general development of the nascent practice (we cannot yet say 'science' or 'art') of social forecasting. And thirdly, they would work in and with all the forecasting which is done in Europe Plus Thirty, to ensure that knowledge about society and social trends, and the probability of social 'surprises', are never overlooked.

The importance of social forecasting as such cannot at present be assessed, but it seems *potentially* so great that Europe Plus Thirty should not rely on the part-time presence of outside people. There should be people in the central team, and the skills of those chosen should reflect the pattern of work to be undertaken. Seminars, out-house contracts, and short attachments should be used in the usual ways.

7. *Education*

Nearly all Western European countries have had broadly similar educational experiences since the end of the Second World War. There has been an enrolment explosion caused partly by population increase and partly by increased participation rates, first at primary and secondary and then at the higher levels of education. The period of rapid expansion was accompanied by severe shortages of many kinds of teachers. Subsequently, since about 1970, educational growth has slowed down considerably in many countries, again partly as a result of slower population growth and partly because young people are showing less enthusiasm for upper secondary and higher education than seemed likely only a few years ago. This slower rate of growth has been accompanied by a tendency to teacher surplus and indeed unemployment.

Other developments have been similar in many European countries. A few may be listed almost at random. There is the movement away from rigid selection at the beginning of secondary school; there is the tendency towards child-centred rather than teacher-centred, subject-centred, or state-requirement-centred models of instruction, and towards the growth of non-traditional subjects, such as social sciences, and of vocational subjects in secondary and higher education. There have been attempts to use the educational system as an instrument of social engineering, as a means of promoting a more equal society and a more 'advanced' economy. There has been the introduction of new methods like television, radio, film, magnetic tape. There has been student militancy in nearly all European countries. And latterly there has been the growing preoccupation with the costs of, and the returns on, education.

Education has a very long-term effect. Most people leave school before they are twenty and live for another half-century. Information, ideas, and modes of thought learned in primary school influence behaviour sixty years later. A teacher in training may teach for another forty years. The pupils he teaches at the end of his career will still be directly influenced a century from now, and of course it only tails off slowly even after that. School-building also casts its shadow forward. Building a particular type of school has a strong influence for a long period ahead on what kind of teaching takes place in it, although wonders can be done in using buildings otherwise than as they were intended.

The past two centuries have seen the industrial and then the scientific revolution, and these exercised a profound influence on the structure and content of our educational system. The school as we know it today has been shaped largely by the industrial revolution, in which the family was split up as a production unit and both parents worked long hours in factories and workshops. The scientific revolution of the twentieth century has demanded scientific and technical professional training, so that secondary schools and universities have been places where students go to learn how to do things and to accumulate factual information, rather than to discover themselves and learn how to think.

Here are four alternative scenarios:

(1) The next thirty years may see a continuation of economic growth after the pause of the early 1970s. Some commentators claim that if it does our societies will become increasingly dehumanised: technocratic and economic interactions will continue to replace relationships between people, the 'protestant work ethic' and competitiveness will become even more pervasive than they are now, and the role of education will increasingly be that of providing credentials for a carefully selected meritocratic elite.

(2) A more optimistic view is that it is only the freedom from want brought about by economic growth that will permit mankind the luxury of improved human relationships freed from the pressures of economic necessity. The education system of such a genuinely affluent society could concentrate on the personal development of its pupils and students and on preparing them for lives of constructive leisure and satisfying work experience, rather than having to provide them with the intellectual weapons needed for success in the rat race. It could also afford to provide opportunities for 'recharging the intellectual batteries' through periods of study and reflection by adults at intervals throughout their working lives.

(3) An alternative view, common at present, is that the Western World is about to experience several decades of slower economic growth – slower at any rate than that experienced since the Second World War. People who welcome the prospect of zero economic growth claim that it would engender other social values than those which predominate today. They speak of a growing tendency 'to do one's own thing', to relate to people in small groups rather than in large impersonal workplaces, and to pursue self-fulfilment in co-operation with others instead of through competition to reach the top of a career structure. Protagonists of this school of thought expect to see increasing participation by workers in the organisation of their work, so that work itself becomes an intrinsically satisfying experience rather than an instrument for producing at once goods and the income to purchase other goods. Education in such a society might correspond to the vision of the 'de-schoolers' and become much more closely integrated with work and leisure activities. Like work itself, the aim of education would become self-fulfilment and not preparation for a life external to the educational system.

(4) But an opposite view of the likely social effects of zero economic growth is equally possible. It may lead not to a more harmonious society but to one in which competition for resources is intensified.

Individuals may struggle all the harder to reach the tops of fewer and smaller economic trees, it may become impossible to make further progress towards equal educational opportunities for all as education has to compete for resources with everything else: with health, transport, social security, private consumption, and so on. Within education, the competition for resources between the various sectors – primary, secondary, higher, adult – already shows signs of intensifying. The reduced education budgets of recent years may be a portent of things to come. The graduate unemployment of the early 1970s in many countries illustrates another danger: reduced job opportunities for those with high educational qualifications can lead to considerable hardship and might result in frustration and anger being turned against existing social structures. This in turn might prove either constructive or destructive.

Europe Plus Thirty could perform a useful function by considering the likelihood of each of the four scenarios outlined above and by exploring the implications of each for education and for society as a whole. In particular, it could examine ways in which the educational system could be used as an instrument for promoting what may be called the optimistic alternative, whether the general rate of economic growth be fast or slow.

A common assumption underlying all these scenarios of the future of education is that the growth of public expenditure cannot go on ad infinitum. Therefore, if its forecasting is to be useful, Europe Plus Thirty will have to have a close look at cost-development.

From the 1950s to the end of the 1960s, education expenditures increased their share of GNP in the developed countries from 2–3 per cent to some 6–9 per cent. This growth in the total share could only take place at the cost of other sectors, and at some point firm financial priorities, which would become even more firm in an era of 'steady state', will have to be established. In the 1970s, and for the foreseeable future, the four sectors of education – pre-school education, school education, higher education, adult or 'lifelong' education – will have to compete keenly for public resources after a period rapid overall expansion.

There exists now a branch of economics – the economics of education – which relates expenditures on education in a wide sense to economic development and growth. This is an important area of study which arose at the end of the 1950s when traditional input factors, such as capital in terms of natural resources and numerical measures of labour, could not account for the whole of the economic growth, and one was thereby left with a 'residual' factor, sometimes estimated to account for as much as 50 per cent of economic growth. Considering that educational expenditure increased from 1950 to 1965 twice as fast as national income, it was natural to assume some kind of relationship between educational growth and the knowledge explosion on the one hand and economic growth on the other. What will be the implications of reassessing the utilisation of resources when the limits to educational expenditure are reached?

In general, education probably ranks lower in public esteem than it did ten years ago. The massive expansion of secondary and higher education in the 1960s has resulted neither in a more equal society nor in more rapid intellectual growth. Instead it has given us unemployment of graduates, student unrest, and a feeling that our schools and universities are growing apart from the rest of society.

There have been three recent claimants for special attention in education policy, all deriving to some extent from the disillusion with the effects of earlier expansion. The first is a growing concern with nursery and pre-primary education. The mainspring of this is the increasing evidence that the roots of educational inequality lie far back in early childhood, and that by the time some children start their primary schools it is too late for them ever to catch up with their more fortunate fellows.

Europe Plus Thirty could usefully devote some effort to a comparison and projection of what the education services and health services of different countries do for children from birth (and even before it in the form of ante-natal classes for parents) to ensure that all children at least start life with equal educational advantages, and to derive forward studies from that comparison. It goes without saying that any such study in Western Europe would take as a starting point the very high value that is put on democracy and individual freedom. It would, for example, be no solution to take children away from their mothers at birth in order to minimise the effects of family background, any more than it was when Plato first urged it.

The second new claimant for attention in thinking about educational policy is at the other end of the educational spectrum: the continued education and training of adults. There appear to be at least two separate reasons for promoting adult education. One is summarised in the common remark that 'the half-life of an engineer is six years' – in other words, that at the end of six years half the knowledge acquired by an engineer is obsolete. Thus engineers – and doctors, teachers, lawyers, managers, and almost all other skilled workers – need frequent retraining in order to bring them up to date. The other is an interest in equality. It is claimed that, given the diversity of human abilities, interests, and rates of development, an increase in economic and social equality would be possible if everybody had the opportunity of attending education and training courses at all stages of their working life. As with pre-school education, there could be a role for Europe Plus Thirty in exploring the extent and nature of the potential demand for 'recurrent' education. Critics claim that such practical matters as house purchase and family commitments will ensure that it never affects more than a minority of adults. Supporters aver that there is a vast latent demand for the right kind of recurrent education properly integrated with the rest of society. An international study of the demand, actual and latent, present and future, among adults for education and training could be valuable to those concerned with policy in this area.

The third new development is the growing clamour for a closer integration between schools and society; here the growth of parent/teacher associations lies at one end of the spectrum, and the 'de-schooling' movement on the other. Europe Plus Thirty could consider the extent to which institutionalised schooling may cease to be judged an adequate instrument for socialising young people and for inculcating the competences they need in the society of today and tomorrow. The immersion of all teenagers in institutionalised schooling has occurred in an era when there have been fundamental changes in the role of the school as an institution, in the society in which it is embedded, and in such previously powerful alternative institutions as the churches and various youth movements. The school does not possess a monopoly of information or of teaching. There are many agents in society that are as 'information-rich' as the school; television, radio, record players, the press, libraries, and various leisure activities. Europe Plus Thirty could consider the likelihood and implications of schools becoming less institutionalised and having more informal contact with society at large; it could focus upon the possible crisis points at which institutionalised education may be dysfunctional with respect to the rest of society, resulting, for example, in university graduates with job aspirations that are unrealistic in relation to the jobs available, or on the other hand in needs for trained people which the universities fail to satisfy. Another possibility that a forecasting body could explore would be the implications of giving teachers the opportunity to alternate between the classroom and the outside world, and conversely giving other workers a chance to become part-time or temporary teachers. There is the basis for a 'de facto social experiment' here (see chapter I.1) in a comparison with the system which has applied for many decades in Chile.

So far we have been considering educational developments that are occurring more or less simultaneously in many European countries; since many countries are facing common problems, all are likely to find that they have something to learn from each other. Certainly much of education must remain a national responsibility – many people in Britain and Germany would claim a local responsibility. But no European country nowadays is likely to pursue an educational policy completely uninfluenced by the experiences of its neighbours. Apart from anything else, international comparisons are one of the favourite weapons of those who are proposing or opposing a particular educational development. It is useful if such comparisons are made on as reliable a basis as possible. But there are also a number of areas in which education is becoming inherently more international, and in which an international approach to the issue is not merely an adjunct to national policies but esssentially *is* the policy of the countries concerned.

The first of these arises from the international market for qualified manpower. It has long been realised that true international mobility of manpower will be possible only when all educational qualifications have international acceptability. In certain high-level occupations international agreements have already been reached, or are very near, on the international currency of qualifications. Further detailed study is needed before we do more than scratch the surface of this problem. Europe Plus Thirty could sponsor forward-looking studies in particular occupational areas and thus help to promote a situation in which all the workers of Europe can find employment where their particular qualifications are most in demand. Such studies should also take account of the general tendency, tersely known as the 'brain drain', for the best-educated people in any country to emigrate to another if they can get better pay and conditions there. This affects not only movement internal to the Community, but also movement into the Community from less-developed countries and out of it to the U.S.A. The flow of engineers, scientists, and doctors into the U.S.A. (about half of them from Western Europe) trebled between 1955 and 1967. One way for 'down-gradient' societies to slow their own brain drain might be the encouragement in them of centres of excellence transcending national frontiers, to which we turn below. The Community has a duty not only to itself in this matter, but also to those down-gradient of it, the developing countries.

A related issue is the international mobility of students. This has three aspects. One is the acceptability of entry qualifications for universities and similar institutions. What is needed in the long run is a European accreditation agency, so that any institution in any country can immediately evaluate the entry qualifications of any aspiring entrant to that institution. The establishment of such an agency would require considerable research into the vast number of educational qualifications provided in the various European countries. The second aspect is financial. European countries finance their higher education institutions in different ways. In some, students pay fees and are subsidised. In others, all facilities are free but students receive no grant. In others again, students can obtain loans to help finance themselves during their studies. If any substantial interchange of students is to develop between countries, arrangements must be developed to ensure that such financial mechanisms do not distort the flows of students. The third aspect is the existence in some countries and some universities of the *numerus clausus*, which leads, and might lead increasingly, to an outflow of students to neighbouring countries.

Another factor which makes education inherently international is the high capital intensiveness of much scientific research. Many research projects require such expensive equipment that it is beyond the reach of any one European country to undertake more than a few of them. And yet if a country does not undertake the research, it has no way of ensuring that its young scientists and technologists can keep up with developments in that branch of science. This is clearly an area for European cooperation, and a forecasting body could attempt to identify the areas in which it is likely to become necessary. Moreover, the argument for European centres of excellence is not confined only to 'big science': it applies also to a certain concentration of training facilities, and this can only be made efficient if it ignores national boundaries. Again, it would be useful to identify in advance areas where international centres of excellence of this sort are likely to become desirable.

A third area for international cooperation in educational policy is that of new educational technologies using programmed texts, magnetic tape, and film. This means that whole courses can be packaged, and bought and sold. Already the British Open University has a flourishing trade in such pre-packaged courses, and so have a rapidly growing number of commercial enterprises. Perhaps there should be a Community standards institute to test the various course materials offered for sale and ensure that they are effective according to various criteria, and that it is reasonable to claim that they could be used in different countries. An even more ambitious idea would be the establishment of a European centre for educational technology which could itself develop new course materials.

Finally, it may be that the Community will in due course wish, as part of its external relations policy, to further types of education in Europe which will be specifically useful to the developing world – to stimlulate a reverse brain drain as part of a coherent drive to overcome the problem and the dangers we touched on in our Introduction.

An essential preliminary for all such developments would be forward-looking studies that reviewed the possibilities and likely developments in curricula and educational technology for the next quarter of a century.

Obviously, forecasting activities in education will have to take identified areas of common concern as their point of departure. The Janne Report of 1973 on Community Policy in Education[1] lists a number of problems which should be recognised by the Community as areas of responsibility. The present chapter has outlined others. Europe Plus Thirty should initiate and develop, for the benefit of the Community, a better insight into the linkages between education and other social sectors, and should be capable of policy analysis and comparison in this matter. This means continuously looking for and analysing the 'educational dimension' of the economic and social problems which the Community has to face.

The Commission has since 1974 had at its disposal an important instrument (Directorate General XII) to deal with educational problems. Similarly, the Council of Ministers has created an Education Committee in order to develop educational policies in a certain number of priority areas. Several other departments (probably most of them) of the Commission, and Committees of the Council, are involved in activities which are directly relevant to the future of education. Coordination between these departments and committees is already taking place, but for reasons due mainly to the nature of large organisations such as the European Commission this coordination is limited. It may be that an independent body such as Europe Plus Thirty, devoted to interdisciplinary and intersectoral forecasting, can provide some impetus for the development of this linkage.

Europe Plus Thirty should also address itself to studies of the institutional development of educational systems with the aim of anticipatory identification of what changes in the structure and content of education would be necessary in order to meet possible changes in society and, conversely, what changes in society are likely to result from present or foreseeable structures and contents of education. It should also conduct or sponsor forecasting studies, on the basis of a systematic collection of statistical and other information (much of which already exists in UNESCO and OECD) about enrolment, trends on the labour market, and changing preferences with regard to education offered.

The content of the curriculum, where changes tend to be even slower than in the structure of the system, is another area which might benefit from forecasting. The common denominator, as far as the Community is concerned, is the growing internationalisation of the

[1] *Bulletin of the European Communities*, Supplement, October 1973.

national systems of education, and the common interest lies in the fact that what happens in Europe in the future will be mainly the result of what its children and students are taught is true or good now. Studies of the curricula at all levels of the education systems should therefore be stimulated in order to lay the basis for forecasting about the teaching of science, civics, philosophy, sociology, history, and languages, and as an input for general social forecasting.

The methods of forecasting about education do not differ essentially from those employed in other social areas. Educational changes occur within general socio-economic change, and this means that educational forecasting must be related to other areas of forecasting.

Assessments of future trends and developments in education should be based on three main activities:

(1) Continous secondary collection of *basic statistics* on

(*a*) demographic trends and population projections, with particular reference to the age-range five through twenty (see II.3);

(*b*) enrolment at various levels of the formal educational system;

(*c*) cost development.

(2) Continuous collection of information concerning institutional changes and innovations in the educational systems, such as reforms in structure, content, and methods of instruction.

(3) Forecasting studies making regular use of panels of experts in seminars and conferences, to obtain new injections of ideas and vision, and to review and criticise the ongoing work.

8. *Science and technology*

The relationship between mind on the one hand and space, time, matter, and energy on the other is the subject of a huge literature, in which we in the West still largely use the thought structures devised in Greece two and a half thousand years ago. Mind subsists in space, endures in time, and consists of or is a function of matter and energy; but still it is able to apply something called understanding to the very extensions it exists in and the very 'things' of which it is made, and there is something about this understanding which enables it to go further and 'control' them, or get them to do things they would apparently not otherwise have done. The question whether the laws of nature are 'truly' the laws of nature or on the other hand only the laws of science – that is to say, whether they inhere unconditionally in space, time, matter, and energy, or whether their inherence is conditional on the activity of that part of those very things which we call mind, and thus on the ability of one mind to communicate them to others, dubbing them 'laws' – this question lies at the heart of any attempt at forecasting about science.

If ever we could describe with certainty the part played in some past scientific discovery respectively by the grasp of an individual mind and by the availability to be grasped of some scientific law which we were later enabled, by that particular act of grasping, to describe as such, we should be able to forecast what type of relationship between what type of mind and what type of (so far unexplained) phenomena would be most likely to produce 'results' in the future. Unfortunately the subtlest book yet written about all this, Arthur Koestler's *The Sleepwalkers*,[1] tends to the conclusion that, far from public policy being able to help the right scientist to the right place, the greatest scientists have only made their greatest discoveries as by-products, unrecognised by their very authors, of enquiries into something else. Forecasting about technology does not pose such arduous problems. Laws and propositions about space, time, matter, and energy, as they are bandied about between mind and mind, sometimes suggest useful things to do, called inventions, applications of inventions, technologies, etc.; and sometimes they do not.

Forecasting both about science itself and about its application in technology must, as usual, be a blend of theory, experience, and imagination. This field is so vast that here, perhaps more than anywhere, the forecasting to be done by Europe Plus Thirty must be related to the powers and functions of the European Commission, which will be its principal user.

The Commission's function in scientific and technological research is limited. The greater part of what it does is done through its Joint Research Centre, a chain of establishments in Italy, Germany, and the Netherlands; this body has been concerned mainly with the vain attempt (to which we return in the next chapter) to develop a European reactor, but it is now diversifying.

At present, only 2 per cent of the public money spent in the Community on scientific research is spent by the Commission; the rest is national. The Community is roughly the equal of the U.S.A. and the Soviet Union in population, education, and wealth. Yet it lags far, far behind them both in scientific and technological innovation, and this is all too obviously because the member countries are still competing against one another as they did a hundred years ago, when all the scientific research in the world was done in Western Europe, and none of it was too expensive to be done on a population base of thirty to

[1] London: Hutchinson, 1968.

133

forty million. To eliminate duplication of work, and to obtain economies of scale, is an obviously rational goal. Habit and pride impede it, but they are on the downgrade.

Two general purposes suggest themselves for the forecasting which ought to be undertaken in this field by Europe Plus Thirty for the Community: to facilitate the rational and beneficial exercise of its existing powers and functions and the formulation of new powers and functions which it might seek to obtain; and to provide informed conjecture about the future course of scientific and technical innovation in so far as that may affect the development of industry, the economy, and society in general. Over industry and the economy, the Community exercises substantial powers.

The evaluation of the results of scientific research, in terms both of direct utility to mankind and of indirect utility in leading to the next necessary piece of research, is a rapidly developing but still rudimentary art. The work done so far usually assumes a single society, within which and for the benefit of which the research is done; the society as a whole is then found to have benefited from it or not. The very first work on the differential benefiting of different social classes within national societies is now appearing; much of it is far from dispassionate,[1] but it is a useful corrective to decades of blind incrementalism. On the other hand there is little work indeed on the differential benefiting of national societies within one region of the world, or indeed within the world as a whole.

There is thus a clear role for Europe Plus Thirty. It should enquire far enough into the question of what sort of research has benefited what sort of people to be able to tackle the question of what sort of research is likely in future to benefit what sort of people. It would then be able to proceed to forecast about the likely effects of given quanta of research being undertaken

(1) by the member states of the Community severally;

(2) by the Community as such because it is bigger;

(3) by neither (because neither is big enough) so that it has to be done on a world or Western-world basis.

Research is an open-ended commitment. Some sectors – high-energy physics, nuclear physics and engineering, radio astronomy, and aerospace are obvious examples – have already become extremely expensive to maintain productively. Other sectors, including oceanography and even some branches of biology, are threatening to join the 'big-science' club. Independent national work? Community division of labour? World division of labour? To take a hypothetical example:

---

[1] Should the assertion that there is no such thing as dispassionate science be debated passionately or dispassionately?

geophysical forays into the earth's crust could be valuable to Europe from several standpoints. They could show the way to geothermal energy reserves, especially for the least physically stable regions of southern Europe; they could advance the technology of exploration and exploitation of fossil fuels, especially for nations with large continental shelves; they could open new options for long-term disposal of radioactive wastes, of interest to every nation with a nuclear power programme. A concerted multidisciplinary effort in geophysics might thus open new options which no single nation or sectional interest would consider warranted the necessary 'critical size' of effort to reach them.

Attractive targets for research, considered in relation to the probable time span of Europe Plus Thirty, are now so numerous that it is difficult to assemble a balanced 'portfolio of objectives' within the means of any one nation. Valuable options may thus remain closed to Europe unless ways can be found to share the expense. The European Science Foundation (which goes wider than the Community) has now been set up to deal in part with such problems.

Some objectives (e.g. in defence) and some commitments (e.g. to high-energy physics) threaten to distort the totality of scientific effort by monopolising a disproportionate and possibly increasing amount of talent and cash. Political patronage can also distort objectives. Here is a field where future changes in social and political structures and values may well affect the development of science itself. We are so used to thinking of the effects of science on society that it is important to remember that things happen the other way around as well.

Besides providing the social and economic forecasting necessary for the exercise of Community functions in regard to scientific and technical research itself, Europe Plus Thirty will have to provide inputs, in the form of speculation and forecasting about the future of science and technology, into the general social and economic forecasting it does. It should undertake technological forecasting in those areas where possible technological developments would or might have such substantial effects on the economies and societies of the Community that the Community institutions would, one way or another, be bound to be concerned.

In a world in which energy costs have so abruptly increased there is little question that the most socially and economically fruitful scientific achievement would be cheap thermonuclear fusion. Cheap fusion power would afford Europe independence in energy resources, a freedom it cannot now contemplate until well into the next century (and then only if high-efficiency fast breeder reactors prove a success). Provided fusion reactor technology could then evolve smoothly from the industrial base now being created for fission reactors – by no means a certainty, for far greater engineering problems, temperatures, and neutron fluxes are involved – fusion could mean a return to cheaper energy and the exploitation of very lean mineral resources, even sea-water.

A technologically less demanding way of harnessing fusion power would be the discovery of an efficient method of converting solar energy into electricity or into food (where a mechanism that merely doubled the present abysmally low conversion efficiency of photosynthesis could, if it were found, dramatically promote growth in crops). Another possibility for a great reduction in energy costs would be the discovery of a simple low-temperature chemical reaction for splitting water molecules to release hydrogen – a clean fuel. An encouragingly large number of reactions has been discovered in the last few years, although none is simple enough to promise cheap hydrogen yet.

New ways of synthesising very complex substances – food is the obvious example – at much less cost in energy and raw materials would be dramatically important to Europe. The breakthrough could come with an understanding of the subtleties of catalysis (including the mechanisms of the living catalysts, enzymes), or from the work of molecular biologists. Only a few years ago very few people would have predicted that the new science of molecular biology would disclose the opportunities now opening in 'genetic engineering', in the tailoring of genetic templates to develop desired characteristics in a living micro-organism. Opportunities within comparatively modest research budgets seem to centre on radical intervention with the behaviour of micro-organisms such as bacteria, having prodigious powers of reproduction. Such nitrogen-fixing organisms might be provided with genetic templates selected so that they synthesise the optimum mixture of proteins to promote growth in animals or plants. It might prove possible to transfer the nitrogen-fixing ability of such organisms to higher plants, giving, for instance, potatoes and wheat the ability to make their own fertiliser, a prospect which has been described as a gift to mankind almost as valuable as fire. Other possibilities are the synthesis of vaccines against virus diseases, or the recovery of valuable minerals such as gold or uranium from lean but inexhaustible resources such as sea-water. Each of these opportunities – crop growth promotion especially – have immense implications for population distribution, jobs, transport, etc. which Europe Plus Thirty would have to explore.

Solid-state physics may open major new options in materials science, where the attraction of materials perhaps ten times as strong as they are today is immense in terms of husbanding natural resources, or in sensor technology where the implications of, say, a new mechanism for detecting and locating submarines at great distance (to supersede sonar, just as radio location superseded sound location of aircraft) could change the pattern of mutual assured deterrence between America and Russia, by making the nuclear submarine vulnerable. If this should happen, the entire political structure of mankind would be called in question.

There is perhaps no better example of an invention whose impact could be profound, but for which identifying the consequences well in advance calls for expertise and imagination of a high order, than the laser, born in 1960. Its promise lies in two quite different directions: as a unique and versatile sensor and as a unique and versatile energy source. Some of the most exciting possibilities today, including laser fusion (microfusion) and laser enrichment of uranium, were not anticipated in the early years of its exsitence. Lasers of increasing energy and diminishing wavelength, including the 'graser' or gamma-ray laser, are almost certain to open fresh vistas, if only indirectly as research tools of unprecedented analytical power.

The question of how to forecast about the carrying-through of scientific discovery into technological innovation, and thence into daily use and wealth, raises once again the difficult distinction, which we touched on in the Introduction, between forecasting and planning. This carrying-forward is being planned all the time in industry, and 'corporate planning' rests on forecasting undertaken for the benefit of industry, not of society at large (see the next chapter). Europe Plus Thirty could undertake systematic forecasting about the costs and benefits of the alternative routes which might be taken by a given scientific discovery through the applied research phase, the development phase, and the prototype phase; through alternative socio-industrial structures, with their different degrees of public answerability; through the different expenditure phases with their related alternative fiscal and subsidy policies; and, lastly, through the alternative mixes of national and Community law, tax, and subsidy, which apply, or might apply in the future, to such alternative routes. At every stage careful distinctions would have to be made between the various parties meeting the cost (internal or external, etc.) and the various parties receiving the benefits. This would be an immense task, and one which would only become justifiable as the Community obtained, or saw an immediate likelihood of obtaining, a measure of power to change or affect those routes themselves.

Certainly one can dream – indeed all of us who contributed to this report have probably dreamed – of a world, or even a European Community, capable of taking our prodigious science and technology by the scruff of the neck and bending it by human will to the service of conscious human aims. We dream of deliberately and actively planning their development in a new partnership between government, research, and industry, so that needs of our battered race may be met in time, so that we may command our future and not follow our past. If it were done, it would be necessary to survey and investigate alternative technological options well in advance and, as a kind of sub-continental insurance policy, to ensure that many of them are pursued as far as the pilot plant or engineering prototype stage, so as to be capable of rapid exploitation if the need arose. Diversity of technological development like this would, of course, be very costly, and it is unthinkable that all the relevant options could be followed up in each industrialised country. If any attempt were made to grip this matter, and to grip it within the world of democracy, it could not (in Western Europe) be made by any one country alone: it would have to be done by the Community.

Nor would it be wise to attempt any such thing, or even a tenth of it, on the basis of knowledge or opinion about what society needs or wants now; it would need to be based on forecasting about what society is likely to want of science and technology in the future, and this would probably be among the most fertile of the sectoral interactions which could be achieved in a closely integrated forecasting instrument.

Much light is thrown on how this could be done by C. F. von Weizsäcker's tripartite division of the history of science.[1] The first phase was the creation by princes of institutions where scientifically minded barbers, builders, and sailors could become something new: scientists. The second phase was that of the autonomy of science, when scientists followed their own noses and always got the money to do it. This was the phase which produced the laws of science, the dignity of science, and the power of scientists. We are now in the third phase, when science and scientific education are so expensive that society has to ration the expenditure and, in doing so, to decide what science shall be done. Times have changed since the first phase; it is no longer princes now, but the diffuse machinery of democracy which has to produce the decision.

As in many of our fields, we think Europe Plus Thirty should spend considerable effort on finding out what the present causal linkages are. How are social demands on science and technology expressed? How are they transmitted, and to whom? What structures and policies exist, and what results do they yield? There are one or two specialist

---

[1] Vividly expounded by Ralf Dahrendorf in 'Science, Policy, and Science Policy', *Proceedings of the Royal Irish Academy*, vol. 75, section C, no. 2 (1975), pp. 33–44.

institutes in Community countries which are well qualified in this field.

Then Europe Plus Thirty must, by the use of task forces, brainstorming, and scenarios, work out alternative future European structures and policies for comparison by the decision-makers on the basis of the knowledge acquired.

It must keep scanning in many fields of advanced technology for those breakthroughs (we gave examples above) which, if they happened, would really change people's lives and would thus demand new policies which might have to be on a Community scale.

Lastly, it should scan current experience of the effects of different subsidy and fiscal policies on the development of innovations (that is, development as opposed to research) and should forecast for the Community about alternatives open to it in this matter.

Technological forecasting of the kind outlined in this chapter has much in common with the process of technology assessment (TA), which is the subject of Part III below.

Those concerned with this work in Europe Plus Thirty should be headed or guided by, or should at least be able to call on the services of, two people, one each in the physical and the life sciences, who by their own work and reputation have access to the places where the absolute frontiers of ignorance are being pushed back. There should be extensive use of task forces, short appointments, and contract work.

9. *Industry*

In dealing with social forecasting, we pointed out that the same vastness and variety of the subject matter which make forecasting about it desirable also make it hard to specify what should be done. The same applies to industry. We in Western Europe are an industrial society; industry is not what we are *for*, but it is what most of us do.

In a field so vast, it is best once more to keep firmly before us the facts that Europe Plus Thirty will be assisting the Institutions of the Community, that what they require assistance in is the formation of policy, and that policy is simply a particular way of exercising powers. No powers, no policy: no assistance needed. The powers the Community now has and those it might acquire must set the boundaries of Europe Plus Thirty's work in this field.

It is therefore useful first to distinguish three sorts of 'industrial forecasting': forecasting about industry for the benefit of industry, forecasting about society as a whole for the benefit of industry, and forecasting about industry for the benefit of society. It is clearly in the last two of these three activities that Europe Plus Thirty must find its role. Forecasting has to be devised which is useful in identifying and pursuing goals. It is probably more misleading than not to think separately of social goals, economic goals, and industrial goals; there are only social goals. Economics are a means of measurement and reasoning, industry is a means of production, and neither of them can in themselves constitute or provide a goal or goals. Likewise with technology: it is not enough to watch technology going ahead and then check to see whether its results are going to be harmful; it is better, having chosen our social goals, to see what technological developments can and should be applied to their achievement. We should be examining not so much the social acceptability of new technologies as the technological possibility of achieving new social goals. Above all, Europe Plus Thirty should speculate about the demands which society may make on industry in the future, and the responses which may be called for from the Community in both industrial and social policy (see II.6).

Though designed for the good of society, such an approach could not but be useful to industry itself. In the past, Western European industry pursued its aims strictly according to economic criteria. It produced goods to be sold on the market, and it was assumed or hoped that the 'social good', whatever that was, would automatically be furthered by firms pursuing their individual goals. These goals consisted of maximising the efficiency of the profit–investment cycle, controlling and defending market positions, and devising and adjusting to changes in the product cycle.

It has for some time been clear that industrial activity in itself does not necessarily produce desirable social results. Increased standards of living may go a long way to satisfying needs, but needs are not only for goods; this becomes clear when the trade-off is between the increased production of goods and environmental deterioration or other external costs, or between 'economic' efficiency and full employment or satisfaction at work. An awareness of this fact has expressed itself in the development of government intervention, of technology assessment, and of an emphasis on qualitative rather than quantitative growth, and in moves towards worker participation in decision-making. People have also become aware that at a certain point technological innovation began to be used not only to increase productivity and welfare, but also as an artificial means to increase the market by shortening the product life-cycle and introducing 'better' new products in as rapid a succession as possible. The filtering-through and resolution of these problems are long-term issues.

In general, this change in attitudes has made it harder for firms to get on with their own business as they see it, namely that of producing profitably. The firm is increasingly torn between its responsibilities towards its shareholders, towards the society in which it operates, and towards its own employees. As a consequence of the confusion over these conflicting responsibilities, industry sees the increasing number of pressure groups (local residents, trade unions, consumers, environmentalists), more or less fostered and coordinated by governments, pushing it in different directions and, as it sees it, hampering it from getting on. The resolution of these often-contradictory demands makes for a climate in which public accountability is increasingly expected. Formerly, in a period of rapid economic growth, these demands, embodied in pressures on the firm, could be glossed over by distributing to all sides more of an ever-increasing cake. But when the workings of technology itself are called in question, and basic resources become scarce and expensive, the situation needs new solutions.

The adoption of Keynesian principles in the post-war period laid the basis, in Europe at least, for the rapid economic growth of the 1950s and 1960s, because it helped to cushion out downswings of the economy. This in turn caused governments to take on the responsibility of ensuring progressive growth. They became more closely involved with industry, because they were the only agencies with the authority to implement the demand policies which could ensure full employment and growth. Three further factors encouraged government involvement: the recognition and open acceptance of industrial development as a prerequisite of national power and independence, the need to direct and regulate 'natural' industrial development in order to create a regional and social balance, and the need to mobilise resources which lay beyond the capacity of the individual firm.

Hence the increasing government involvement at the national level; hence also the Community's attempts to make these involvements compatible first with the ideal of fair competition and now with a groundwork for possible economic and monetary union. Thus, even though the Community treaties do not explicitly mention industrial or technology policy, the fulfilment of their overall aims makes such policies inevitable. The need for close cooperation between industry and government in forecasting has long been evident, because of the increasing involvement of governments in devising policies for the reform of society as a whole and consequently in changing priorities for the goods and services that society needs. The need for close cooperation between member governments and the Institutions of the Community is in turn becoming increasingly apparent as the Community pursues both its established aims and those towards the definition and adoption of which it is struggling.

The European Community, and especially the Commission, is not starting from scratch in all this. The earlier interventions in industrial policy, the 'partial communities' of the ECSC and Euratom, have yielded countless lessons of the highest value. Coal and steel were chosen, back in the fifties, as a gauge of courage and wholeheartedness; they were felt to be the backbone of European industry. Their 'communitisation' did not yield the results hoped for, and it led in particular to the coal crisis of 1958 and the over-production of steel in 1969, because European coal and steel were not considered, or not sufficiently considered, as part of the energy sector as a whole or as part of the development of the world economy. Euratom (as a 'communitisation' of another part of energy production and of the R & D therefor) also failed to yield the hoped-for result – this time, probably, because a mistake was made about how industrial innovation can be procured and diffused, particularly in a field so intimately connected with military security. One cannot create an establishment, order it to innovate, and then, when it has innovated, order it to secure the adoption of its innovations on the shop floor. Life works more independently and more inconveniently, and above all it works in a way which can be better understood by forecasting about what may happen and better influenced by making decisions only after prolonged forecasting and analysis of the surrounding landscape. So the European innovations in nuclear energy were made where they would have been made anyhow – that is, nationally – and a European nuclear industry did not materialise.

The past experience of the Common Market, then, has shown the difficulties of seeking economic union without a broader industrial policy. The general aims of an industrial policy can only be to ensure a suitable framework for industrial development with the European market and for the application of Community regulations. But the economic forecasts which should have helped industry tended to become ends in themselves and not instruments to modify and guide decisions. The three programmes prepared by the Committee on Economic Policy (1966–70, 1968–70, 1971–5) were very general attempts in this direction but would have had to be more precise to enable them to be translated into policies and sectoral decisions.

To what extent the Community will increase its involvement in industrial policy is itself a matter of forecast. Effective Community action in the industrial field will only be obtained when it is possible to formulate a 'Community plan'. But while waiting for this eventuality, the Community will no doubt continue to fix general goals for industrial policy and for technology policy. These might include the easing of restraints on rationalising industry across frontiers, common approaches to fiscal and taxation policy, the development of a Community approach towards non-member states, concerted action towards foreign investment, and the development of regional industrial policy.

The Community might also wish in the future to develop a greater role in the exercise of public control over the multinational corporations. At present there is an ambiguity in our attitude towards them. On the one hand, they are obvious generators of wealth and very big generators of innovation. On the other, they are by their very multinationality able to 'play off' against each other the governments of the countries in which they operate. As long as it is national governments which, in the last resort, take decisions on labour conditions, land-use planning, pollution controls, safety standards, infrastructure investments, regional grants, water charges, etc., a company with the capital and the organisation to create production capacity where it likes is bound to seek the country where these decisions are most favourable to it, and national governments are bound in turn to be tempted to compete in offering favourable decisions. The result is by no means always to the good of a balanced Western European economy, especially from the regional point of view.

It is true that standardisation and coordination in these matters would leave the Community as a whole still in a state of unregulated competition with the rest of the world, and thus liable to be played off against, say, Japan or Eastern Europe. But that is true of many other things as well, and we imagine that an end to investment-snatching as between the member countries would be regarded as progress, and that attempts to achieve this will continue and in the end succeed.

So what should Europe Plus Thirty forecast about in the industrial field, and how? To begin with, it will not be alone. There is already a great deal going on: technological forecasting, technology assessment, techno-economic forecasting. Most of it is done by firms and industrial research associations for their own purposes – forecasting about industry for the benefit of industry. Some is done by governments, including much forecasting about society for the benefit of industry. It is fortunate that organisations already exist which can help to provide the inputs for Europe Plus Thirty's activities, such as the European Industrial Research Management Association (EIRMA) and the yet more recently established Federation of European Industrial

Cooperative Research Organisations (FEICRO). Both names are self-explanatory.

It would be impossible, or at least not cost-effective, for Europe Plus Thirty to attempt a detailed comprehensive model, whether conceptual as such or conceptualised onto a computer, for European industry as a whole. Its approach should be more problem-oriented, more based on brainstorming and scenarios, though of course always in the presence of the biggest data base practicable. In what follows by 'vertical' we mean single industries, and by 'horizontal' we mean phenomena, information, and problems which affect several industries or all.

(1) Europe Plus Thirty should produce guidelines (stemming from a generally informed view of the future of Europe as well as from the present long-term policies of the Community), and afford methodological control, for 'vertical' strategic forecasting and assessment exercises concerning certain industrial sectors or group of sectors, particularly those where there is or is likely to be a Community policy, or which are already somewhat integrated at Community or higher level.

(2) It should organise task forces, or repeated seminars, for such vertical exercises and should take part in them to ensure a high quality of forecasting and assessment work from the professional and methodological point of view.

(3) It should also organise and direct task forces for dealing with 'horizontal' issues: the issues should be carefully defined (by Europe Plus Thirty) and should be problem-oriented rather than sector-oriented.

(4) Finally, the general forecasting and assessment output of Europe Plus Thirty – the 'teleonomies' – should include whatever material can usefully be put into them from the outputs of the studies mentioned above.

The task forces should include people from industry itself who are concerned with technological forecasting and technology assessment, and possibly people from other bodies involved in the same activity. Both in the vertical and horizontal task forces, there should be people from the trade unions and, whenever they exist, from consumer associations; from their presence could come much mutual education.

Among the 'vertical' sectors tackled (2) should be some of the high-technology ones, such as electronics, 'informatics', and drugs, and also some sectors from our present mainline industries (e.g. cars, chemicals, machine tools, food processing, textiles). But the bulk of the work would probably fall on the 'horizontal' task forces (3). Some of the following issues could be selected for analysis and forecasting in this way:

(*a*) The problems of regional distribution of industry.

(*b*) Labour, capital, and energy intensiveness.

(*c*) Technology transfer, particularly the question of what kind of technology, in view of the role that the Community can play in the development of the Third World.

(*d*) World 'division of labour'. What are the present trends in the distribution of industrial innovation, high-technology industry, intermediate industry, low-technology industry, and menial drudgery, as between the U.S., Japan, the European Community, Eastern Europe, and various sectors of the developing world? What would be the consequences for Western European and world society of their continuation and of various alternative modifications? Could policies be adopted?

(*e*) The question of *Mitbestimmung*, thus bridging with social forecasting.

(*f*) The relation between manufacturing industry and the service sector. What macro-economic trends are emerging, and what would be the consequences for society of their continuation or modification?

(*g*) Forecasting and speculation about the dispersion of power in our midst – whether power for good or for ill, we do not say. The most obvious area is the rise of the multinational corporations. At the moment, as is very well known, some of them have bigger turnovers than the state revenues of middle-sized nations, and the trend appears to be continuing. What would or might be the political and social consequences for European society and for our external political and economic environment of its continuation or its reversal? What would be the prerequisites and effects, social, political, and economic, of alternative policies in this field?

(*h*) A contention well worth elucidating and deepening would be that which holds that it is enough for a government (or for the Community) to forecast, plan, and regulate only the development of bigger firms, since the smaller are conditioned and determined by what happens to the big ones. Is this true? If so, what are the conclusions to be drawn for policy formation?

(*i*) Again, what is the relative role of large and small firms in innovation both technological and social? Do small firms have a special role in jumping around trying out new things in the interstices between the industrial giants? What would happen if they were gradually squeezed out?

(*k*) And lastly, what might the future hold for the humanisation of industrial work? This concerns the movement, most advanced so far in Scandinavia, away from the inexorable production belt and towards a more craftsmanly organisation by work teams, and the opportunity for the individual worker to identify himself in a personal way with his product. This car was made by John, Henry, and Mary . . .

10. *Energy*

The Community lives now and will live for a long while yet with permanent energy difficulties, because of the conjunction of three historical trends. The first is that industrial societies have become addicted to high levels of energy use. Industrialisation and the rising material standards that go with it have depended on the substitution of one form of capital resource – energy – for other forms, especially labour, time, and land. This process accelerated sharply during 1950–70 on the back of ultra-cheap and assured oil supplies, with the result that most production and consumption patterns have become 'locked in' to patterns of high energy use that will not be at all easy to undo. Good examples are transport and settlement patterns, mechanisation and automation of both the manufacturing and service sectors, and the whole food production chain from the farmer to the urban housewife with her desire for packaged convenience foods. The solidity of these patterns is shown by the many recent estimates that energy consumption in most production and consumption activities can be lowered only by 10 per cent or so without making major structural changes or reforming highly ingrained attitudes.

The second trend is the growing difficulty of meeting this dependence. The escape from Middle East oil while also maintaining high levels of consumption inevitably calls for the massive expansion of very demanding technologies such as offshore oil, coal conversion, and nuclear power with their formidable requirements for capital, skilled manpower, materials, public acceptance of risks and environmental impact, and, in the case of nuclear power, requirements for infallible people and unbreachable security measures. Other less demanding technologies such as natural gas and geothermal, solar, and wind power tend either to be short-life resources or low-rate sources, creating their own sets of difficulties. It is now increasingly recognised that the real limits to the level of energy supply and/or to their possible rate of increase will be set not by purely geological or technical considerations but by the combination of an extremely wide range of social, political, and environmental factors.

The third trend is the growing recognition of global inequities and the consequent pressures for a new and more just international economic order. The energy profligacy of the North and the crippling impact of higher fuel prices on many countries of the South are one major cause of these moves to forge a new global relationship. Another is the move within the industrialised nations themselves towards new paths of development which are more relevant to non-material needs, and which distribute material requirements more fairly. If these adjustments are to be realised, the present disparities in energy consumption – approximately sevenfold between the richest and poorest sectors in individual European countries, and approximately tenfold between the averages for the EEC and the Third World – may have to be among the first fixtures to dissolve.

Given these trends, the wise management of energy will in future require an extremely broad and searching outlook. Clearly, the energy future is peculiarly uncertain. The constraints, and the opportunities over the longer term to escape those constraints by choosing other paths, are both very large. The general management process involves many judgements between risks and benefits, costs and advantages of many different kinds – some quantifiable, others not. Energy policy also has innumerable interactions with nearly all other social areas and issues, including fundamental questions of ethics, preferences, and ultimate goals. At this level of complexity, any process becomes political as well as – or more than – economic or technical.

At the deepest level, energy calls up far-reaching questions about the nature of industrial societies and their future directions of change: indeed, the radical transformations of the world energy/economic scene since the winter of 1973/4 have prompted widespread heart-searchings of this kind.

These introductory remarks point to the extreme difficulty of energy forecasting – at least of forecasting over a reasonably broad front with realism and credibility. Yet the attempt must be made: the energy future is too important to be left to trend extrapolation, as in the past. The rest of this chapter therefore reaches into this thicket of difficulties to pick out key priorities for energy forecasting. When these have been reviewed, the chapter ends by drawing out their implications for Europe Plus Thirty, and for the place of the latter among other European energy initiatives.

Since energy forecasts which cover a reasonably broad field must include a very wide range of social factors, they should be intimately related to large-scale social forecasts. Indeed, to an important extent energy forecasts are themselves social forecasts. For example, any projection which shows a large increase in electricity production implicitly assumes, because of economies of scale, the building of large power stations. If it assumes that power-station waste heat will be used for industrial or domestic purposes, then it also supposes the development of large industrial–urban clusters around the power units, or the location of the latter in existing clusters. With five to ten thousand megawatts per unit, or more in the case of 'nuclear parks', this assumes an extreme degree of centralisation. (Conceivably the development of small-scale nuclear fusion stations could reverse this situation, but such stations are still conjectural.) Meanwhile, low-energy-demand scenarios or those based on large-scale use of 'income energy' (solar, wind, etc.) immediately lead to massive changes in settlement patterns, the organisation of work, and so forth – and are in fact usually based on the desirability of such changes for social rather than energy reasons.

This point may seem obvious but is normally ignored. The great bulk of energy projections and forecasts (a) are based on and confined to rather narrow technical and economic considerations and (b) are extrapolatory rather than normative. For both reasons they tend to assume that the future will be much like the present, with some sectors 'bigger' and others 'smaller', and they therefore see no reason for questioning the social assumptions behind either the present energy pattern or the future projection.

A first priority, then, is to relate energy forecasting to all other social considerations and sectors: to attempt fully integrated forecasting. This is easier said than done; but it is precisely because hardly anyone is taking this all-sector, multidisciplinary approach to the longer-term future that Europe Plus Thirty was conceived.

A EUROPEAN APPROACH

One of the most striking facts about the European energy scene is the large differences between EEC nations in some rather basic parameters. Some of these are shown for the year 1970 in Table 2. These differences raise many important questions for the Community as a political entity, not least of which is the prospect of sharp divergencies in the energy policies and priorities of member countries, with all that these imply for common standards, common research efforts, trading relations, and so forth. To reduce the risk of this a Community energy strategy – and hence Community energy forecasting – is a necessity.

Useful forecasts and models of the energy sector must clearly be based on a proper understanding of past developments and the present patterns of energy usage. Yet such an understanding hardly exists for many important factors. For example, there is no satisfactory causal explanation of the disparities in the first three columns of Table 2. There is no satisfactory causal explanation of past energy growth patterns. Why, for example, did total energy consumption in the UK increase by only 30 per cent between 1900 and 1947? On a per capita basis, the increase in the half-century was a mere 2 per cent, from 4.08 to 4.15 tonnes coal equivalent per year. The usual explanation – that coal was progressively used more efficiently while other inherently more efficient fuels such as oil were substituted for coal – is not sufficient, since it ignores important factors such as the large-scale supplanting of horses (and hence land) by machines. Without information of this kind, trends and saturation effects are not easy to estimate. Lacking information of this sort, extrapolations are usually based on correlations rather than causes, notably the correlation between GNP and available or net energy consumption. This relationship varies very widely for different countries, even at the same level of development (see Table 2). Very little has been done to explain this variation.

Table 2

	Energy per capita (tce)[a]	Energy growth per capita (% p.a.)[b]	Ratio GNP to energy (UAs per tce)[c]	Import dependence (%)[d]
France	4.2	4.9	678	71
West Germany	5.6	4.3	557	48
Italy	3.0	8.6	580	82
U.K.	5.5	1.0	396	45

SOURCE: *Eurostat* (published by the Community Statistical Office).
[a] 1 tce (tonne coal equivalent) = 28.8×10^9 joules.
[b] Average annual percentage growth 1960–70.
[c] Units of Account (1970 U.S. dollars) per tonne coal equivalent.
[d] Fuel imports minus exports as percentage of total consumption.

Similar doubts apply to changes in this relationship: that is, the percentage increase in net energy use for each percentage increase in GNP. This coefficient has been close to 1 for many years for nearly all developed countries and is therefore widely used as a basis for forecasting. Such a grossly aggregated figure, based on correlations and not on causes, is hardly an adequate basis for forecasting or planning. It is anyway likely to change considerably. Little is known about the relationships (elasticities) between energy prices and both supply and demand. Much work on these factors is now under way, especially on monitoring the effects of the recent and dramatic price changes. And very little is known about precisely where and why energy is used, when by 'use' one means both direct and *indirect* consumption. The indirect consumption (e.g. the requirements for making machinery or providing materials) is often a very large fraction of, and sometimes greatly exceeds, the direct consumption. Without this information it is impossible to evaluate the true energy costs of any good or service, any production or consumption activity, or any movement of these energy costs through technological changes, conservation measures, and so forth.

Fortunately, many of these important gaps are likely to be filled during the next year or so following the recent and phenomenal upsurge in energy studies, including energy analysis. How soon or how fully this information can be incorporated into energy forecasting is another matter. An important role for an independent 'centre of excellence' such as Europe Plus Thirty will be to see that it is fully used, whether by in-house or contracted-out studies.

The energy scene is full of critical issues that are shrouded with uncertainty or are highly controversial, or both. In some cases expert opinion is sharply polarised, even inflamed. Among the more important of these conflict areas are several nuclear issues (safety, waste storage, plutonium containment, etc.); the size of fuel reserves (including North Sea oil and gas); potentials for energy savings and the degree of disruption likely to be caused by vigorous conservation measures; and costs and timings of new supply technologies.

An early step in any forecasting programme must be to mount a systematic and aggressive assault on these disputed issues, starting with those of immediate relevance to policy-makers. Means must be found to help experts resolve more clearly what they agree upon, where they differ, and what further research is needed to narrow areas of disagreement. Until this is done a large forecasting programme hardly seems possible, since it demands some kind of mutual agreement about constraints and other inputs or at least about the range of contingencies which should be allowed for. Nor is it possible in the meantime to begin a meaningful and informed debate on energy issues between non-experts, including concerned citizens, politicians, and even ministers and commissioners. If the experts are fighting it out in the dark, what chance is there for the rest? Yet, as we saw above, energy digs so deep into society as a whole and raises such fundamental questions of ethics, preferences, and goals that a widespread and informed debate on 'energy futures' is entirely necessary – at least for societies with any pretence to being democratic.

Mounting such an assault requires a concerted effort simply to speed up and facilitate communication between experts, who possess much valuable information which now circulates slowly and erratically (or not at all). But an even more valuable and practical approach would be to initiate a series of task forces or intensive seminars on critical issues, bringing together experts with widely differing opinions, providing them with ample library facilities, research assistance, and computational back-up, and – as it were – locking them up until results are achieved. Previous experiences with this technique have proved remarkably effective both in establishing the areas of consensus and differences among experts and later in communicating these findings to the public at large.[1]

With energy, the main strategic problems to be solved are (1) how to conserve energy, (2) how to increase indigenous supplies, (3) how to develop new supply technologies, (4) how to keep today's supply patterns going without economic collapse, and, more controversially, (5) how to make a strategic withdrawal from high energy dependence, perhaps at relatively short notice.

While each of these problems demands its own forecasting approach, most of what needs to be done falls under three main headings:

(1) *Supply developments*: identification and timing of fuel reserve appreciation/depletion and of global export/import patterns; identification, costs, and timing of supply technologies, both new and existing; prices.

(2) *Demand developments*: by sectors and overall in response to changes in technologies, costs, and prices; energy availability; deliberate energy-saving measures from simple technical, fiscal, or legislative 'fixes' to deeper structural changes. Study of wants, needs, necessities, and unwanted consumption (e.g. planned obsolescence of goods, some private transport).

(3) *Interactions*: changes in supply and their impact on other sectors (capitals, balance of payments, skills, materials, land use, environment, safety, etc.). Impacts of demand changes on other sectors (labour, manufacturing output, capital, balance of payments, need for anticipatory planning, etc.). Identification of feedback loops between all energy and social sectors, time delays, critical phases and 'gaps' (e.g. over- or under-supply at future dates). Broader consequences of alternative supply technologies and demand patterns.

Even this incomplete list of target areas add up to a formidable forecasting commitment. Nevertheless, while necessary, it is very far from being sufficient. The innumerable uncertainties of the energy

---

[1] *Man's Impact on the Global Environment: Report of the Study of Critical Environmental Problems* (SCEP) (Cambridge, Mass.: MIT Press, 1970). *Inadvertent Climate Modification* (SMIC) (see p. 89, n. 1).

future, the extreme openness of this future to change, and the tight connections between energy and all other social sectors, adds up to a severe problem of credibility for *any* attempt to forecast from the present more than, say, ten to twenty years ahead. Yet as stated above, forecasts of this time scale or longer are urgently required now.

Here as elsewhere, extrapolation can only be the handmaid of forecasting. For the longer-term view we require leaps *into* the future. Here scenario techniques are supreme. Energy scenarios are easily quantified and hence can be 'back-tracked' to the present. This allows trends and decision points for getting 'from here to there' to be identified. With energy-demand scenarios one can distinguish futures requiring mere technical 'fixes' (with little or no change in life-styles) through the spectrum to full-scale changes in social structures and attitudes. This helps to bring political judgement to bear on desirability, feasibility, etc.

Implications for non-energy factors are normally easy to identify since they are often the starting point for constructing the energy scenario itself. For example, in transport, measures that save energy also advance many other social benefits (e.g. a switch from private cars to public transport in cities can reduce energy consumption and, by clearing the roads for public vehicles, help improve public services so that most people have access to a swift, flexible, and convenient transport service). Scenarios are much easier for non-experts to understand and to question, and are less easily misinterpreted, than are complex dynamic models. This is especially important in the energy field, where the wide-ranging debate has already begun.

Though much used, scenarios in the energy field mostly focus on the consequences of single 'events': for example, the impact of major technological developments (e.g. a breakthrough in cheap solar or fusion power); the impact of major public or government actions (e.g. heavy fuel taxation, a ban on nuclear breeders); or the impacts of extraneous forces (e.g. an oil cut-off). Broader scenarios are needed. For example, the 'extreme ecological' scenario of the Energy Policy Project of the Ford Foundation (U.S.A.) postulated a possible halving of energy use in the year 2000 from present levels.[1] Imaginative proposals for individual sectors of use (urban transport; food production; domestic heat, light, and power) show potentials for savings of the same order. Such ideas need to be explored systematically and thoroughly, even though some may now seem eccentric, uneconomic,

---

[1] This scenario was abandoned in the final publications of the Project (e.g. *A Time to Choose: America's Energy Future* (Cambridge, Mass.: Ballinger, 1974). A less extreme 'zero energy growth' scenario nevertheless gave a 50 per cent reduction in energy use in the year 2000 compared to a 'historical growth' projection, and involved only relatively minor changes in consumption patterns, life-styles, etc.

unlikely, or plain impossible – academic fantasies. The fact is that one cannot judge their value until they have been explored properly. Some possibilities may not seem at all uneconomic under broader cost–benefit accounting or in different economic conditions. A full appreciation of all alternative options and their implications changes our perceptions of what is realistic and desirable.

Above all, it seems premature to judge these alternative future possibilities until they have been matched with the deeper undercurrents of social change, motivation, and behaviour now at work in all industrial societies, or, equally important, until they have been tested by exposure to public opinion – something that has never been done in a systematic way. It is very significant that many 'utopian' proposals for energy futures match rather closely some major undercurrents now being revealed by future-oriented social studies: for example, the Swedish 'To Choose a Future' programme.[1] These include the expectation of or desire for a greater integration of education, work, and leisure; a dissolving of the tie between income from work and standard of living; substantial decentralisation of living patterns, organisational structures, and decision-making processes; a stronger 'sense of community'; greater income redistribution combined with a slowdown of growth in the consumption of goods; greater solidarity with the poor world.

Some economic problems pertinent to the energy and raw-material sectors will also have to be examined. Particularly:

(1) When mineral resources are exploited down a gradient of decreasing quality, outputs of residuals and inputs of capital, labour, energy, and other resources normally rise. It is usually assumed that higher prices will cover these higher costs. Yet as *all* finite resource stocks are depleted, their scarcity value and market price also rises. At what point do these effects combine to produce rapid 'resource price inflation'? What are the implications for resource allocation over time – i.e. between the present and the future? What are the implications for poorer countries, where higher prices are already imposing intolerable strains?

(2) Economists often answer these questions by saying that new technologies will increase 'efficiency' of resource stock conversion and use (e.g. breeder reactors rather than uranium burner reactors), enlarge the stocks by new finds, or discover how to use new stocks (e.g. fusion reactors). The critical uncertainty is, of course, the rate at which these can be introduced successfully. But technical progress

[1] 'To Choose a Future: a basis of discussion and deliberation on future studies in Sweden' (Stockholm: Royal Ministry for Foreign Affairs in cooperation with the Secretariat for Future Studies, 1972).

is not a free good: in fact it is very costly when one includes all components of research, all required substitutions of technology and capital, and all changes required by consumers. Very few of these costs are reflected in the accounting, though they do appear as an increase in GNP. What are the true costs? And what implications do they have for the main argument?

(3) Economists are sharply divided on the 'optimum' rate for depleting a resource in the ground. Some have used theoretical arguments to show that present extraction rates are below the optimum: we are using resources, including oil, too slowly.[1] Others produce a strong theoretical case for conservation. Much depends on the number of factors considered (boundary conditions), the future discount rate, how one values present capital stocks of goods, knowledge, etc. Can economists sort this out? Should depletion strategies, which depend ultimately on the value placed on the options left open for future generations, be decided by economic means, or by political (ethical) judgements?

A vast amount of energy forecasting and modelling is now being done in Europe and around the world by commercial and industrial interests, by energy industries and institutions, by universities, and by governments. The European Commission itself has major proposals for an energy research and development programme ('Energy for Europe').[2] These proposals include a fairly ambitious scheme for energy modelling/forecasting which covers many, though not all, of the priorities set out in this chapter.

Most of this work is inevitably rather rough and tentative. Conditions have changed so abruptly since the winter of 1973–4 that old assumptions and methodologies, such as the former (and never remotely justifiable) reliance on single trend analysis, have had to be scrapped. Forecasting has had virtually to start afresh. At the same time there has been a wide recognition that the data base for forecasting is inadequate.

Nevertheless, one can expect a fairly rapid build-up of competent forecasts and models on narrow fronts (sector and sub-sectors) as the iterative process of model-building, identification of weak data, improvement of data, and building of better models gets under way.

[1] J. A. Kay and J. A. Mirrlees, 'The Desirability of Natural Resource Depletion', paper presented to Environmental Economic Study Group/Institute of Environmental Science joint Conference on Natural Resource Depletion (Royal Institution, London, January 1974).

[2] European Commission, DG XII, 'Energy for Europe: Research and Development' (Lindner Report) (Brussels: SEC(74) 2592 final, 17 July 1974), and 'Draft Proposal[s] on Common Research and Development in the Field[s] of Solar Energy ... Geothermal Energy ...Hydrogen as a New Energy Vector ...Systems Modelling on Energy' (n.d.).

Progress on wider fronts – as discussed in this chapter – is likely to be slower, but one might expect the emergence of some valuable models and scenarios and a rather more rapid emergence of important ideas and data for incorporation into them.

It is in this wider work that a Europe Plus Thirty instrument has an extremely valuable – indeed, unique – role to play. It will have no need to get involved with narrowly technical research or forecasting; it should concentrate on broader techno-economic forecasting about alternative energy patterns and policies, and above all on forecasting about the possible relations between those alternative patterns and alternative patterns of change in the society, economy, and external relations of the Community as a whole.

The major contribution of Europe Plus Thirty to energy problems can perhaps best be summed up by three characteristics: integration, vision, and emphasis on longer-term goals and alternatives. A major role should be to apply multidisciplinary and generalist 'excellence' to checking, questioning, balancing, integrating, and enlarging on longer-term and wide-ranging forecasts from an energy point of view. In other words, it should concentrate on exploring the bridges between specialised sectors as they relate to energy: for example, by looking at the energy implications of forecasts and alternatives in transport or urban design on the one hand, and at the impact of existing energy forecasts on particular sectors of society, such as the poor, on the other hand. The work would involve sifting and synthesising studies produced outside, making in-house studies to fill important gaps or to combine existing studies in fresh ways, and contracting work out to other institutions. The general aim should be to apply a specifically Western European angle to the exploration of alternative options and goals: for example, to improve, rework for Europe, and extend the 'first cut' alternative strategies of the kind that were produced for the U.S.A. by the Ford Foundation Energy Policy Programme and are now being developed for a range of countries by the Workshops on Alternative Energy Strategies (sponsored by the International Federation of Institutes for Advanced Study). It is here, in the design and verification of broad and long-term goals rather than in yet more detailed analysis of short-range problems, that energy forecasting is weakest and that the policy-makers and people of Europe most require help.

11. *Materials*

There can be no doubt about the necessity for forecasting in the materials sector[1] nor about the need for a common European forecasting effort. In the broadest sense, the materials situation of the Community is similar to that for energy. Like other major consuming regions, the Community is perilously immersed, through its great dependence on many strategic materials, in a worldwide shift in the balance of who controls raw materials and reaps the benefit of ownership. This shift has deep historical roots and is likely to intensify rather than diminish.

At the same time, the Community is caught up in a second unforgiving historical trend, that of progressive resource depletion at a time of unprecedentedly high rates of consumption and dependence on these high rates. Regardless of who owns resources, the adequacy of many materials and the various costs of getting most materials from the ground and into useful products (including financial, energy, environmental, and land-use costs) are likely to be constraining or disruptive forces of major and increasing magnitude.

There are, of course, substantial possibilities of damping these trends by reducing consumption of critical materials. Policies range from providing developing (producer) countries with greater help and technical collaboration to increasing domestic production and applying a host of materials-saving measures. However, many of these moves will cost money, will take time, will involve massive research and development programmes, and in many cases will lead to deep conflicts of interest. They certainly call for more purposive action than a mere reliance on automatic market price adjustments.

While it has not recently erupted with quite the violence of the 'energy crisis', the materials challenge nevertheless amounts to a major discontinuity and points to a new era of considerable instability and uncertainty. This alone is sufficient reason to make intensive forecasting efforts and to make them on a common European basis. But this argument gains extra force when one considers the Community's response to the challenge so far. Unlike other highly industrial and

---

[1] The materials considered in this chapter exclude water, energy, and agricultural commodities. They include all metals; constructional materials such as stone, sand, and gravel; and mineral fertilisers (phosphates and potash). Owing to shortage of space none of these materials can be considered individually in any depth but are used only as examples of more general issues.

import-dependent regions such as the U.S.A. and Japan, the Community has not yet developed an overall strategy to cover immediate problems for its internal materials system or its relations to external suppliers. (No region has developed an adequate long-term strategy.) Instead, member nations have acted alone – making their own investment decisions and agreements with producer countries – with all the known risks of distorting prices, international relations, and world trade generally.

In most respects, the priorities for materials forecasting are the same as those for energy discussed in the previous chapter. In the most general sense, forecasting in the materials sector is more difficult than for energy. There are many more materials to consider than there are fuels. They have very different 'criticalities', dependencies, possibilities for substitution and recycling, and consumption growth rates. There are many more actors in the game, including producer countries and their 'monopolistic' organisations, mining and processing organisations, and manufacturing and other corporate interests. Market speculation often plays havoc with prices, creating great instabilities. Compared with energy, there is a much more complex structure of manufacturing and end-uses, with subtle balances of supply and demand, prices, technical suitability in both manufacture and use, consumer preferences, marketing, lobbying, and legislation controlling why some materials are favoured over alternatives, all having innumerable impacts within and without the materials sector. Finally, much forecasting work is already done by industrial and corporate interests and by institutions responsible for particular materials or groups of materials: collection, validation, and integration of data from this motley crowd of interested and sometimes antagonistic parties is both more difficult and more necessary than it is for energy.

As a result of all this, it is perhaps as difficult to make a credible and comprehensive model for *one* material, such as lead or zinc, as it is for any major fuel, such as oil or coal. A general priority, then, is to begin with intensive studies of small sectors and intersectoral areas, building to a better understanding of the existing materials system, rather than to attempt immediately large-scale, long-term dynamic modelling.

For most minerals the spectre of *geological* exhaustion on a global scale seems fairly remote. One can reasonably suppose that, for the next few decades at least, technological improvements and price effects will continue to upgrade presently unknown or unproved or uneconomic resources into the proved, economic, and workable category at a rate to match 'reasonable' increases in consumption. This cornucopia theory is almost certainly valid for iron, aluminium, magnesium (from sea-water), chrome, nickel, limestone, sands, gravel, phosphates, and potash. It is more disputable for other key materials – notably lead, zinc, and copper – since reserve estimates of these 'igneous emplacement' metals are hard to make and vary considerably.

But acute shortages within twenty to forty years can be foreseen for some materials, notably helium, mercury, silver, and perhaps tungsten. It is an open and much-argued question whether these impending scarcities can be avoided (e.g. by substitution), at what cost, and with what impact on other sectors. In the longer term there could be some very serious scarcities indeed, which would lead to vast upheavals (or the intervention of as yet unknown technological innovations). A good example is phosphates, on which all high-yield agriculture critically depends. World phosphate consumption is some 20 million tonnes, rising at 8 per cent annually, and must increase about 2.7 times faster than agricultural yields, owing to inefficiency of uptake. In largely urban societies, it is progressively lost and, unlike nitrate, can be recovered only by very expensive tertiary sewage treatment, with a theoretical maximum efficiency of 90 per cent. Assuming that a future population of 10 billion is to be fed at adequate standards, annual phosphate consumption could be in the region of 100 million tonnes. Total known and potential world reserves are put by the U.S. Bureau of Mines at 45 billion tonnes, giving a 450-year supply. But most of these reserves are thought to be very low-grade; known reserves are highly concentrated in the U.S.A., Morocco, and the U.S.S.R.

Apart from the need for more systematic and integrated studies of resource inventories, a major priority here is to respect the Law of the Minimum. This law (which does not apply to energy, where all sources are theoretically substitutable) says that if you have less than the minimum amount needed of any essential, it does you no good whatever to have surpluses of every other essential. What essential will we run short of first? And what materials are 'essential'?

There is a world of difference between materials reserves and available supplies. First and most obviously, many reserves are concentrated in only a few nations. Availability and price are therefore dominated by political and socio-economic considerations and hence by the extent to which producer countries can and will exert monopolistic pressure in the manner of the OPEC oil producers. This has already occurred or is occurring with several commodities (notably phosphates, copper, and bauxite), while producer cartels or looser associations have been formed for silver, mercury, and tin and are expected for iron ore. Others may follow.

The outcomes of these forces are extremely hard to forecast. They depend on many complex and interacting factors to do with political determination and cohesion among producers, degree of monopoly supply and consumer dependence, possibilities for and time required for consumers to substitute or otherwise reduce consumption, stock-piling questions, dependence of producers on the consumers' advanced technologies, and so forth. Pressures may also take many forms, from a price or tax increase to nationalisation of foreign mining facilities and upgrading of ores in the producer countries (with heavy price penalties for consumers).

In this situation, the most valuable approach to forecasting and policy assessment is the application of risk analysis to identify critical dependencies. Risk analysis is specially designed to help choose the best out of several complex alternatives through estimates of the costs and probabilities of various events occurring. Critical dependencies are commodities for which the impact of scarcity or price disruption is sufficiently high to warrant an 'insurance strategy' – that is, a package of policies to cushion consumer countries against later disruptions by paying a penalty immediately. Examples of penalties are a rapid introduction of substitute technologies at otherwise uneconomic levels or dealing with several suppliers even if this means paying higher prices.

Hardly less important than these geopolitical supply questions are a wide range of other possible constraints and uncertainties on the supply side. The mining and production of materials, especially at lower and lower ore grades, can involve heavy costs in terms of pollution, land degradation (including wilderness, scenic areas, and competition for recreation space and building land near cities – especially in the case of sand, stone, brick clays, and gravel extraction), energy consumption, and the disruption of communities and creation of depressed regions when short-lived mining operations are abandoned. Factors of this kind already create fierce conflicts in parts of Europe and could loom larger as basic value system and perceptions change.

By and large, technological development and economies of scale have held constant the real costs of mineral production despite an overall trend toward the working of lower-grade ores. It is not at all clear – indeed, it is hotly disputed – how far this will apply in future. Some estimates show a very sharp cost increase with decreasing ore grade: for example, a rise from £1,000 to £7,000 per tonne of metal as one goes from 1.0 to 0.1 per cent average ore grade for non-ferrous metals.[1] Total accounting, to include the social and environmental costs mentioned above, might sharpen this trend appreciably. To make

[1] B. F. Roberts, 'Management Policies for Non-Renewable Material Resources', in *Proceedings of the Conference 'The Conservation of Materials'* (Harwell, U.K.: March 1974).

matters worse, it is not clear what effect such increases would have on our economies. One opinion is that they would be slight, since the cost of raw materials is a small percentage of GNP and of the price of most finished goods. Another view is that they can induce massive inflationary effects.

Even with 'low growth' demand forecasts – that is, assuming an approach to saturation of per capita consumption in the developed world but increasing consumption in the developing world – annual production figures nevertheless rise steeply. These can lead to remarkable figures for the rates at which metals 'must' be found, mined, and processed, and for the magnitude of these operations. For example, one such forecast for lead points to the need for a discovery rate rising from 9.5 million to 54 million tonnes per year between 1970 and 2020 and to the need to find by the latter date 800 million tonnes in excess of the present known reserves of 90 million tonnes.[1]

The present economic and political struggle for materials may benefit producers in the short to medium run but will continue to hit hard the many poor countries without raw materials to sell – the so-called Fourth World. If technologies are developed which allow mining of much lower-quality (and hence more common) ores, these would give great advantages to the rich, industrial countries, since they are likely both to control the technologies and to have plentiful low-grade ores for their own uses. All poorer countries, including today's producers, could be hit hard. If this does not happen, then the rich countries may well use more or less subtle economic measures to dominate the producers – or they may even be tempted to revert to cruder military adventures. Even if they do not contemplate such steps, they may well be believed by the producers to be about to do so, with political results which are not hard to foresee. A very wide range of scenarios can be built on arguments of this kind, with considerable utility to political and general forecasting, both as regards the adoption of optimum policies and as regards the avoidance of pessimum ones.

Even if one neglects the vagaries of supply constraints, the growth of demand for materials is an exceedingly exacting and uncertain area of study. For example, the most comprehensive recent set of mineral demand forecasts (published by the U.S. Bureau of Mines)[2] shows a consistent upward trend for all non-energy minerals, with world growth rates ranging from 3.8 to 5.6 per cent per annum, but has high, medium, and low estimates for the U.S.A. in the year 2000 spread by factors of up to three. Allowing for the development (or non-

[1] Ibid.
[2] *Mineral Facts and Problems* (Washington: Government Printing Office, 1970).

development) of the rest of the world gives a much greater range of uncertainties.

Similar problems afflict the study of other demand/growth parameters. As with energy, the per capita consumption of many metals varies widely even between countries at similar stages of development. It can also progress very erratically: for example, the former levelling-off of per capita copper consumption in the U.S.A. and Germany has recently given way to sharp increases. Another important measure – the quantity of metal used per unit of GNP – also reveals wide variations between countries and over time. Intensity-of-use studies of this kind do show that consumption per unit of GNP has a strong tendency to slow down and flatten out as GNP rises; but longer-term forecasts of GNP are so uncertain that they are little help beyond the ten-year horizon. Nevertheless, these studies do show that many simple trend extrapolations are probably giving inflated figures for future demand.[1]

Ideally, forecasts of demand should of course not be based on correlations of this kind but on causes; that is, on detailed scrutiny of where and why metals are used within particular production/consumption sectors. But even this is of little help in longer-term forecasting, owing to uncertainties about future growth rates in the various sectors, possible substitutions, and other technology-related or price-related effects.

In principle, as we noted, there is large scope for reducing the consumption of materials or consumption growth rates. Opportunities range from the technical to the broadly social. Perhaps the most obvious is more efficient use – that is, less material per unit of the product, or smaller products, or better materials specifications (for instance, for preventing corrosion), or design modifications to make recycling easy at the end of the product's life. Then there is what can be done in the manufacturing stage: for instance, precision casting and forging instead of machining. Product lifetimes can be increased by design changes; products can be made easier to repair and maintain; and the 'throw-away syndrome' can itself be made obsolescent by the reduction of obsolescence in the product. There could be a conscious social and political effort to make second-hand goods markets more efficient. Things which are not at present recycled could begin to be: treatment of domestic rubbish, chemical wastes, phosphates and potash in sewage. Critical materials could give way to less critical ones for a given use: for instance, in Britain the present trend is that one and one-half million tonnes of metal in new production are replaced each year by half a million tonnes of plastics. Some uses could very well be

[1] D. B. Brooks and P. W. Andrews, 'Mineral Resources, Economic Growth, and World Population', *Science* 185 (July 1974), pp. 13–19.

sharply reduced, for instance packaging and advertising, and, lastly, the number of useful products required by a given society could be reduced by greater sharing or communal ownership (launderettes, public transport, communal living patterns, etc.).

In practice, all this might be hard to achieve. By and large, the more technical design and reclamation measures are already used vigorously whenever they are profitable and/or do not undermine engineering standards. If they are not used, there are normally good reasons. These reasons are themselves compounded from very many complex factors, including the availability and costs of labour, alternative materials, capital equipment, sites for waste disposal, energy, and the like – and, not least, consumer preferences.

How these will alter naturally under new conditions, or what effects deliberate policies would have, are extremely important but also extremely intractable questions. This is partly because the basic data and the general understanding of the materials system and its ramifications are still inadequate. For example, extending product lifetimes clearly has enormous direct and indirect implications for employment and for the structure of manufacturing and service industries. Conversely, the throw-away syndrome is not merely an expression of senseless consumer prodigality but reflects perceptions about the value of time, 'convenience', novelty, desire for genuine product improvements, and the high cost and unreliability of equipment repair services. Interactions of these kinds are extremely hard to evaluate now, let alone to forecast about.

Again, recycling can obviously occur only when an artefact is finished with: the level of recycling is therefore mainly a function of previous consumption levels and the lifetimes of goods. But for most materials and for most nations, time series on sales, the average and range for product lifetimes, penetration of the potential market, materials content of products, and the like are so poor that one cannot even say how efficient present recycling is, let alone forecast about future efficiencies or the quantities of recycled materials available. It is even less clear what effect recycling and longer product life will have in holding down resource consumption because of the unknown effects that will be exerted by 'first-time' owners/consumers entering the materials acquisition–use–disposal–recycling chain.

But perhaps the largest area for uncertainty in materials forecasting or management lies at more fundamental levels. While all these techniques can clearly buy time in the face of a resource challenge, studying them does nothing to answer many deep, underlying questions. For example, if existing economic forces have led to 'wrong' answers on materials by not providing incentives for conservation, what forces can provide such incentives? Will those forces arise naturally (through price pressures etc.)? And if not, by how much can, and may, they be deliberately engineered? Whether natural or engineered, can they provide sufficient anticipation of future events, bearing in mind the long lead times and high inertia of the materials system? More fundamental still, given that Western economies and individual organisations within them have so far depended for stability on continued expansion (because of demands for profit, investment to meet competition, etc.), is it possible to make the transition to a resource-conservative economy without a major change in present economic systems and value structures? How and when could these come about? As a sharp example of this point, one might instance the throw-away syndrome. Many would say that eliminating it is impossible because of the dire employment implications. Many others would reply that it is dehumanising and dangerous to base a society on the premise that human effort should be used increasingly to produce things designed to be thrown away. How might external events or changing value structures affect these arguments over, say, thirty years?

As with energy, forecasting in the materials sector demands an extremely broad attack. On one flank, one finds that the most basic technical data are inadequate or inappropriate. On the other flank loom persistent questions about the ultimate goals and the very survival of industrial societies. In the centre, there are great complexity and uncertainty, and few ground rules either for forecasting or for making sensible policies under these conditions. What one can hope to do in the present turmoil of events is to assess the options for, and the implications of, immediate strategies in a long-term 'options open' context and to reassess these longer-term options regularly, hoping for new trends and patterns to emerge following the recent discontinuity. Exploratory work on longer-term scenarios is also vital, as and when adequate data and broad agreement on assumptions are forthcoming.

For these reasons, the unique value of Europe Plus Thirty and its methods of work could be much the same for material resources as it would be for energy (see chapter II.10). The major difference is one of time scales for longer-term forecasting. While there is almost enough material now for constructing in the energy field the wide-ranging, integrative forecasts that are so urgently needed, in the materials sector this task might have to wait upon adequate sector and sub-sector analyses. Europe Plus Thirty could play a leading role in identifying what work of this kind is being done and in coordinating further work, so as to cut the delay. As soon as possible, it should feed the data which are 'adequate' into its general forecasting programme.

12. *The environment*

Of all the sectors treated in this Part, 'the environment' is undoubtedly the most heterogeneous. The word itself, used in the way we now use it, is of recent adoption. In the European languages it only came to this immensely broad sense in the late 1960s, when it reached bureaucratic consecration in the Ministries of the Environment in several of our countries.

We divide the subject into four parts: (1) the physical environment, both land and sea, including pollution; (2) the biosphere, including wildlife and flora; (3) the man-made environment, particularly cities, and land-use planning; and (4) society's response to the challenge of environmental change.

All these concern all the member states of the Community, but the Community has become concerned with them only gradually and pragmatically, as its territory came to be perceived as a suitable social and geographical unit for resolving these problems.

More thoroughgoing Community powers could arise in a number of fields which do not lend themselves readily to treatment on a national, regional, or local level. Clearly forecasting would be useful in both cases, but it would be the concern of Europe Plus Thirty only in the first.

There could be forecasting about the impact of new technological developments on the physical environment. This is closely related to the TA which should always accompany any major innovation and to the elaboration of the schemes of technological development on the basis of which research decisions are taken in big industry and in public bodies. There could be forecasting about the impact on the physical environment of the spread of productive techniques that are not new but that have been hitherto little applied, or not applied in this or that specific area, and about the spread of new products or new habits of consumption (public or private, of goods and services) which sometimes derive from a technological innovation but which are in many cases based on traditional techniques. There could be forecasting about the effects of new administrative arrangements, new laws, and new regulations, whether they are intended to affect the environment or something else.

In our second group of problems, the impact on the biosphere (wildlife and vegetation) of the increasing 'rationalisation' of agriculture is also amenable to forecasting, and so is the impact on the living

164

environment and on the system of watercourses of the drift from the land and the abandonment of areas formerly used for agricultural purposes. Where this happens, the effects may be contrary to the effects of the changes taking place in the areas of modern and intensive agriculture: the depopulation of rural areas leads to an increase in formerly threatened animal species, while agricultural rationalisation leads to the disappearance of species, though the species affected are not the same in the two cases. Similarly the hydrogeological confusion brought about in many Mediterranean regions by the abandoning of agriculture leads to diverse and sometimes opposite effects.

In the third group of problems, forecasting should cover the quality of life in the man-made environment – that is, it must seek to introduce an element of foreknowledge into the management of urban and regional planning. Forecasting about urban planning is not a job for Europe Plus Thirty: it is best done nationally, and city by city. Forecasting about regional land-use patterns and especially about regional infrastructure investment could be a job for Europe Plus Thirty when the region in question crosses national frontiers.

The mobility of the European population will probably be extremely high in the next thirty years, and the growth of urban zones and changes in land use very rapid. Two problems exist here about which forecasting might usefully be done at Community level: first, the impact of the redistribution of population densities and of land use on the physical environment destined to house new urban developments (air pollution, weather, sea coast, noise pollution, etc.), and second, the impact on people's lives of the shape and size of the various alternative urban infrastructures (e.g. the ghettoisation of the elderly or of women, school choice in poor areas, etc.).

It should be possible to forecast usefully about the socio-political impact of environmental change. Naturally, given that in this case we are talking about changes in society, this is really part of social and political forecasting, because it talks about the relationships between the balance of society and the balance of the natural environment.

Forecasting could also be undertaken concerning the impact on production and consumption (and thus again on ways of life) of changes in environmental conditions. This type of forecast has so far always ended by showing the political and psychological bias of its author. When we are faced with the possibility of a given change in environmental conditions, we have to choose a priori between two hypotheses that can be made about society's way of reacting. The first assumes that the capacity for reaction is unable to go beyond what might be called the 'patching up' of an increasingly threatened environment. The second assumes that society has some capacity to confront the risks and the cost of radical transformations in a timely and organic manner. The span of these hypotheses is naturally wide. But the idea that society *is* capable of rising to the challenge posed by environmental change can give rise to very different forecasts of the impact of such change on the production and consumption systems and on ways of life.

The already-established long-term policies of the Community may bring about changes in the way of life which influence land use and sea use as well as the quality of the environment throughout the Community. There is no doubt, for instance, that the Community would be interested in advance knowledge of the probable environmental impact of Commission directives about agriculture, about the free movement of workers, about regional development, and about the mobility of labour.

Some environmental changes have, in turn, a social impact which affects Community objectives favourably or unfavourably. The most obvious example is the efforts of the various member countries to update their national legislation on water pollution by industrial waste.

The lack of uniformity in controls, standards, and rates of application of anti-pollution legislation bids fair to bring about not only distortion in international trade but also a threat that it may be exploited by one or other of the member states to produce 'pollution paradises', more or less camouflaged by the justification of regional development, which are already common enough in the Third World. This lack of uniformity in Europe could lend itself to protectionist manoeuvres which run counter to Community aims, and the Community has therefore a strong interest in the present tendency towards the development of trans-national rights where trans-frontier pollution is concerned, of the concept of 'additionality' where pollution havens are established, and of the principle that developing countries must be compensated if they are required to take environmental measures which put up the price of their exports. In all these cases, it is in the Community's interest not only to study the problems but also to look into the future development of those which lend themselves to nationalistic exploitation.

Sometimes the Community has the opportunity to react to environmental change and the ensuing transformation in the modes of production, consumption, or life in general in a way different from that in which the single state might react – that is to say, in a more timely and organic way. When this happens (and here political judgement comes into play) the Community could intervene promptly with initiatives of its own. Three examples are river basins, the environmental effects of energy use, and sea-use planning.

The control of inland waters aims at protecting them against pollution and at their regeneration so as to satisfy or reconcile the needs of the conservation and flow of the water itself, of drinking water for the population at large, of river transport, of the biological life of the rivers (particularly fish), of recreation and sport, and of the protection of natural beauty.

The uses of water are numerous and irreplaceable. Indeed, so crucial is water that any map of population or industry is mainly a map of river valleys: they are where people live. The interdependence of all elements of a river basin is its main feature. The best system of control cannot be achieved without an overall policy extending from upstream storage, for reserves and flow regulation, to purification downstream of built-up areas or industries, passing through the distribution networks and discharge of waste water in the intermediate zones. This interdependence, recognised by all states, naturally applies equally to the great river basins that cross frontiers, like the Rhine, and it is impossible for partial and national solutions to achieve proper control of these huge systems, whose banks house the greatest concentrations of population not only of the European Community, but also of the whole of the European continent. They constitute a fundamental resource, as fundamental as coal and iron once were when the Community was in its infancy.

The stakes for the future consist in forecasting the population of these basins, their economic development, and, from that, what developments are needed for the water to render maximum service to the peoples along its banks and what form of regulation can be devised to share the costs of these developments justly among the countries which derive different benefits from the water.

The effects of energy production, transport, and use pose many problems for the environment: among them are the pollution of the seas by oil, of the air by industry and domestic heating, and of both air and inland waters by water cooling in power stations.

As far as pollution control is concerned, the most urgent problems are probably those caused by the peaceful use of atomic energy – that is, the heating of fresh water and sea water, and the stockpiling of radioactive waste in conditions which must be totally safe even in the extremely long term (up to 40,000 years). These, and the problems of ionising radiation and accident risk, are obviously more justly and expediently solved on the Community level than nationally. And of course research into new forms of energy and new techniques of utilising energy (geothermal, wind, and above all solar) necessitates forecasting about their possible environmental effects.

In the last twenty years, there has been a revolution and a boom in the exploitation of the sea. It is now not only a means of communication but also an increasing source of biological and non-biological resources for the life of man. From the exploitation and organisation of the water surface, we proceeded to that of the water mass, and now to that of the resources on and under the sea-bed itself.

Moreover, the rapid development of technology has lessened and blurred the distinction between zones above and below sea level. This phenomenon can be seen not only in the identification of a 'continental shelf', a 'continental rise', and a 'continental slope' – zones of transition between land above sea level and the deep sea-bed – but also in the extension of political organisation typical of dry land to the sea and its bed, with the consequent crisis in the law of the sea. Today, the concept of 'coast' (defined as that zone above sea level whose organisation and use is influenced by proximity to the sea, plus that part of the land below sea level, and its superjacent water, whose organisation and use is influenced by the nearby land) is changing its meaning. The possible modes of exploitation of the submerged zone increase further, and faster, than do those of the land above sea level (thus making the marine influence on the organisation of space above sea level broader, more changeable, and more complex). The 'frontier' between land and sea is blurred and at the same time is charged with increasing political and economic tension.

The coastal zone below sea level, some few of whose possibilities are only just being glimpsed, will probably be organised and exploited in the future not so much by the use of new technological developments as by a new knowledge about the marine environment. Indeed, our knowledge of the lunar environment is more complete and systematic than our knowledge of the submerged portion of our own planet.

Commercial fishing was considered in chapter II.4 above. It interacts with everything else which may be done at sea. The desalination of sea water is today the main extractive activity from the sea water itself, and the shortage of fresh water in dry Mediterranean countries makes it foreseeable that desalination will increase. It will probably be flanked by other exploitations like that of magnesium; the U.S. derives most of its magnesium from sea water.

Mining as intense as that on dry land is conceivable on the sea-bed (where vast reserves of certain minerals lie about, particularly manganese nodules) or below it. There is no reason to believe that the marine subsoil is any less rich than the dry land's subsoil. Although extraction promises to be costly, several large firms and governments are planning to start as soon as they can obtain some security of tenure in the international sea-bed. Techniques of offshore mineral extraction have so far been developed mainly for oil or for particularly valuable minerals; in South Africa there has been some extraction of offshore diamonds. The resources under the sea-bed can be exploited down to several thousand metres (in the case of oil). The technology for deep-sea oil drilling and extraction is at the very limits of materials strengths and of human endurance. It was developed in the Gulf of Mexico and refined in the Persian Gulf, and it is now forced to take a quantum leap to withstand the howling gales and towering seas of the European North. The results are still far from clear.

Sand and gravel, which have long been worked in the beds of rivers and in land that was once covered by water, are now being worked out to sea and causing coastal erosion. Sea transport is no longer just a surface activity but tends to be organised along 'traffic corridors' situated on the sea-bed, not only in the case of the transport of energy (or information) along cables but also in the case of transport by pipeline. The planning of submarine space must therefore take into account this new network of submarine energy-ducts and systems of pipelines in general which not only carry natural gas (sometimes liquid) or other fluids but also can transport several fluids without mixing them, or a pumpable substance like grain, or even solids like coal or iron ore mixed with a fluid (slurry). Despite some experiments, the possibility of the submarine transport of substances lighter than water contained in plastic bags with ballast and pulled by submarines, still seems remote. In the near future it is therefore likely that transport will remain concentrated on the surface and on the sea-bed. On the surface it is likely that the network of routes will become increasingly dense and intricate, while on the sea-bed, which today is criss-crossed in all directions by transmission cables, an equally complex network of pipes may rapidly be formed, to the potential detriment of trawling. This will lead to a very high demand for access to the coast. Even today it is obvious that the coastal areas are the real bottlenecks in the transport and communication network of surface and sea-bed, to the point where the movement of ships, and particularly of fishing and pleasure craft, is obstructed in various ways.

In the future it is likely that the demand for forms of recreation which use the sea surface will increase more rapidly, putting further pressure on the navigable zones nearest the coast, as well as on ports whose size, frequency along the coast, physical structure, and organisation will gradually have to change fundamentally – given that (unlike commercial shipping, whose harbour time is short) pleasure craft must lie idle for most of the time and so require enormous mooring areas.

All this competes with the use of the sea for refuse disposal. Both organic and inorganic liquid refuse is discharged from the sewage systems in the densely populated and industrial zones surrounding Western Europe, except for a part of the French Atlantic coast, and for Britain, where it is mainly treated first. Some solid and liquid waste, because of its toxicity, is sometimes transported in lighters to very deep parts of the sea far from the coast. Oil is discharged from ships and from land: it amounts, in the Mediterranean alone, to between a million and a million and a half tons a year, of which more than two-thirds are deposited in the open sea from tankers or other ships. Lastly, waste is carried down the rivers, particularly between the mouth of the Seine and the Baltic.

The sea is used not only to discharge heat but also to dump dangerous substances. At present it still appears necessary, especially for densely populated countries like England and Wales, the Netherlands, and Belgium (which are the densest three in the world), to use the sea to get rid of part of the radioactive waste from nuclear power stations. It is still also the safest graveyard for surplus war stores that cannot be deloused. Floating or fixed oil storage tanks are beginning to appear, equipped with moorings, helipads, football pitches, etc. Sea space has already been used and may increasingly be used in future for noisy airports and for burning refuse. Equally, civil aircraft fly supersonic mainly over the sea. Lastly, it is once again the sea which is already beginning to provide the space for tomorrow's gigantic power stations, especially where the coastline is already over-used, as it is in Italy for instance.

Naturally, in the face of all these demands on the sea, the need to protect the systems which permit animal life in water, and thus in the entire planet, has grown and will grow enormously. It is reflected in the demand now so clearly expressed at UNCLOS III for each coastal state to have an exclusive economic zone going out 200 nautical miles, as we discussed in chapter II.4 above concerning fisheries.

There will obviously be conflicts. They pose problems of choice – for regional planning, and for the organisation of the surface, the water mass, and the sea-bed – which must be solved in a way that is conceptually like (even if technically unlike) the way in which problems of the dry part of the European continent are solved. The day of sea-use planning, of *aménagement des mers*, of *Seeraumordnung*, is already upon us. Like all planning, it will rely on, and be symbiotic with, forecasting.

The field is vast, pregnant with great gains and great losses, even great disasters; and the study of it is, in comparison with those potentialities, still derisory. The European Community could move into this new policy field before, or as soon as, its member states.

The choice of the areas of environmental forecasting in which

Europe Plus Thirty should actually work, at least at first, is extremely difficult.

Two fields are suggested for the starting point. They are pollution control mechanisms and sea use; both these are clearly of interest to the Community as such. Europe Plus Thirty should forecast about the economic and environmental effects of alternative systems of pollution regulation, since they will directly affect the economic competition among member states which lies so close to the heart of the Community's purposes. For inland waters, for the air, and for land, what would be the economic, social, and environmental effects of the general adoption of alternative systems based on (1) single emission-point or dumping-point licensing, (2) generally applicable body-standards,[1] and (3) pollution charging? And what would be the effects of different methods of enforcing and supervising their application?

For sea use, what would be the effects of alternative Community policies for the regulation of conflicting interests among economic sectors and among member states, and how could such alternative Community policies be related to those likely to be followed by other nations and groups of nations in the world after UNCLOS III?

Naturally Europe Plus Thirty should be ready to start work in other fields as they appeared appropriate or might be demanded by the development of Community policy.

13. *Transport*

Transport, in all its forms, absorbs about one-fifth of the economic resources and roughly one-quarter of the energy expended annually in the Community. The economic importance of its future development is therefore immense. But, unlike some other industries, it also has enormous consequences of a non-economic nature. It occupies a large, and increasing, part of people's spare time. It is the greatest menace to the environment, both in urban areas and in the countryside. It exercises a decisive influence on the distribution of population and industry within cities (urban form), within countries (regional structure), and to a lesser extent within Europe as a whole (see chapter II.12 above). In many subtle ways it dictates the style of life and the opportunities open to different social classes. It is one of the

---

[1] Body-standards are regulations of the following type: nowhere in inland waters shall there be a cubic metre of water which contains more than so many parts per million of such-and-such a substance.

greatest causes of premature deaths (60,000 per year in the Community) and of serious injuries.

During the last hundred years, and especially the last thirty years, the use of transport has grown at an extraordinary rate and has radically changed the life of Europe in many ways, both for the better and for the worse.

All industries need to look ahead, but usually not thirty years ahead. It is not necessary to look further than you think events will be affected by decisions which must be taken now. The long-acting decisions are usually investment decisions; even so, much investment has a life of less than ten years or, alternatively, consists of equipment which can be readily disinvested in if it is no longer required. Of course, a thirty-year forecast may be useful to an industry whose horizon of interest is limited to twenty-five or twenty years; and even to those with shorter horizons the first half of the forecast may be valuable if it gives the greater detail and accuracy that are normally required of short-term forecasts.

Unlike other industries, transport investment consists of two totally dissimilar parts: infrastructure and vehicles. No important vehicle has yet been invented that can operate without major additional fixed plant such as roads, railways, canals, stations, locks, docks, airports, tunnels, and bridges. All these are extremely costly, long-lasting, and inflexible (i.e. they can hardly ever be used for any purpose but that for which they were intended). Investment decisions in infrastructure are therefore very long-acting. The lead time in infrastructure investment, the time between the decision to build and the opening ceremony, is normally at least seven years, after which the new facility is likely to be a permanency. There are very few examples of transport infrastructure being scrapped, and certainly not within thirty years. The normal time horizon for a major transport planning study is therefore twenty-five to thirty years, and it ought to be longer.

For the makers, buyers, and operators of vehicles the position is quite different. The life of most road vehicles and aircraft is rather short – ten years or less; the life of a ship is typically thirty years; the life of trams and railway rolling stock should be about twenty-five years but in practice is often much longer. But the main difference between vehicles and infrastructure is that vehicles, being mobile, are easily disposable on the second-hand market, which infrastructure is not. Vehicle operators, whether they be road hauliers, bus companies, airlines, or shipping firms, consider at the moment that they have little economic interest – as distinct from academic interest – in long-term forecasting. Five years is their likely horizon, or ten at the outside. And their main interest will be not the smooth trends during that period but the cyclical fluctuations which are not the main interest of long-term forecasting.

Lastly there are the suppliers of equipment, the motor, aircraft, and shipbuilding industries and other engineering industries which manufacture rolling stock, new types of transport, earth-moving equipment, concrete, steel girders, road rollers, and so on. Some of the specialised activities of this great ramification of supporting industry need long-term forecasting: for instance, the construction of a new shipyard, or the approval of an aircraft prototype development. But most of it – including the motor industry – considers that it does not.

Greater long-term forecasting resources probably have been committed in the transport sector than anywhere else. The reason for this is simple. Transport planning in the last thirty years has been predominantly road planning, both in towns and between towns, and huge amounts of money have been available for roadbuilding. The lead was set by the United States where motor revenues were hypothecated by law for road construction. In 1962 the Federal Highway Act made Federal grants for highway construction conditional upon elaborate 'land use and transport studies' which consisted largely of long-term demand forecasting models. The first of these 'scientific' studies were made in Detroit and Chicago in the late 1950s, since when every major city in the U.S. has followed suit. Studies of this kind were strongly encouraged by the U.K. government (which in 1963 offered to pay half the cost) and also spread to other European countries. Normally these studies have been based on extensive surveys followed by computer analysis and projection, requiring about three years and the expenditure of one or two million dollars. The London Transportation Survey, completed in 1969, was the biggest up to that time, taking seven years and costing about four million dollars, but it has probably been exceeded since by New York.

There are few major cities in the non-communist world, including the developing world, which have not by now indulged in a large, long-term transport planning study of this kind. Similar methods have also been applied – with modifications – to regional transport planning, and to such well-known cases as the U.S. Northeast Corridor, London–Glasgow, Paris–Lyon, and, currently, the European Intercity Transport Study which is being carried out by the OECD. The unprecedented efforts put into this field have led to a highly sophisticated forecasting technology supported by a large variety of computer programs. A new professional group has sprung up – the transport planning technicians.

In common with forecasters in other sectors, transport planners and policy-makers have to base their forecasts upon forecasts about population, employment, trade, and income. They have to know, for instance, not just the overall growth rate of the population but also its distribution, age, and household structure; they have to know the type of employment, the reduction in working hours, the growth in holidays, the types of commodity traded, the distribution of income, and so on, just as forecasters in all those fields have to know something about transport. With international studies, there are difficult problems in defining and establishing real income as distinct from monetary income; varying costs of living and styles of living, and exchange rates that bear little relationship with purchasing power, make the measurement of real income a difficult task. On all these questions, which are fundamental to the demand for transport, the transport planner looks for help from outside the transport field. But he can seldom find it, even for the short term, and practically never for the thirty-year horizon. A major requirement for all long-term transport planning, therefore, is a reliable source from which the best possible forecasts about these non-transport variables can be obtained.

Special mention should be made of car ownership. The future growth of car ownership and car purchase is obviously of crucial importance to transport planners and to the motor industry; it is also of interest to many other bodies. Many forecasting methods have been devised and innumerable forecasts made, both long- and short-term. In the past the growth of car ownership was often grossly underestimated, but modern methods are more reliable. They are based on greater disaggregation of the market, requiring extensive survey work, as well as a more refined use of the aggregate methods formerly relied upon. Nevertheless, there is still great uncertainty about the levels at which various markets will become saturated and car ownership will level off. Saturation will probably be reached in some parts of Europe within the next thirty years. The possible impact of transport policy on these saturation levels is also uncertain.

The lion's share of transport forecasting has been given to inland transport, and especially to urban transport. Quite a lot has also been done in the aircraft and aviation industries, but the depth of the research has been less and the results are of dubious quality.

Nor should inland waterways be forgotten, as they so often are. An American study of 1972[1] estimated the following distances in miles per ton of goods and per gallon of fuel: pipeline 300, waterway 250, rail 200, road 58. The additional advantages of inland waterway transport in safety and quietness are obvious.

In the shipping and shipbuilding industries the forecasting effort

---

[1] Oak Ridge National Laboratory, USA.

has been very much smaller. The methods appear to be limited to broad analysis of time series within a ten-year horizon. In shipping, and also in aviation to a large extent, one is involved with intercontinental transport, not confined to Europe, even less to the Community.

We turn now to the particular needs of the Community. One of the original goals of the Community was to produce a common transport policy, but so far there is little to show for it, perhaps partly because the original six countries did not constitute a very coherent area for transport planning. The absence of Switzerland and Austria was (and still is) one major gap. The presence of major corridors into the external areas of England and Spain was another. The absence of Europe's premier airport, London, was another.

With the accession of the U.K., Ireland, and Denmark, the position is more favourable but still not satisfactory. The area which makes best sense for a common transport policy is the whole of Western Europe, bounded by the Arctic snows to the north, the Atlantic Ocean to the west, the Mediterranean to the south, and the Iron Curtain to the east: this is the natural transport area from which the physical links and the traffic flows with outside areas are minimal. The desirability of coordinating transport over this larger area was acknowledged nearly twenty years ago by the establishment of the permanent European Conference of Ministers of Transport, (ECMT), but this too did not lead to a European transport policy.

At present many branches of the transport industry engage in forecasting, according to their needs, either through their own staff or through consultants. In a few countries official forecasts of car ownership – i.e. forecasts adopted by government departments – are published and are widely used within the industry. But this seems to be the only way in which official forecasting is regularly made generally available. Nearly all other forecasting is carried out in a piecemeal way, by small groups or individuals working independently and with little cooperation from others.

Hitherto the initiatives of the Community and the ECMT have been limited to matters of organisation and regulation, e.g. pricing policy, weight limits, standardisation, working conditions, etc. They have not entered into the planning of the infrastructure. But the joint establishment in 1973 of the European Intercity Passenger Transport Study (being carried out by the OECD for the EEC, the ECMT, and twelve member countries of OECD itself) is a hopeful sign.

Year by year, transport in Europe is becoming more international. Trade, tourism, and personal travel are growing faster across frontiers than within them. As the national barriers to movement gradually come down, the flows of people and goods across frontiers will continue to increase. As the efficiency of transport improves and people's incomes grow, average travel distances will increase, adding further to the international character of the system. In thirty years, assuming that Europe continues on the path towards greater unification and prosperity, the need for a common transport policy will be greater than it is today.

The need for a Community or European policy grows out of the need for national transport policies. The growth of interregional movement within a country makes a national transport policy increasingly desirable; and the growth of international movement similarly calls for an international transport policy.

It is likely that if any such policy were adopted, it would adopt goals something like these:

(1) to connect the national road, rail, air, and waterway networks efficiently and to plan their future development in cooperation (this is specially relevant to the creation of new systems of high-speed ground transport, if they emerge, and to the reorganisation of the European air network);

(2) to facilitate the easy movement of passengers, goods, and vehicles between the various national parts of the coordinated networks;

(3) to avoid, reduce, or overcome the many undesirable side-effects of nearly all transport systems (e.g. accidents, noise, pollution);

(4) to reduce the frustration and delay which affect the users of present transport systems, whether by better technology or by better human management;

(5) to develop and manage the transport system in support of Community policies concerning regional aid and energy conservation;

(6) to find, by international cooperation, ways of spreading peak demands for transport so as to reduce congestion on roads and at airports;

(7) to coordinate and undertake research and development towards the foregoing objectives, especially (4).

Community objectives will presumably relate to long-distance inter-city transport and not to urban traffic, country roads, village bus services, or railway branch lines.

One may conclude simply that a need for a Community (or European) transport policy exists and has long been recognised, and that this need relates to long-distance transport of passengers and goods by road, rail, air, and water (including ferry links) and concerns not only the management and control of the system but also the development of infrastructure. In all these areas long-term forecasting could be useful, and in the last it is essential.

The preceding section suggested that one of the desirable objectives of a Community transport policy was to coordinate research and development in order to promote the other transport policy objectives. Large resources are devoted to transport research and development, both by governments and private industry. The field of study is enormous, ranging from hydrodynamics to traffic engineering, from supersonic aircraft to travelators, from hovertrains to skid-resistant road surfaces. The high cost of aircraft development has already forced European manufacturers into international consortia for projects like Concorde, Airbus, and Europlane. In the railway field important new developments are taking place in at least five European countries, sometimes with rival projects under way within the same country. In both industries, air and rail, numerous and costly projects have been abandoned in recent years. There are no doubt some advantages in competitive research like this, but it can be overdone.

In transport more than in most of the fields we are considering, very costly research projects must be directed towards chosen goals, and this requires a study of long-term needs. They must be designed to overcome not only current problems but also those expected, in the light of long-term forecasts, to be important in the future.

Community transport policy is not yet far advanced, and long-term forecasting could (among other things) help it to get off the ground. The purpose here, as in the other fields where Europe Plus Thirty would be working, should be to indicate the magnitude of future problems and the likely impact of policies (and new technologies) designed to help solve the problems. A secondary purpose could be to provide an official source of forecasting for the many small forecasting units working independently in different branches of this vast industry. The forecasting should concentrate on long-distance traffic and main-line hauls, i.e. air links, intercity rail links, national and interregional highways, principal waterways, and ferries. The area studies will have, for some purposes, to include all of 'Western Europe' (including Yugoslavia, Greece, and European Turkey), regardless of which countries are or are not members of the Community.

A European forecasting model could not be simply the sum of component national forecasting models: the arguments of chapter I.4 above apply with full force here. National models are not able to deal efficiently with international movements: the only way to do this would be to build a comprehensive international model, which would be the Community role. Hence the Community model would provide the external data needed by national models. In fact no national models yet exist, although several countries are moving towards them.

Europe Plus Thirty should also work closely with the inland waterway forecasting undertaken by the UN Economic Commission for Europe in Geneva.

14. *Communications*

Europe, like every other region of the globe, is criss-crossed by the flow of world information and permeated by the ferment of its own.

Despite the search for economic and political unity, the European Community will no doubt try to retain the diversity of its cultures. The maintenance and enjoyment of this variety will require great efforts of education and comprehension. The general system of communications between the members (individuals, societies, institutions) of the Community may well need to be even denser than in the more homogeneous culture of the American 'melting-pot'. This has already been touched on under the heading of education (see II.7 above): the electronic demand could be large.

The energy crisis, which is just one aspect of our failure so far to manage planetary resources in the necessary double solidarity – geographical (all the continents) and temporal (including our descendants) – may force us to limit the growth of physical movements of people or objects and to supplement them by transfers without the movement of matter, which is the purest form of communication. Much communication between people could take place by the intermediary of electronics, in order to economise on time, money, energy, and raw materials. Urban congestion points in the same direction. Why *go* to work? Why not work at home, with electronic communication, audial or audio-visual, with your colleagues and with the papers and data? The advantages, and the disadvantages, are obvious.

The development of communication is prodigious: the numbers of messages transmitted, economy of energy, miniaturisation of components and lightening of materials, ease of dialogue between the human being and the technical network; all that is well known. What is less well known is the *rapprochement* of the sectors of data-processing and of telecommunications, the techniques having increasingly numerous points in common, and industry tending to work in the two sectors simultaneously.

The growing use of communications satellites raises the question of whether the geostationary orbit may become overcrowded. On the other hand, the number of channels which each satellite can carry will increase in the decades to come.

Recently acquired scientific knowledge opens the way to future techniques that one can already imagine and whose utilisation can be programmed. Among them are transmissions through highly transparent optical fibres, use of phased light for data-processing and telecommunications (laser and holograph, for instance), and possible roles for superconductivity.

To return to the humdrum: the postal service. The need to transmit documents seems likely to persist and to develop, despite the development of new techniques. The written word is important and does not seem likely to become less so in the future. But the spectacular deterioration of Western Europe's postal services over the last twenty years is cast-iron evidence of incorrect development planning, and thus of bad forecasting in the past. Speculation about the future of the mails is dominated by the tension between man and machine. The work is boring, so people don't like to make a career of it. But magnetic coding of addresses, and automatic sorting at the other end, seem in practice to give, if anything, worse results. An area of study to open up would be research into what sorts of work people will be willing to do without striking, going slow, etc. because the work is so soul-destroying. Technological fixes could well be concentrated on the phases of the work where they are really needed.

The telephone works very badly in some countries, but this fault is not congenital, as its effectiveness under other administrations (especially the U.S.A., so far) shows. The main R & D effort must therefore go into bringing the worst parts of the European network up to the standard of the American one. This requires no forecasting. But two possible future applications of existing technology might do so.

Besides sound, the wire can transmit an image, a 'facsimile'; there seems no reason why letters should not be sent visually by wire and read in the original handwriting. Certainly the number of bits of information per page is considerable (of the order of a million, and even four times as much if one wants to transmit the details of a drawing or photograph). This is certainly a limitation, but it should not prevent the development of this elegant means of instantaneously transmitting a perfectly personal letter. One can imagine the use of terminals for the sending and receiving of such letters in post offices. Not only is the speed of the transmission ensured but also the authenticity of the document received. (Could this mean the end of registered letters, or even of notification by the servants of the court?)

There also exists a simpler system, well known and requiring little information (less than a tenth of what the previous system requires): the telex. It still requires considerable improvement, but if the cost of use can be reduced it might well spread to use by private individuals.

Hertzian technology has made possible television and radio. It is also used in telephonic transmissions, but the user cares little whether the message he receives is transmitted by wire, a carrier wave, or a satellite. The question for the future is the way the sending of messages to a large number of receivers will develop. Two possibilities are emerging. Firstly, on the technical level: Hertzian space is near saturation, and the obstacles to radio waves in towns are numerous. Hence recourse to cable distribution. Secondly, on the social level: a need is emerging for messages sent not to everyone but to a more or less restricted group interested in a single category of messages. It is clear that one cannot occupy the TV screen, which is meant for everyone, with local information about a district or a town. Hence, again, recourse to cable television.

Television also has an important limitation: it is only a receiver. It is difficult to say how far the need for feedback from the viewer is felt; but we already know that it is urgent for educational TV, and it is easy to list cases where it would be convenient or pleasant, especially in the matter of public participation in politics.

In these technical areas, there is much forecasting in each country. The forecasters often meet at international conferences, and there seems little reason for Europe Plus Thirty to become involved in this technical sector. Nevertheless, one cannot forget that the Community has not even succeeded in unifying its own TV standards. The lack of advance consideration here is worrying. When we adopted the American definition scale, we ignored the difference in the current frequencies: 50 Cycles in Europe, 60 in the U.S. This difference is enough to bring the mechanical interference vibrations which are produced in medium-quality receivers into the spectrum of audible frequencies, at least for the young. If Europe Plus Thirty can play any role in preventing that sort of mistake from arising again, it certainly should, though it would involve a dive into detail which would normally be outside its sphere.

The Commission, and other relevant bodies, are now working on various plans for European information and data-handling networks. Europe Plus Thirty would have an interest in the way they were set up, since it would clearly be among the users. It is possible, though we are by no means sure about this, that Europe Plus Thirty might be able to undertake some useful forecasting about the alternative ways these networks might develop.

All in all, forecasting in this field is not so much a matter of technology forecasting as of demand forecasting: what will people want? The question itself shows the obvious interdependency of this field with those of society, industry, education, transport, and, on the data-handling side, health.

Europe Plus Thirty should seek to discover the probable impact on communication needs of different industrial and commercial policies, data-processing and documentary policies, and cultural and educational policies – and, not least, the impact of different degrees of economic and political integration within the Community.

Communications is the last of the fields (the others having been climatology, demography, health, and education) where Europe Plus Thirty should rely almost entirely on the services of one or two outside correspondents or part-time members of its team. So much is going on anyhow that this will be the best approach. As in the other fields mentioned above, seminars should be called from time to time and the inputs of technical knowledge (extensive) and numerical data (rather small) should be arranged and secured on a continuing basis by the specialist correspondents of the central team.

15. *Economy and finance*

If we want to ask to what extent long-term forecasting is possible and desirable in the economic and financial fields, one way to do it – one that is methodologically tolerably legitimate – is to go back twenty or thirty years and try to see whether the economic and financial events that have since taken place could have been forecast. This kind of exercise is certainly not optimal as a test for our purpose; it might very well be the case that twenty or thirty years ago enough elements of the last twenty or thirty years were already present to allow us to predict their permanence over that period. To borrow a mathematical concept, we might already have had a base to span the field constituted by those twenty or thirty years. But it might equally be the case that, if we place ourselves at the beginning of the next twenty or thirty years – i.e. today – we do not possess enough elements, we do not possess a base to span the next two or three decades. If so, it would be because the present does not necessarily always contain the future. Discrete changes may divide historical periods: two twenty- or thirty-year periods, for instance, may have, as regards economic and financial structures, an equal base of essential features; a third such period, immediately before or after them, may be totally different from the other two.

Extrapolation of previously evidenced trends would, if we were extrapolating the third period from the preceding two, yield thoroughly indefensible results, while the same exercise, if used to forecast the second period using trends evidenced in the course of the first, would be very successful.

All this becomes extremely clear when we reflect on world economic and financial events over the last fifty years. The post-war years have differed radically from the pre-war ones, particularly in some of the respects that can be considered 'essential'. Certainly one can detect several permanent trends throughout: the decline of the British economy and the rise of the American economy were well under way more than half a century ago. But how could one forecast that the 'economic constitution' of the Western World, dictated by the U.S. in 1944–5, would have been so successfully and quickly enforced in its vital parts, like currency convertibility, free trade, free capital movements, and the international division of labour? Had we extrapolated what had passed in the West starting in 1929, then autarky, rationing, planning, inconvertibility, etc. would have been more likely to be forecast.

The job would have been radically easier, and tremendously more successful, in the middle fifties. Then, a simple extrapolation of the previous ten years of U.S. economic history and its projection onto Europe, for instance, would have missed very little of what actually happened. This would have been the 'analysis by precursive events' described in chapter I.1 above. Future production and consumption patterns could have been predicted very closely by looking at what they had been in the U.S. in the relevant previous period; once it was proved that the 'economic constitution' dictated by the U.S. was enforceable, the phenomena of trade liberalisation, international capital movements, and the spread of multinational corporations could all have been correctly forecast.

What could not have been forecast were the relative places in the economic power scale that individual European countries have occupied. An ordinal scale could probably have been arrived at with respect, for instance, to GNP per capita, but not a cardinal one. The relative placing of Britain and France would have been an impossible job. It would have been equally difficult to assess the relative positions on such a scale of countries like Belgium, Holland, and Austria, even as late as 1958. One was sure that the U.S. would remain on top, and equally sure that traditionally fast-growing countries like Germany, Japan, and Italy would carry on growing fast. But who could have guessed that France, Belgium, the Netherlands, and Austria would become fast growers?

On the whole, however, forecasting world economic and financial trends would have been a successful exercise, especially if the people doing it had focused on industries, products, trade flows, and economic and financial institutions, rather than confining themselves to forecasting the relative growth rates of the various countries. The 'automobile economy', with its accompaniment of related industrial growth, motorway-building, and suburban sprawl, could have been forecast extremely easily in 1955 for the whole non-communist developed world. That forecast would have entailed forecasting also the relative decline of railways and of the coal-mining industry, the decay of urban centres, and the gradual disappearance of a commercial sector based on high labour intensiveness.

In general, once full employment and trade liberalisation were adopted as the basic policy objectives in most developed countries, it was pretty clear that this would entail the gradual disappearance of most labour-intensive activities from the industrial sectors of those countries, and their removal to developing countries. If we interpret recent economic history in this light, most of its features appear to follow from this premise. What could not have been guessed was the temporary appearance, around 1960, of cheap energy that has made the replacement of labour as a means of production so much easier in the Western economy. Once this was assured, however, the pattern of the last fifteen years of growth in Western countries could have been inferred. We knew full employment and high wages were the norm, we knew low-cost energy was available; other things being equal, an economic structure based on substituting energy for labour could have been inferred.

If we now remove low-cost energy and maintain high wages and full employment, what can be substituted for what? We may be near a turning point; long-term forecasting may be very difficult if we start in one year and much easier if we start the next year, if the corner is turned between these years and the interpretative key for the next decade or two appears. This is a general proposition.

Long-range forecasting can score a high percentage of hits if it is restricted to those aspects that can be considered 'safe'. With the considerable lengthening of the gestation period of most capital projects, both private and public, ten- to fifteen-year forecasts are becoming increasingly possible. For instance, when a big motorway scheme or railway scheme is launched, the transport policy of a country is determined for the next two decades at least. Similarly, when capital projects are started in fields like chemicals, steel, or automobile production, fairly reliable estimates can be made of a country's growth pattern for at least a decade, and the probability of their being upset by 'extraneous' events can be assessed. And the same can be said about important institutional changes, like new legislation concerning the financial institutions or the fiscal structure of a country. Because of the vagaries of demand management, it is much more difficult to give appropriate time parameters to these structural trends. But, although the pace may be hard to forecast, direction is much easier to detect, and fortunately long-range forecasting is more about direction than about pace.

Nowhere does supranational long-term forecasting have a greater advantage over national forecasting than in the economic and financial fields. When 'supranational' implies a forecasting agency of the EEC, this is very true indeed. The integrated economy of the EEC is quite capable, because of its sheer size, of making dependent many of the economic variables which a national economic forecaster must consider independent. It is not too much to say that EEC trade *determines* world trade in manufactures, that EEC agricultural policy has a heavy influence on world agricultural production, that EEC energy requirements and energy policy strongly influence world trade in energy products and even world energy production (the EEC countries put together are by far the largest importer of energy products).

It is also more and more clear that the EEC is the economic partner that the Third World and the socialist countries will most frequently have to deal with for political as well as economic reasons. Most socialist countries are in Europe, and this determines a 'geographical premise' to intense economic relations. As to the Third World, it is the sheer importing power of the EEC that induces the Third World to maximise economic relations with Europe.

But if we look at the economic forecasting and, more generally, the economic research which the Community carries out at present, it strikes us that it is not conducted on the assumption (which would be a very realistic one) that the EEC is an integrated economy, nor has it as its main research target the identification and description of the *mode* of integration followed by the EEC economies since its inception. The EEC input–output matrix, developed by the Community Statistical Office, is so far only a rationalisation and summation of the member countries' individual input–output tables. This is, of course, a necessary starting point, but a lot more must be done.

The European Commission also possesses two medium-term forecasting models, COMET (Community Medium-Term Model) and METEOR (European Model for Economic Transmission Effects and Balancing Operations). METEOR should in fact be a short-term forecasting model, but since it uses annual data as input it can hardly be seen as serving that purpose. Both these models are based on the interaction of national models, more or less identically constructed along Keynesian lines. The interaction takes place in only one dimension, the international trade dimension. In this fashion, the individual economies of the EEC are handled on the same level as other national economies like the U.S., Japan, and the Third World countries. The METEOR model consolidates the EEC countries into one block and links this block to other large ones: North America, Japan, the Third World. But the consolidation is obtained by summation of import demands and export supplies expressed by the national economies.

Neither model, because of its nature, contains a built-in mechanism of structural modification that is capable of affecting the representation of the individual member countries' economies and reshaping them into a representation of an integrated EEC economy. In both COMET and METEOR (as in any short-term model) the EEC countries interact all the time, but this does not change the structure of their economies. In addition, one can say that although interaction among the EEC economies is analysed in the trade dimension, it is not analysed in the factors of production dimension. But even the trade dimension remains in both models at too aggregated a level. What matters in economic integration is intra-industry specialisation, as Verdoorn proved in 1957[1] and as several other writers have reiterated more recently. Of intra-industry trade there is no analysis in either METEOR or COMET; but it would be scientifically incorrect to put this type of question to models like COMET and METEOR. We have dealt with them here only to show that entirely new instruments are needed if the Community wants to engage in long-term economic and financial forecasting.

Europe Plus Thirty, being a long-term EEC forecasting agency with access to data collected by the national authorities of the member countries and by international organisations, would be in a unique position to forecast economic and financial trends. It would be based at the heart of a very homogeneous and integrated productive system, composed of countries whose economies are 'mixed' and where planning is a respected tradition, especially if we consider this concept in real rather than nominal terms. Europe Plus Thirty, if it were to concern itself with forecasting in as many fields as are considered in this book, would enjoy an extremely wide potential for economic and financial forecasting.

But in order to do so, it should equip itself with adequate instru-

---

[1] See his contribution to *Economic Consequences of the Size of Nations* (IEA Conference Proceedings, Lisbon 1957), ed. by E. A. G. Robinson (London: Macmillan, 1960).

ments. It should, in particular, work together with the Community Statistical Office (CSO) to transform the EEC input–output matrix, developed by the CSO as a summation of the member countries' individual input–output tables, into a more truly integrated European input–output matrix. This ought to be done, in our opinion, by having regard to the basic fact that, because of the process of integration, the European economy has already become divided into a productive 'centre' and a 'periphery'. The centre must be geographically located and so must the periphery, so that we obtain a concept of 'centre' and 'periphery' that cuts across national boundaries. Moreover, it must be a concept based on production and exchange relations in the sense, for instance, that the centre expresses most of the demand for, and supply of, investment goods; this means that if individual modern industrial activities are located in geographically peripheral areas – Sicily or Scotland or Brittany – these activities are still part of our definition of the 'centre'. The periphery, on the other hand, is charac-terised by the fact that it neither demands nor supplies investment goods. It demands finished consumer goods, and it mostly imports them from the centre and pays for them with the proceeds of the sale of primary commodities and agricultural goods, with the remittances of its emigrants, and with the proceeds of tourism.

In addition, the CSO, in conjunction with European Central Banks and finance ministries, should proceed to construct a matrix of European financial flows.

Both these jobs present difficulties. Nevertheless, if the economic and the financial matrices became available, the economists of Europe Plus Thirty would have at their disposal an enormous quantity of material to be used for long-term forecasting. The matrices would, moreover, provide an invaluable instrument to be used in the shaping of the EEC's industrial, financial, energy, and regional policies, and in progress towards economic and monetary union. All the inputs to the matrices would have, in fact, not only quantitative and qualitative dimensions but also a locational dimension. The matrices would, signally, make it possible to study the intersectoral shifts that have taken place in the EEC economy in the last two decades, and the changes in the inner structure of each sector, and to forecast the nature and the breadth of future changes. Moreover, a careful analysis of the information contained in those matrices would greatly improve our knowledge of the nature of technological change in the various sectors of the EEC economy.

This activity would also have an important by-product: it would show the actual levels which European integration has reached in the econ-omic and financial fields, which are very high but are perhaps not very well known by the public or even by the governments of the member countries.

The Community has so far lacked a complete view of its economic life, taken as a whole. Its statistics are the summation of national statistics, often not homogeneous. What is missing is a structurally interdependent approach, an interrelated analysis of products, markets, and inputs, and of the financial activities that correspond to economic activities. If this type of activity were to be initiated by the proposed Europe Plus Thirty, it would yield very interesting results without great delay and without engaging an excessive amount of human and financial resources. Most of the census and assessment jobs just outlined could be done by competent task forces.

Another task force could study the basic problems of trends in relative price structures. This essential field of analysis was sadly overlooked until macro-events like the recent rise in raw-material prices brought its more lurid aspects to everybody's attention. A spate of research has been initiated, but it does not look as if its results will do much more than scratch the surface of the relative price problem. Under this heading, the study of the inflationary process would find an appropriate and theoretically sound location. Studies of inflation have, at least recently, tended to look at this phenomenon as if it were exclusively determined by monetary causes, by wage pressures, or by the incontinence of public finance: Europe Plus Thirty should study inflation in its proper relative price context, and it should not forget that inflation is only one of the phenomena that result from the changes in the relative price structure.

Equally important is the study of trends in relative wages, and of the whole subject of the modes in which production is organised, since the legal, social, and technological 'modalities' of the organisation of production combine to change the relative uses and relative prices of productive forces. Tendencies toward concentration as well as de-concentration can be detected and must be studied and explained. The study of trends in relative prices and wages, in the structure and technology of production, and in the concentration and diffusion of productive processes in the EEC should be accompanied by a related study of the trends in the placing of the EEC economy within the world economy. This would involve a deep enquiry into the path of development of economic relations between the EEC and its associated countries, the socialist countries, the U.S.A. and Canada, Japan, the other developed countries, the oil-producing countries, and the 'poor countries'. By 'economic relations' one should understand not only visible trade but also invisible trade and investment flows, technology transfers, and the administration of 'aid'. It is through this enquiry that

Europe Plus Thirty should make its contribution to the development of Community aid policy.

The modes of international division of labour should be closely analysed so that the formation of 'hierarchies' and dependence patterns could be detected and their future developments forecast (we touched on this also in chapter II.9 above). Similarly, the process of 'internationalisation' of capital, labour, and production should be given detailed attention, in order to see whether any 'European' pattern becomes evident or, if not, to enquire why. The same type of analysis should be conducted at the intra-Community level, in order to detect the appearance of centripetal or centrifugal forces and intra-regional specialisation and dependence patterns within the EEC.

Europe Plus Thirty should also seek to forecast about the mode of development of financial and monetary structures. This would involve a study of the structural development of European financial institutions and policies. Here, a straight extrapolation of previous U.S. financial history on European data would have yielded extremely poor results throughout the post-war period, while it is quite probable that doing it the other way round – i.e. extrapolating previous continental European trends on U.S. and British data – would have proved more successful. This is simply because the continental European financial systems had to face, both before and after the Second World War, the two basic problems of capital scarcity and inflationary financing, which the U.S. and Britain, with their low rates of inflation and of real investment, were spared until the mid-sixties.

Unfortunately most analyses of continental European financial systems have started from the premise that the U.S. and British financial systems were the models that should be imitated. This has condemned their results to irrelevance, which justifies a reconsideration of the whole style of European integration in the financial and monetary fields. Especially important, when this exercise is taken up by Europe Plus Thirty, will be to make public finance the linch-pin of financial analysis; and this is again the opposite of what Anglo-American financial analysis has traditionally done. The activities of the state (in its widest sense) as a financial intermediary could well be the point of departure of any European financial forecasting.

If this point of departure were chosen, the relevance of European financial forecasting would be tremendously enhanced, especially to forecasts of the structure of European monetary integration, of the activities of non-European multinational corporations in Europe, and of those of European multinational corporations in Europe and elsewhere. Trends in banking, private and social insurance and pension systems, housing finance, and consumer credit (and thus consumption) would be much easier to forecast, as well as the relative weight and patterns of activity of nationalised industry within the European economy.

More generally, Europe Plus Thirty should combine all its findings in the economic and financial fields with the findings of its other sections in an attempt to construct a progressively less naive 'Welfare Accounting System' for the Community as a whole and for its component parts. The greatest difficulty to be faced, when constructing such a system, is that social indicators (like environmental decay or rehabilitation, the number of pupils in secondary schools, the extent of educational recycling, crime rates, wealth and income distribution) cannot without drastic recourse to value judgements be expressed in a common standard of value and aggregated to form a sum that can be added to or subtracted from the money GNP. But it would be just as useful to know, for instance, that production of such-and-such goods and services has been so much in any one year, *and* that the index of atmospheric pollution in the same year was so much in such-and-such places, and to compare both figures to previous years or to other countries, or to extrapolate them into the future. What can usefully be done, moreover, is to calculate trade-offs, e.g. of the relative cost to a community of reducing pollution, increasing education, or raising health standards by certain amounts.

The same reasons that go against putting excessive faith in the GNP indicator also go against trying to pyramid all welfare indicators into a portmanteau figure for 'Gross National Welfare' or some such phrase. What is of paramount importance is to convey to the citizens of the Community and to their representatives the notion that the socio-economic system, in its general functioning, produces this conglomerate of goods, services, processes, and social and environmental phenomena as its output, and that this production process cannot simply be reformed by eliminating its negative outputs, because if that is done the positive outputs will be affected as well. The inner structure of this complex production process must therefore be elucidated, so that the mutual relations between its components can be identified.

The problems involved in this type of social accounting are enormous, but once again this does not mean that the job cannot be contemplated. The identification of the variables that enter the system will be made harder by differing national standards, and the related problems of weighting – of translating quality into quantity – do not diminish just because the exercise is conducted on a Community basis. But it is certain that only if an attempt is made to construct this type of accounting system can we know in what direction the Community is going, understand what rewards national and Community efforts are reaping, and begin to assess and compare the aims the Community might rationally reach for.

Chapter I.2 above spoke of the need for coordination of all the forecasting work, and the research relevant to forecasting, which is done by and for the Commission. The days of partial analysis, if they ever existed, must be gone forever. Nowhere is this truer than in the economic field. The facets of economic and financial forecasting suggested in this chapter are, in our opinion, among the most interesting and fruitful. But it is clear that Europe Plus Thirty could not reasonably take up all of them at the same time. Perhaps the best starting point would be the forecast of the constellation of relative prices that will prevail in the European economy, as a result of the effects of the energy crisis and of the crisis in the concept of 'growth for its own sake'. This aspect of long-term economic forecasting would also be the most relevant to the other forecasting of Europe Plus Thirty. But a long-term forecasting programme may embrace a span from four to twenty or even thirty years. In such a time span things change profoundly, new problems arise, corners are turned; so it would be unwise to crystallise a forecasting programme from the start. Europe Plus Thirty must be capable of responding quickly (though not superficially) to changing events and insights.

16. *Defence and disarmament*

As the European Community is at present constituted under the Treaty of Rome, defence and disarmament are not among its responsibilities. It would therefore be understandable if Europe Plus Thirty were to devote no more than passing attention to them. But this would not necessarily be right. The role of Europe Plus Thirty will be to explore possible futures, using the techniques of forecasting and technology assessment; and a future in which the Community could find itself more directly concerned with defence is certainly a possible one. Nor would it be possible for Europe Plus Thirty to forecast about the European economy or about European technology without taking account of the impact of defence, or about European politics and external relations without considering disarmament.

There is no way of decoupling defence, deterrence, and disarmament from the other great issues of our time, any more than there was in the past. We can list those issues: political and trade relationships with our Eastern neighbours and with America; the maintenance of a sound economic base here in Western Europe; the provision of food and other resources at a time when a century of unprecedented growth shows every sign of overstraining the world economy; our relations with the Third and Fourth Worlds nearer home; the growing sense of disorientation, the lack of cohesion and purpose which has begun to affect industrial society, and the disbelief, perhaps growing, in the need for any defence at all; the general direction of our technological innovation; and, last and most important, the relations between the member states of the Community itself.

Europe Plus Thirty should not go so far as studies of the mechanics of defence: that ground belongs to NATO and the national defence industries. There is no point in redoing within the Community what is already being done elsewhere, and many large specialist areas can be eliminated.

But there are some important matters, impinging directly on the growth of common Community policies in the fields of foreign affairs, technology, and economics, which cannot be tucked away into the defence 'black box', and which will have to enter into Europe Plus Thirty's general forecasting if it is to be realistic.

Then there are the possible changes of the military/political pattern in Europe and the rest of the world: these include the arguments about disarmament, nuclear proliferation, and deterrence; scenarios of European politics and of moves towards East–West detente; the political circumstances in which the Community might begin to acquire defence and disarmament responsibilities, or at least to take defence and disarmament more explicitly into account; and the use of defence expertise and materiel as bargaining counters outside Europe. All these would affect the future of NATO and hence of the Warsaw Pact.

First and most important is the impact on national economies of devoting different levels of resources to defence. This includes both the economic and technological impact of defence technology and defence production on the European industrial base, and the possibility of greater international sharing of defence industrial effort and the form that could take.

This ground can be examined in considerable depth without using classified information; there is no shortage of published data. Defence is served now – as it has been throughout history – by very strong intellectual forces, drawn in by the fascination of watching 'real power' at work, or by the challenge of solving difficult problems, or simply by patriotism. There is also a substantial extra-governmental group of specialists – historians, political commentators, economists – who contribute serious academic studies, and who help in this way to maintain the standards and objectivity of governmental work. But, as always, the way in which the arguments are assembled and the weight given to conflicting considerations depend on who is writing and for whom. Besides being a necessary part of its general forecasting, work in this field by Europe Plus Thirty would help develop a specifically European analysis of the fields we are discussing, and this we think is to be desired.

Military–political scenario-writing needs to be undertaken in order to spell out the range of possibilities which could confront the Community. To be useful, scenarios need to be in some detail: unless sufficient colour is given to the picture, it will not stimulate thought and so eventually action. The effort required for this kind of work is not large, but it needs to be of high quality. Those undertaking it will have to understand Western European, Russian, and American political realities, trends in strategic deterrence, the use of nuclear and conventional weaponry as local deterrents, the long-term political and economic implications of the 'limits to growth' debate, etc.

The time at which Europe could become more responsible for its own defence is obviously relevant to any future defence studies. As already noted, the Treaty ignores the issue. But a more unified Western Europe (if one is eventually created) which consciously planned on looking in perpetuity to another power of comparable population and wealth for its defence is not among the most likely long-term developments. If the Community were to involve itself with defence, that would be bound to have an effect on the future of NATO. Already, indeed, some movement in this direction can be discerned in the creation and recent extension of the Euro-Group of Defence Ministers.

The existence of this group is relevant to the forecasting about defence which might be undertaken by Europe Plus Thirty. It started in 1968 as a kind of dining club for European Ministers of Defence when they happened to be together for meetings of the NATO Council. Its membership is smaller than that of NATO: the United States and Canada are not members, nor are Iceland, France, and Portugal (which had been preoccupied with colonial problems). The membership also differs from that of the Community, Ireland being neutral. Norway, Greece, and Turkey are in NATO but not in the Community. The Euro-Group has met so far in the NATO buildings in Brussels. Germany and Britain tend to take the leading roles; the chairmanship rotates, and Britain provides a small secretariat.

France is not a member of the Euro-Group, though she remains a member of the NATO Committee of Armament Directors. In order to associate France in some way with a European defence initiative, the idea has been floated of reviving the Western European Union (WEU). But its membership is even more limited than that of the Community (Britain, France, Germany, the Netherlands, Belgium, Luxembourg, and Italy); and Germany does not regard it as the most useful organ for policy decisions because the Treaties of 1954 which gave it birth also imposed on Germany and France a stringent system of nuclear weapons inspection and control which Germany has observed and France has ignored.

The Euro-Group was originally intended to work on the improvement of the European end of NATO in general. In practice it was concerned at first mainly with armaments and the defence industry (see below), but it has recently made a tentative start on a study of longer-term issues. This involves entering sensitive territory which cannot be usefully explored without making judgements about the likely future of European defence and disarmament, and hence about Atlantic relationships and progress towards detente. The importance of the Euro-Group in relation to the work of Europe Plus Thirty is, clearly, that a great deal of defence forecasting on behalf of Europe could develop naturally out of its efforts.

At this point it may be convenient if we give an impressionistic account of the way long-term defence forecasting is done in NATO and in several of its member countries. It is often done under four headings: economic, political and military, demographic and educational, and technological.

Under the *economic* heading, the likely growth in national resources is examined both absolutely and in comparison with that of allies and potential enemies, with the likely proportion of those resources which will be available in the public sector, and with the share of that sector which defence might get. Realistic assumptions have to be made about the cost of equipment and manpower and about such things as the likelihood of burden-sharing and collaboration with allies. The economic contribution of the defence sector to other sectors can also be estimated: e.g., the training of airmen, engineers, and craftsmen, and the development of the uneconomical technologies, like exotic fuels, which later have a civilian application ('fall-out').

Secondly, the possible future *political and military environment* is examined. Developments in international relationships which might have a substantial effect on the size, plans, structure, equipment, deployment, and mobility of the armed forces are identified: in superpower relationships, the American commitment to Europe and the possible emergence of a more integrated Europe in the Western Alliance; likely progress on arms control; the possible development of China and Japan as military powers; the stability or otherwise of the Third World and of national or European interests outside Europe; and the threat of civil disturbance in Europe and elsewhere.

Thirdly, forecasts are made about *demographic and educational developments* and *changes in social attitudes* which may affect recruiting, manpower structure, and manpower costs of the armed forces and may perhaps act as a major constraint on future defence planning. The armed services may have to face over the next decade or so changes in their social environment and in their own social function at least as fundamental as have occurred in any previous period in history.

Lastly, possible longer-term trends in *technological developments* are analysed, and their significance for defence. The objectives and capabilities of the relevant areas of Soviet and Western technology are compared, and trends of promising research wherever these may occur are identified. In particular an attempt is made to identify developments which could upset or change the current offensive/defensive balance, or which would offer wholly new concepts of weapons systems or military activity which would entail the elimination of particular classes of weapons or military activity.

The issue of *deterrence* is nowhere of greater significance than on the European mainland, since only there do the two superpowers face each other in an embattled posture. As weapons technology moves ahead (and there is no sign of its letting up), the theories underlying our concept of deterrence will need periodic re-examination, and Europe Plus Thirty should aim to master the arguments. In the not very distant future it is possible that the need for political thinking on this issue may be sharply increased, through foreseeable developments leading to the increased proliferation of nuclear weaponry, an ever-increasing danger of nuclear war by accident, and fresh risks – in this age of subversion and guerilla organisations – of nuclear or other blackmail. And most important of all will be the possibilities of disarmament and detente. A future containing an unrestricted arms race for evermore would not be the same as a future containing even limited disarmament, and the difference would have considerable consequences for the economy – and major ones for the society and politics – of Europe.

The bill for European defence – not counting the American contribution – runs at about 3.2 per cent of the gross domestic products of the Nine (excluding Ireland). In money terms this amounts to around $35,000 million in total (at 1974 prices). Industrially the significance is even greater than this already very large figure would suggest. Defence is a major consumer of the Community's technical effort: it can, for instance, account for 25 per cent or more of a country's industrial technology. It is, moreover, the most advanced 25 per cent, and it captures the imagination and allegiance of some of the best recruits but makes little direct contribution to the health of the civilian economy. Some such lopsidedness is unavoidable as long as we have defence; but the economic side-effects need to be assessed and brought out into the open, for the Community just as for an individual country. The commitment of defence technologists on the present scale is more than a peripheral issue, and a more planned distribution of defence resources might be expected to play an important role in the future economic policies of the Community. Quite apart from technological implications, defence ties up, in a necessary but largely unproductive activity, many of the best of each nation's young people, so that the opportunity cost of lost productive employment has to be added to the direct cost if the true effort is to be fully appreciated. All of these factors merit regular economic appraisal in the light of forecasts of 'possible futures'.

As more European joint production agreements are set up, and as more trans-European companies are formed to carry them out, the process of European collaborative arms production will seem increasingly natural. Already there are a dozen or more good examples of what can be achieved. By, say, 1990 it would be surprising if Western Europe were not physically able to provide the industrial base for a defence and deterrent effort of its own. By then it could certainly create its own satellite reconnaissance system, and so avoid remaining dependent on America, as it was during the 1973 Israel–Arab war, for some kinds of information – information, moreover, which would be of critical importance in any disarmament or arms-control process. All these possibilities would be proper elements of scenario-writing in Europe Plus Thirty.

For such reasons Europe Plus Thirty should not arbitrarily exclude anything from its purview simply because it has to do with defence or disarmament and because these matters do not figure in the Treaty of Rome. They must be part of its forecasting work because they are part of European life: politically, industrially, and above all economically. Lack of mention in the Treaty has not prevented the Community at all levels, up to and including summit meetings, from talking about this matter or that, or from laying plans for Community action. Defence and disarmament should therefore be part of the normal work of Europe Plus Thirty, like anything else. Data and scenarios should be integrated with the normal inputs of the economic, industrial, technological, social, environmental, materials, and educational forecasting which Europe Plus Thirty undertakes. And it goes without saying that its technology assessment should not create artificial frontiers between the defence and civil applications of a given technology, product, or process.

17. *Politics and institutions*

Of all the areas dealt with here, the political and institutional is the least amenable to forecasting: the nature and function of political institutions themselves make this the case. Every social system nourishes a number of institutions, whose function it is authoritatively to regulate the demands and conflicts which arise within it and, in the case of national systems, to monopolise the use of force. These institutions we call political because it is their purpose sometimes to be, and sometimes to develop and provide, decision-making mechanisms. We have to distinguish between institutions in the economic sphere (e.g. firms, trade unions), the socio-cultural sphere (e.g. churches, mass media, etc.), and the politico-administrative sphere (government institutions themselves). Here we will concentrate on institutions in the politico-administrative sphere; they are set above the others because they regulate and control them. But we have to keep in mind that political institutions are always interdependent with the other spheres: they can never be examined outside the context of other institutions. It is the purpose of politico-administrative institutions to prepare and bring forth decisions which are important to the order and shape of the whole of the social system, as well as to the development of individual sub-systems.

All political systems have to solve one basic problem, namely how to adjust political order to changing social demands. It is typical of political institutions in the West, to which the countries of the European Community belong, that they do this by balancing conflicting interests within the framework of regulated and more or less accepted procedures. The criteria by which we judge such institutions are legitimacy and efficiency. By 'legitimacy' we mean consensus: acceptance of the legality of institutions, and a consequent readiness to submit oneself to their authority. By 'efficiency' we mean the ability of institutions adequately to fulfil the role assigned to them.

There is only a limited typology of political institutions in the modern history of the West; institutional innovation has not been especially noteworthy in recent times. So, while the basic forms of political institutions have remained rather constant, their relationship with each other and with society in general, their tasks, and their internal structure fluctuate according to the particular problems which come up, when the need for order has to be reconciled with changing social demands. We are here considering institutions that either influence the political 'input', by which we mean the demands of social forces which arise in problem situations, or else are concerned with handling input in order to create legislative and administrative 'output'. While all political systems have these two characteristics – input-oriented structures (parties, pressure groups) and output-oriented institutions (government, civil service) – the relationship between them is constantly changing. On the one hand there can be quite a strong executive facing a 'weak' parliament and on the other a 'strong' parliament facing a government that is nearly unable to act. And there can be institutions in the economic and social sphere that have such a dominating influence on the politico-administrative system that it is unable to go against their wishes.

The above is necessarily a somewhat schematic and simplified account of the matter, and in practical experience its outlines are no doubt often hard to perceive through the dust and heat generated by the conflicts between entrenched power systems. This is particularly the case where an institution (for instance among great companies or trade unions, or in the press and television), having acquired the power necessary for the exercise of a function to which there is general consent, uses it to exercise another function to which general consent is lacking.

The development of political institutions and their capacity to meet the demands on them is determined less by the logic of their own internal development than by the tasks and problems which are imposed upon them from the socio-economic and cultural spheres. An internal dynamic of political institutions about which we might forecast thus exists only to a very limited degree; we cannot say much about the future development of political institutions 'as a separate subject'. Forecasting institutional change presupposes a knowledge of the problems and developments in other spheres of the social system, to which the political system always has to react, to find an adequate response.

Let us take an example. If critical developments occur in an area which is of prime importance for the existence or further development of a society – energy scarcity, high unemployment, a lack of skilled workers – it is the duty of the politico-administrative institutions to cope with the matter. They must adapt themselves to fresh exigencies. This process can lead to the internal re-organisation of a political institution (administrative reforms). Sometimes an institution which serves a particular purpose begins to serve a different one. Sometimes it is itself supplanted as the chief servant of its own purpose. Institutional change is determined partly by the nature of the problem and partly by the will of those in charge of the institution. Institutions are partly secondary phenomena which relate to primary causes (so that their internal logic or inherent laws are of secondary importance compared with those of the economy or of population dynamics) and partly instruments for the exercise of power, which can be guided and manoeuvred by each succeeding generation of persons in charge of them. It is obvious that the task of forecasting as it attaches to each of these two aspects of political institutions is different.

Political predictions have mostly been wrong. Some sociologists and philosophers at the turn of the nineteenth and twentieth centuries predicted new forms of government based on the domination of scientists and technocrats. This was the spectre of the technocratic state, which is still with us today and is still only a spectre. Marxists predicted the breakdown of capitalism and with it the bourgeois state. They denied that capitalism could in the course of its development become flexible enough to resolve most of the contradictions which were supposed to bring it down. In Germany many liberal intellectuals and politicians didn't give Hitler a chance; conversely those who believed in him were unable to foresee his early ruin. Authors such as George Orwell foresaw, against the background of contemporary experience, a totally technological society in the hands of unscrupulous power fanatics; but this was less a prediction than a device to warn humanity against a frightening political possibility. Orwell did not repeat Cassandra's mistake: his warning of doom was credible, was believed, and has, so far, been accordingly falsified. At the beginning of the 1950s many social scientists and even more politicians in Europe were convinced that a federal Europe could be created within a few years. The Treaty of Rome was signed in the hope that a European political community would come about as a by-product of economic integration. General expectations and forecasts always tend to be based upon an evaluation of present conditions; they influence one's own assessment and interpretation of the future. Such forecasts often tell us more about the present and its appraisal than about the probable future. 'Every forecast is the projection into the future of a certain understanding of present reality. This shapes its structure, direction and results.'[1]

We must distinguish between forecasting the development of political events and institutions, which is not very fruitful, and postulating or drafting new political institutions as part of hypothetical alternative futures, the problems of which may require new or adapted institu-

---

[1] Klaus Scholder, *Grenzen der Zukunft* (Stuttgart: Kohlhammer, 1973), p. 71.

tions as tools for their solution. Political theory and practice are full of examples of how to construct new political institutions; whenever we have to reorganise things or feel the need for new political forms, there is no lack of such designs. This book is itself concerned with the outline of an institution to cope with certain new tasks, and it takes into account the reality of the present political scene. In what follows, we are talking about the construction of new institutions at Community level. The corresponding activity at national level, where the ground is thick with instruments of entrenched power grown up over the centuries, would be different.

If you want to achieve a political goal, such as a united Europe or a European economic and monetary union, you must necessarily presuppose the establishment of certain institutions. Their function would be to achieve the chosen goals through institutional mechanisms. Theoretically, it is rather easy to answer the basic questions when setting up institutions: you always need a body to elect, appoint, or delegate members to an institution; every institution that has powers of decision needs a controlling institution; every new institution needs to be sensibly integrated into the network of existing ones; and so on. In theory, therefore, it is not difficult to design institutional structures. But practical questions remain: How do we achieve desirable institutions? Has historical experience been taken into account? Has the relationship between existing institutions been correctly gauged? It is not very useful to sketch an institutional model of, for instance, a federal Europe, if it is not accompanied by a realistic assessment of the present political situation from which one can deduce whether within a foreseeable period it is in fact possible to reach that goal. Political forecasting in this sense – namely, dreaming up institutions and constitutions – must be accompanied by a practical analysis of the real power relations which would either facilitate or hinder their creation. Quantitative methods are of only limited use in political and institutional forecasting. In this area the 'simple methods' and 'intuitive methods' mentioned in chapter I.1 above are of most use. They can be supplemented by analytical methods such as rough cost–benefit analysis, so that one can estimate quantitatively some of the advantages of a particular political strategy.

But above all, it is important that the people working in this area should understand the functioning of political institutions.

Thinking in a non-committal way about the formulation of political strategies should include seeing how far political institutions within the European Community are capable of responding appropriately to any given problem, considering the powers and information available to them, asking whether new institutional arrangements could be made to meet a particular situation better than existing arrangements can, and comparing various alternative changes.

If it should be found, or urged, that we do need new institutional provisions, then one should ask what preconditions would enable existing centres of political decision-making to produce or permit an institutional solution to the problem in question.

One can well imagine the development of scenarios in the field of political institutions. Their purpose would be to canvass alternative institutional designs for appropriateness and for ability to solve problems. In most cases, one can think of alternative institutional possibilities, whose advantages and disadvantages can be discerned by testing them against specific questions. An examination of the conditions under which such possibilities have a chance of success is just as important as thinking them up in the first place; when Frederick the Great had read *Perpetual Peace* by the Abbé Castel de Saint-Pierre, he wrote in a letter to Voltaire: 'The thing is more practicable; all that is lacking for its success is the consent of Europe, and a few similar trifles.'[1]

Designing institutional arrangements always implies a realistic assessment of the chance of success. This means that those who will be working on this for Europe Plus Thirty should have not only a fertile imagination but also a good background in history and a wide knowledge of current affairs.

A general and diffuse task for Europe Plus Thirty could be to canvass different pictures and institutional forms for possible political alternatives. This is a matter of 'tangible utopias' (*Konkrete Utopien* in the sense of Ernst Bloch):[2] tangible, in that they align themselves on, and arise from, existing reality. Tangible utopias belong to identifiable moments in the chain of possibility. By starting from given technological, economic, and political possibilities, one could offer specific scenarios for future European policies in certain areas. If one has a picture of a possible future, or the possible future development of a sector, one can try to sketch what institutional conditions would be necessary to reach it, what institutional shape such a trajectory would imply, and thus what institutional changes and innovations would be necessary.

Another task would be to consider alternative institutional responses to emerging problems. If we want to bring about a particular line of development in Europe, we look first for emerging trends; then we examine the present political situation, and then think how the institutions which we have could best produce the necessary policies. If we

---

[1] Quoted in F. H. Hinsley, *Power and the Pursuit of Peace* (Cambridge, 1963), p. 45.
[2] Ernst Bloch, *Das Prinzip Hoffnung*, 3 vols. (Frankfurt: Suhrkamp, 1969).

think they could not, then we think of more appropriate institutional structures. Sea-use planning, as was argued in II.12 above, is a field where institutions are required, are almost entirely lacking, and should be devised.

Europe Plus Thirty will come into being at the time of the most profound political change in the institutions of the Community since it came into existence: we refer to the decision of the European Parliament at long last to apply the Treaty of Rome and proceed to direct elections, by national electoral law in 1978 and by a single Community electoral law a few years later. The institutional upheavals caused by this decision will (unless the decision is overridden by *force majeure*, and probably even so) create a demand for fertile and informed speculation about the forms and effects of new arrangements within the Community. So will the moves towards economic and monetary union and even towards a European government, which are now being canvassed in the Tindemans Report and elsewhere. If it is ready in time, Europe Plus Thirty could meet a large share of that demand.

The 'political' people in Europe Plus Thirty should be mainly responsible for keeping all the other work in touch with political reality. They must keep a sharp lookout for any postulated development which may be held to be physically or economically possible but which would entail a political impossibility: for instance, the prolonged acceptance of subjugation by a population able to fight, or the infinite prolongation of the inability of a population to fight (this refers to the world outside the Community).

The political forecasting of Europe Plus Thirty should in general by no means be confined to the Community as such. It should look downwards to the member states, outwards to other international organisations, and upwards to the United Nations. It would obviously not be appropriate for Europe Plus Thirty to develop scenarios for the internal political development of single member countries; that would be politically counter-productive. But it will be impossible for it to develop scenarios for the Community as a whole without making some assumptions about the internal development of single countries, and those assumptions must be both well informed and explicit. This will perhaps be politically the most tricky area of its work, and it will require tact and skill. It will be necessary – indeed it will be the mainstream of its work – for Europe Plus Thirty to produce scenarios for the Community as such, and, as we have said earlier, we think these should range over a spectrum the width of which is determined only by political possibility and not by political aspiration. For instance, besides 'a little more, a little less' scenarios about European integration, the spectrum should obviously encompass extreme ones too, from a unitary federal state within thirty years (which one cannot say is impossible) to the total disappearance of the Community as a political and economic entity, and a reversion to the unmitigated singularity of nine sovereign states, within less time than that (which one cannot say is impossible either). Economic and other forecasting will also be needed about the addition of new member countries and the departure of existing ones; the choice of scenarios here is itself a political one. Scenarios will be needed in the political field, no less than in the economic, for relations with the rest of the world. The forecasting imagination must range freely over possible developments: for instance, changes in the U.S., in China, or in the Soviet Union and Eastern Europe; changes in the structure and role of OECD or OPEC; the possible establishment of an international ocean regime; the growth of terrorism; and so on and so forth.

Most important of all, though no doubt not most immediate, it must range over possible developments in the United Nations. We touched on this in our Introduction: no part of the work of Europe Plus Thirty is likely to be more useful than its speculations about how the European Community will fit into a shrinking world. And it goes without saying that Europe Plus Thirty should also review and assess its own political utility and efficiency.

It is important that Europe Plus Thirty, in this area more than any other, should never urge particular policies on the Community as such, or on its member states.

PART III
TECHNOLOGY ASSESSMENT

The phrase 'technology assessment' tells its own history. At first there were just crafts or trades. And then the craftsmen became so clever and knew so much that it became necessary to have a word for all the sorts of things they did, and the word 'technique' was invented by the French (they drew it from the old Greek '*techne*', which just means 'craft'). From it we got the adjective 'technical'. This word is full of unspoken meanings. If you say something is 'technical', you immediately place it halfway up the hierarchy of thought. If you look at it from below, as 'ordinary' people may do, it describes something secret and difficult: 'I'm afraid that's too technical for me.' If you look at it from above, it describes something menial and unimportant: 'Now we can leave it to the technicians to get on with.' Techniques, technicians, and technicalities are above the heads of the masses and beneath the notice of philosophers and scientists. This fact, in due course, was reflected in the education systems of Europe.

But time marched on, and people began to notice that different techniques had attributes in common. Techniques as such became an object of analysis and study, and the word 'technology' was coined, meaning 'the study of techniques' or 'writing about techniques'. That is still its true meaning, but a corrupt meaning gradually appeared and has now superseded the true one in all but the most rigorous discourse: the corrupt meaning makes 'technology' synonymous with 'techniques' – all techniques collectively. Technological innovation is, if one ponders, no different from technical innovation. But the techniques themselves had flourished so wonderfully, both in number and in intrinsic complexity, that a word of only two syllables was no longer important enough – it had to be four.

'Technology' came to describe that whole sphere which lies below science but above the common man. Institutes of technology were founded and drifted upwards in the scale of intellectual values. One would not now expect to stumble across anything which was not understood at the Massachusetts or California Institutes of Technology, yet they proudly keep their roots and their name in the old word for the middle ground, a word which simply says 'crafts'.

Since the Second World War, we have come to look more critically at our marvellous new creation: it has brought us not only wealth and convenience but also disgusting weapons, pollution, and, we feel, a certain dehumanisation of life in general. Were we perhaps not the sorcerer at all, but the sorcerer's apprentice who, after he had taught brooms to carry buckets, could not stop them and flooded the castle? It was time to pause and think; and so another need, another attitude, found its name. Technology Assessment (TA) was born. The English word 'assessment' and the corresponding words in other European languages go back to the process by which government officials used to judge people's ability to pay tax. When we assess a situation, we judge whether it is good or bad, just as the medieval assizes used to examine a man or an institution to see how much tax they were 'good for'. We are now beginning to pick up fresh new technology as it appears, to shine the light on it, to examine it from all sides, to go into its history and expectations, to discuss it over and over, to report upon it, in an attempt to make sure in advance that it is not going to hurt us.

The activity of TA requires three parties. First, it requires a proposer, an inventor or innovator, a producer of something new – namely, the new technology. Second, it requires those to whom he intends to sell it, the people or the public. And third, it requires a judge. It is the third party, the judge, who interests us.

For the activity to have meaning, there must be this element of adjudication. There must be two parties applying to a third for a judgement. Broadly speaking, the first party applies for a permission, and the second party, the public, applies for reassurance. The people no longer took for granted the assurances given to them directly by big industry that this new thing or that would be good for them; too often they had been fooled by assurances which later turned out to be false. Technological innovation, people felt, could no longer be left to the uncontrolled interplay of consumer and producer.

TA is not an idea which struggles for want of written definitions. A dozen or so, some vague, some incoherent, some naive, most far too long, are available. For the purposes of the European Community the following may serve: Technology Assessment is the advance evaluation of potential and unintended social, environmental, and other effects of the application of existing or foreseen technologies. Ideally, the assessment of a technology should anticipate and evaluate the impacts of a new technology on all sectors of society. So far, however, only a few such full-fledged technology assessments have been conducted. Instead, there is a long history of partial assessments, generally limited to impacts on the economy and, more recently, on the environment.

Technology Assessment emphasises the secondary or tertiary effects of new technology rather than the primary (intended) effects, because in the long run the unintended and indirect effects may be the most significant, because undesirable secondary consequences are often unnecessary and may be prevented by proper planning, and because the intended effects have usually been extensively studied in the planning stage. In building a bridge, dredging a canal, introducing enzyme detergents, or electrifying a railway, the first-order effects – those intended as the primary goal of the effort – are generally explicitly planned for and costed out in the initial plan. Technology Assessment focuses on the question of *what else* may happen when the technology is introduced.

The tension between technology and society arises mainly from three things: the side-effects of technology, its increasing complexity, and the lack of public involvement.

The unwanted and often unforeseen side-effects of technology are obvious. Some are direct, such as pollution and general environmental deterioration and a loss of work satisfaction in repetitive industrial manufacture. Others are more subtle and indirect, such as the increasing frustrations and difficulties of urban life, increase in crime and violence, and a growing sense of irrelevance in contemporary education. Perhaps these latter can be attributed to technology; perhaps not at all.

Technology was until recently seen as the weapon by which man could win his struggle with nature; this was the view of the Age of Reason. Largely successful in the industrialised world in winning this Pyrrhic victory, technology now appears to be rivalling nature, its former adversary, in the range of ills it imposes upon man: ills which are insidious and not immediately apparent in the short or even the medium term. Their impact is unevenly distributed across society. Since the future must always be unknown, risks have to be incurred in innovation; the problem is to 'calculate' them and as far as possible distribute them equitably. We need, if we can, to foresee these effects and to reduce the damage they can do. If they may be irreversible, the need is that much greater.

All this calls for more public control and participation. Technology is not 'out of control'. What is true is that political institutions have been slower to advance than technology, since a certain inertia hampers institutional innovation. The public is in the dark, and it is rather afraid. More people probably now fear what more technology might do *to* them than want more technology to do things *for* them.

The argument so far could be expressed in economist's language as follows: TA is concerned with identifying external costs in advance, so that the public power can take whatever measures are open to it to see that they are reinternalised, in the form of on-cost expenditure necessary for the avoidance of harm, and thus fall on the direct beneficiaries (producers and consumers) of the goods or services produced and not on society at large. If the external costs are of a kind that cannot be reinternalised, the question of outright prohibition of the venture arises.

Before turning to the possible application of TA in the European Community, it may be useful to consider where and how it is already done.

The idea of Technology Assessment emanated in the second half of the 1960s from the U.S.A., and it is there that the theory, methodology, and practice of TA are most developed. The U.S.A. is also the only country in which the efforts to create a specific TA institution within the legislature have so far been successful. After five years' discussion in Congress, the President of the United States was able to sign the Technical Assessment Act in October 1972, by which an Office of Technology (OTA) was set up under Congress, with a governing council – the Technology Assessment Board – made up half of Senators and half of Representatives. Its aim is 'to provide early indications of the probable beneficial and adverse impacts of the applications of technology and to develop other coordinate information which may assist Congress' (TA Act, Section 3c). In other words, it is to give Congress something to allow it to hold its own against the intrinsically superior information base of the executive.

In various European countries – particularly Sweden, the Netherlands, and Germany – there have been attempts, so far unsuccessful, to imitate the American example. In the Federal Republic of Germany a proposal put forward by the CDU/CSU opposition faction in April 1975 was rejected by the government majority in the research and technology committee of the Bundestag.

Even after the establishment of the OTA, most governmental TA in the U.S. remains in the executive. Many government agencies undertake or finance TA and TA-like activities: for instance, the Department of Transportation, the Department of Commerce (and its National Bureau of Standards), the Department of Health, Education and Welfare (and the Public Health Service), the Department of Agriculture, and the National Science Foundation. The number of groups and institutes with contracts is increasing inside and outside the government.

The National Science Foundation (NSF) funds much TA under its programme 'Research Applied to National Needs'. By dispersing contracts as widely as possible, the NSF hopes to discover the suitability of institutions for given project areas. So far, university groups have been preferred.

The National Environmental Policy Act of 1969 requires all federal agencies to include in every recommendation or report on proposals for legislation and other major actions of the federal government from which significant environmental effects are expected a detailed Environmental Impact Statement containing, among other things, information on the environmental impact of the proposed action, on any adverse environmental effects which cannot be avoided should the proposal be implemented, and on possible alternatives to the proposed measures. The Environmental Impact Statements can be regarded as partial TA analyses. They are reviewed by the Council on Environmental Quality (CEQ), which monitors controversial actions and identifies problem areas. Several thousands of Environmental Impact Statements have now been received by the CEQ.

In the course programmes of many American universities, TA and related subjects are coming to be recognised. For example, George Washington University has since 1970 offered a master's degree in science, technology, and public policy, and, more recently, a special one-year course on TA.

In Japan, TA has developed in the executive. This is mainly due to the striking environmental deterioration which followed the forced pace of industrialisation. The main organisations supporting these efforts are the Science and Technology Agency (STA), a coordinating group under the Prime Minister and the Ministry of Trade & Industry (MITI). Since 1971 STA has had a rapidly increasing budget for TA. By 1973 studies had been undertaken among others on the following subjects: agricultural chemicals, high-rise buildings, computer-aided instruction, technical systems in a new town, synthetic paper, offshore atomic power plants, and earthquake alarm systems. Studies on technical systems in a new town and on offshore atomic power plants, as well as the compilation of a TA manual, have been commissioned from the private Nomura Research Institute of Technology and Economics.

MITI announced its industrial and technology policy for the 1970s in May 1971 and recommended the inclusion of TA as an instrument of government policy to guide and watch over industrial technologies. Also in 1971, MITI itself, through its Agency of Industrial Science and Technology, started a TA study programme, which was to provide basic information for the application of TA to industry. It included atomic-powered steel-making, the fuel cell, technology for traffic control, automatic vending systems, and micro-wave ovens. Like the STA, MITI uses not only an in-house capacity but also outside contractors and consultants.

In Sweden, TA is largely determined by the strong environmental awareness of that country. The Prime Minister's Secretariat for Future Studies published in 1973 a report on nine studies with a TA character; it was worked out according to a recommendation of the Advisory Group on Control and Management of Technology of the Committee for Scientific and Technological Policy of the OECD. Four of the nine studies in question were environmental, and most of them were undertaken with the cooperation of several institutions, mostly governmental.

In the Federal Republic of Germany, the research and technology policy authorities – e.g. the Ministry for Research and Technology (Bundesministerium für Forschung und Technologie – BMFT) – have for years formulated recommendations and performed tasks which resemble TA, even though the words themselves are rarely used. For instance, it is government policy that projects which are competing for government money should be compared with respect to their probable effects on society, and that projects which could profoundly change the environment or living conditions should be examined and continuously assessed from the viewpoint of the social sciences, and if necessary be suspended. The efforts of the Opposition to create a parliamentary TA institution are not supported by the Government; but the BMFT has offered to submit its TA studies to the Bundestag and also, before contracting studies out, to give the Bundestag the opportunity of expanding the subject matter.

Certain systems studies on the development and use of nuclear energy can be seen as preliminaries to TA activities. These were encouraged in the middle of the sixties by the Ministry which was then called Education and Science. They were carried out mainly in the nuclear research centres at Karlsruhe and Jülich. These studies are today being continued within the programme of 'Applied Systems Analysis' of the Arbeitsgemeinschaft der Grossforschungszentren. They comprise four projects: (1) man, energy, the environment; (2) resource exploitation and resource safeguards; (3) communications and society; (4) transport, land use, the economy.

Transport and communications have also been starting points for TA and TA-type activities in Germany. Among the most important research and development institutions in this sphere are those of certain major industrial firms, which maintain a large systems-analysis capability. Some of these are increasingly involved in the development of new systems for city and intercity transport and are undertaking studies which are not limited to technical and economic aspects, although the profit motive is still in the foregroud.

In the non-profit sector the Institut für Systemtechnik und Innovationsforschung (ISI) of the Frauenhofer-Gesellschaft for the Promotion of Applied Research in Karlsruhe, the Studiengruppe für Systemforschung eV (SfS) in Heidelberg, and the Battelle Institute eV in Frankfurt deserve mention. The ISI is doing a TA of a planned refinery extension in North Baden. The SfS has prepared a report, commissioned by the German Bundestag, on problems and methods of TA and on possibilities of institutionalising TA in the Bundestag.

In France there has for some time been intensive government activity in evaluating technological projects and their consequences. Emphasis has been upon environmental protection and land use. As far as environmental protection is concerned one can mention, for instance, the Reports of the Agences Financières de Bassin, which were set up to look after the six great hydrographic areas of France; we can regard these as technology assessments for water-supply policies. As to TA in the stricter sense, it has been reviewed by the working group Evolution des Techniques et Techniques Nouvelles au regard de l'Environnement (Group D) of the Inter-Ministerial Project Group for Environmental Problems, founded in 1972 (Groupe Interministériel d'Evaluation de l'Environnement). In 1973 it took stock of TA activities in several countries. Among other things it found that out of the 490 French studies reviewed (of which only a very modest number were 'real' TA studies) pollution was the topic in 18.4 per cent, followed by transport and town planning, each with around 13 per cent.

TA and TA-like activities in land-use planning (aménagement du territoire) are mainly concentrated in the Délégation à l'Aménagement du Territoire et l'Action Régionale (DATAR). In 1968 DATAR founded the long-term project SESAME (Système d'Etude pour l'Elaboration du Schéma d'Aménagement de la France), which was to prepare an overall master plan of French land-use policy, and to which is attached a sub-group on technological forecasting (1969). This technological forecasting group was charged with the threefold task of identifying technological innovation that could be important for land-use planning, of studying criteria for the judgement of technological innovations from the angle of land use, and lastly of making detailed studies on some specific innovations. The Centre d'Etudes et de Recherches sur l'Aménagement Urbain, the Bureau d'Informations et de Prévisions Economiques, and the Bureau Central d'Etudes pour les Equipements d'Outre-Mer have all made contributions on these topics.

In Britain, there is a TA capacity in the executive: the Programmes Analysis Unit (PAU). PAU, which has existed since 1967, is financed jointly by the Department of Industry and the Atomic Energy Authority, and its studies are generally confidential. It has a staff of around thirty scientists. The Central Policy Review Staff under the Cabinet, founded in 1970, whose tasks embrace the study of general policy issues such as the energy supply, regional policy, etc., may sometimes come close to TA. Its reports are not published. The National Research and Development Corporation, a public institution founded in 1948 which deals with the transfer of research results into the industrial sector, is in its own estimation continually concerned with TA.

Some public inquiries can be termed British TAs *sui generis*. They are held on the initiative of the responsible ministers and deal with technological failures (ex post TA) or, more often, proposals (ex ante TA). The best known perhaps was the public inquiry into the siting of the third London airport. Its recommendation was not accepted, and no third London airport is now to be built in any case.

The Select Committee on Science and Technology of the House of Commons formulates opinions on current science and technology policy. In its work it frequently takes outside advice.

Within the university sector, the Science Policy Research Unit of the University of Sussex and the Technology Assessment Consumerism Centre of the University of Manchester (TACC) deserve mention. TACC has undertaken a TA of the British bread industry.

There is not much information on the – certainly few – TA studies and TA capacities in the other European Community countries. The TA activities of certain large industrial corporations like Montedison in Italy and Novo Industri in Denmark have become well known.

As to the methods used in TA, two levels have to be distinguished. The first is the work plan for the TA exercise itself: this will divide the problem up into its parts and suggest a certain temporal sequence (with iterations) for the solution of these component problems. The second level comprises specific analytical techniques for solving the component problems.

Among the best-known TA work plans is that developed by the American MITRE Corporation.[1] It goes as follows:

SEVEN MAJOR STEPS IN MAKING A TECHNOLOGY ASSESSMENT

Step 1: *Define the assessment task*
  Discuss relevant issues and any major problems
  Establish scope (breadth and depth) of inquiry
  Develop project ground rules

---

[1] The word 'societal', which appears in this quotation, is one used by American sociologists instead of 'social'. They think that their thoughts about society are of a different order from other people's and must therefore be marked by a different word. We await the arrival of societology.

Step 2: *Describe relevant technologies*

Describe major technology being assessed

Describe other technologies supporting the major technology

Describe technologies competitive to the major and supporting technologies

Step 3: *Develop state-of-society assumptions*

Identify and describe major non-technological factors influencing the application of the relevant technologies

Step 4: *Identify impact areas*

Ascertain those societal characteristics that will be most influenced by the application of the assessed technology

Step 5: *Make preliminary impact analysis*

Trace and integrate the process by which the assessed technology makes its societal influence felt

Step 6: *Identify possible action options*

Develop and analyse various programs for obtaining maximum public advantage from the assessed technologies

Step 7: *Complete impact analysis*

Analyse the degree to which each action option would alter the specific societal impacts of the assessed technology discussed in Step 5

Some of these steps are further sub-divided and have been supplemented by 'checklists'.[1]

In the TAs which have been carried out so far (since the end of the 1960s) a whole series of methods have been used, for instance:

Cost–benefit analysis

(Computer) simulation

Trend projection

Operational research

Group consensus procedures, including Delphi

Behavioural experiments and observations

Historical analogy

Cross-impact analysis

Morphology

Scenario-writing

Relevance-tree procedures, and analytic methods of evaluation based on the relevance tree

Participation techniques, for instance procedures working with the aid of television and computers

All these are well known in the social and economic sciences and are used in policy planning; they were not developed for TA, and it is unlikely that a standard tool-kit will ever emerge. Most of them have already been described in chapter I.1 above.

The impacts of technology often cross national borders. The under-

[1] M. V. Jones, *A Technology Assessment Methodology: Some Basic Propositions* (McLean, Va.: MITRE Corporation, 1971).

standing that one nation's technology may affect another, and that liabilities flow therefrom, goes back at least to 1941 and the U.S.–Canadian case of the Trail Smelter, where gaseous effluent from Canada damaged U.S. fruit trees: the Canadians were held legally responsible. The damming or pollution of international rivers, pollution of the seas, cloud-seeding and weather modification in general – all these exemplify international effects. Satellites and supersonic transport are vigorously objected to for different reasons by countries which did not make them; and as to agricultural innovation, it has already been suggested that trade patterns are being distorted by the 'green revolution'. The exploitation of resources for energy, the exploitation of the ocean and the ocean floor, and the use of the air and of space itself are clearly enterprises where the indirect effects have to be examined internationally, and the question of whether the European Community as a whole should abstain from, or regulate, certain technological developments will require consideration of the secondary effects, which means TA studies.

What should be the function of Community TA in relation to national TA and to the activities of the other international organisations in this field? Is there a risk of duplicating the activities of national systems on the one hand and those of world agencies on the other?

The role of TA in Europe Plus Thirty should be creative as well as responsive, but it can only be so to the extent that its work is tied in with the powers and functions of the Community. One of the most important purposes of the social assessment of technology is to examine a much wider range of options than is usually the case in the narrowly defined functional framework of present national and Community mechanisms. Developing a broader function at Community level would have several advantages. The first is that many technologies are simply too international in impact to be evaluated only at national level. Another is that since member countries have their present primary commitment to greater economic cooperation, they might benefit from the use of this cooperative tool to produce a more truly balanced social development of the Community as a whole. The third and most obvious is that there is economy of scale and avoidance of duplication in doing the work once, at Community level, and not several times over, at national level. There is no danger of duplicating the activities of worldwide organisations, since they do not yet exist. But in this matter, as in others, liaison should be maintained with OECD.

The goals of the Community must be the starting point for TA, as they must for forecasting. For example, the Community aims to develop its own poor regions. Technological initiatives in particular sectors might adversely affect the balance between regions, and that should be avoided. It is particularly in this context that Europe Plus Thirty might possibly help the European Investment Bank (EIB). This Bank is described by Articles 129 and 130 of the Treaty of Rome.[1] Article 130 reads:

The task of the European Investment Bank shall be to contribute, by having recourse to the capital market and utilising its own resources, to the balance and steady development of the common market in the interest of the Community. For this purpose the Bank shall, operating on a non-profit-making basis, grant loans and give guarantees which facilitate the financing of the following projects in all sectors of the economy:
  (a) projects for developing less developed regions;
  (b) projects for modernising or converting undertakings or for developing fresh activities called for by the progressive establishment of the common market where these projects are of such a size or nature that they cannot be entirely financed by the various means available in the individual Member States;
  (c) projects of common interest to several Member States which are of such a size or nature that they cannot be entirely financed by the various means available in the individual Member States.

To evaluate applications for loans, the majority of which in the technological areas are for 'infrastructure' – transport, power distribution, civil works, etc. – the Bank has an internal staff including seven engineers with support staff, as well as bankers and economists. The project evaluations, in number perhaps eighty major and some two hundred minor ones per annum for a total loan value of around 1,000 million Units of Account (UAs), are in many cases minor or partial TAs. They may be performed to a greater or lesser degree by the Bank or by the applicant, and the amount of assessment done by the Bank itself will also vary depending on whether a member nation or an associated country is involved. A wide range of activities is supported, from rubber plantation in the Ivory Coast to the production of synthetic rubber in Turkey, from hotel-building in Gabon to large-scale support of electrical production and transmission, and transport and infrastructure in general, within the Nine themselves. Not many of them are in the advanced technology sphere; perhaps the most advanced so far has been a synthetic-protein plant in Sardinia, but even that was the second of its kind.

As with the World Bank, the impacts most often considered in the assessment process (other than the economic) are environmental. Improvement of the physical environment is directly supported, for example, in depollution projects for the Rhine. Assessment often takes the form of comment and answer, technical modifications then being

[1] See *Treaties Establishing the European Communities* (Luxembourg: European Communities, 1973).

agreed. But in contrast to the World Bank, the EIB's assessment staff does not include sociologists, or technologists other than engineers.

Europe Plus Thirty might be able to offer a TA service to the European Investment Bank. It could be offered either direct to the Bank, especially in areas where there is no Commission policy, or to the Commission, which has to approve all EIB projects over 2m UAs, including credit lines to intermediate institutions for the financing of smaller projects down-line.

Another Community institution which could possibly make use of TA is the European Court of Justice. If the Court becomes more involved in industrial and commercial litigation with a high technological content, it is conceivable that cases might arise where the issues of fact to be determined could require a consideration of the long-term effects of a particular application of technology. In such cases the parties, or failing them the Court, might seek an expert report from or through Europe Plus Thirty.

The Directorates General of the Commission have expertise and supporting data in fairly narrowly defined areas, and they are inevitably concerned with nearer rather than further horizons. They often lack the means, more than the will, to perform broadly based 'horizontal' technological assessments. There are indeed places within the Commission where parts of the assessment process have been fairly well developed, but a focus would certainly help. Here are some of the Community aims and powers which might be furthered by the comparative examination of technological initiatives and their indirect effects.

Harmonisation of national regulations is pursued mainly for the promotion of trade, but the function might also be interpreted as covering the incidental disbenefits of industry and trade. In the context of the full social assessment of technology, both aspects are relevant. An example of the control of disbenefits may be drawn from the transport sector. Community harmonisation was applied, with considerable public discussion, to the axle-loading of lorries and to the level of noxious exhaust emissions. Both of these could with advantage have been the subject of advance TA.

The increasing public and political demand for environmental protection in recent years has given rise to national regulations which, unless they are 'harmonised' out of it, risk distorting trade by the imposition of higher burdens on industry in some countries than in others. The main purpose of the Common Market being to avoid such distortions of trade, it is clear that the Commission will need increasing research and analysis in fulfilling its harmonisation function. This research and analysis will be, in effect, TA. Article 92 of the Treaty of Rome is no doubt the main provision governing this case, but Article 36 also bears on it. This allows exceptions to be made to the aim of reducing of quantitative restrictions on trade flow (as set out in Articles 30 to 34).

Article 36 states:

The provisions of Articles 30 to 34 shall not preclude prohibitions or restrictions on imports, exports or goods in transit justified on grounds of public morality, public policy and public security; the protection of health and life of humans, animals or plants; the protection of national treasures possessing historic or archaeological value, or the protection of industrial and commercial property. Such prohibitions or restrictions shall not, however, constitute a means of arbitrary discrimination or a disguised restriction on trade between Member States.[1]

In deciding on a member country's claim that a certain prohibition or restriction is or is not permitted under this article, the Commission is already in fact undertaking some sort of rudimentary TA. The systematisation and development of the necessary analysis could be useful.

In the initial stages, TA for the Community can be largely based on a careful and thorough documentation and evaluation (as to relevance, authenticity, acceptability, and the like) of data already available. The purpose would be not only to give more information to policy-makers but also to improve the quality of what they get. In many cases, a painstaking analysis of existing information would be adequate to spell out incipient dangers and drawbacks threatened by emerging technological developments. But it is also clear that if technology assessment is to probe the future in order to fulfill the wider objectives – if it is to act not just as a screening device for eliminating potential hazards, but also as an early warning system and as a means for systematically evaluating secondary and indirect consequences and allocating limited technological resources with minimum waste – then the act of assessment demands more than just documentation of existing information. Here we come back to the starting point of this section.

Appropriate parties to request TA studies would include the European Commission, the European Parliament, member governments, the European Investment Bank, and possibly the European Court of Justice. A choice would then have to be made among the requests according to some criteria. Flexibility will be important. Community policies will be evolving over the years; so will technology. Groups affected by this technology or that will alter in their composition and their size. Public opinion and public reaction are volatile with respect

[1] *Ibid.*

215

to technology, and they are highly pertinent to the choice of assessment subjects and to the way the assessment is done. It is therefore important to frame the selection criteria in such a way as to allow adaptation to take place, and not to set up too rigid a sieve. The characteristics relevant to the choice for assessment of a particular technology, product, or process are relatively easy to enumerate but difficult to define precisely in terms of limits and thresholds. Criteria for choice, related both to forecasting and to relevance to Community objectives, can be derived from the following questions:

Is the subject proposed for TA being researched, or being developed, or being applied...or is it on the point of submerging us all? Another way of putting the question would be: How much is known about it? There is a direct relationship between known data and likelihood of implementation. The nearer to use, the greater the chance of successful prognostication of the impacts, but the less the chance of affecting events.

What possibilities exist, and at what point in the invention–development–use chain, for modifying or controlling the application?

Is the innovation or technology need-oriented, and how was the need determined? Is it a market-expressed need, or was it expressed in a more conscious manner? Is it publicly or privately promoted or sponsored? Is the enterprise European? Is the market European?

Will the impacts (these should be, and frequently can be, estimated roughly in advance) be mainly political, economic, social, or environmental? There is a dilemma here: if the impacts can be roughly outlined ahead of the TA, is this a reason for doing a full study? If they cannot, is that a better reason?

Are the impacts likely to be latent socially, environmentally, geographically, over time? Are they likely to be severe? Short-, medium-, or long-term?

Are the effects likely to be reversible? If so, at what level? What are the costs of attempting reversal at different times? This point has been developed many times in relation to environmental – or, more strictly, ecological – impacts. It is clear that where changes are irreversible they should be made only if the benefit is major and is unobtainable by other means. The extreme ends of such scales are easily handled: disastrous impacts have their immediate responses, both public and official, and trivial ones have none. In general, TA will have to deal with the less clearly defined middle ground.

There is likely to be some difficulty in drawing the line between the work which has to be done in order to decide whether to undertake a TA, and the TA itself: indeed, TA is only one of many fields in which one may find that, in considering whether to do something, one has already done it. Jesus Christ had something of the sort to say about adultery.

So the above list will, in practice, have to be handled rather summarily.

The two major criteria for undertaking a TA would seem to be the probable magnitude and the irreversibility of the effects. It is finally a value judgement whether, if the choice is possible, greater weight is given to the numbers affected or to the irreversibility. In many cases the distinction cannot be clearly presented; certainly, no mathematical procedure can be devised to arbitrate between the two. Where the possibility of irreversible damage exists, it should be a strong argument for assessing the subject, as opposed to passing it over in favour of another.

Besides the characteristics of the technology itself and of its impacts, we must consider the methods which can be used in the assessment. Many techniques have been proposed or used – cost–benefit analysis, cost-effectiveness, games theory, relevance trees, systems analysis, and so forth, as above. If a first examination of the subject suggested that well-tried techniques existed to deal with the problem, that would be a favourable indication. Conversely, many of the more important and interesting problems presented will have no obvious path to their solution. Some of the effort of the assessors must be reserved for problems which are less amenable to quick results but which give useful basic insights into methodology.

The TA function of Europe Plus Thirty could also coordinate and even improve the TA of member countries. In this it might follow the arrangements made for national R & D programmes, which, beginning in 1976, are to be automatically communicated to the Commission from their moment of conception. Such a procedure could only be built up slowly and tentatively. There is an enormous amount of TA and quasi-TA done in the member countries, and an over-ambitious programme could completely swamp Europe Plus Thirty. But if things were encouraged to develop in this direction it could only lead in time to economies of scale and the avoidance of duplication.

It is clear that many business people fear that TA may stifle innovation. In American polemics, the letters TA have been alleged to stand for 'technology arrestment'. Recently, however, there seems to be a growing consensus in business circles that high priority must be given to the social and environmental effects of technology.

Although legislation usually lags behind technical developments, various branches of industry are already required by national law to investigate the external effects of their activities and products. Consumer watchdog bodies are set up. Recent court decisions (e.g. in Germany) indicate that producers carry the responsibility for their products and have to show proof that their products are 'harmless'. Such decisions will lead to more careful analysis of production processes and products, and this might stimulate the use of TA in industry. There is a clear possibility that a company that assesses its own business goals and technology not only in terms of traditional economic cost–benefit and market analysis but also in terms of social costs and environmental consequences – in a word, of externalities – might even get an advantage in the market place.

The link between forecasting and technology assessment is both clear and strong. The tie is in fact so close that, as the concept of technology assessment wins wider acceptance, technological forecasting and planning studies are not infrequently equated with assessments. The formulation of economic programmes would be hamstrung without some understanding of likely future economic trends. Similarly, the development of policy for controlling technological change – and that is what TA is about – would be much more difficult if it lacked a sense of future trends in technology.

In the initial stages, Europe Plus Thirty must deal with current and prospective impacts of technology large enough to be important, yet of a size which is capable of being dealt with so as to produce an outcome usable for policy formulation. Its work can and should develop in parallel with the development of the Community's actual powers to affect events in this field.

PART IV
EUROPE PLUS THIRTY:
A NEW INSTRUMENT

To carry out the tasks outlined so far, to seek if possible to integrate them into the teleonomies which were described in the Introduction, and to make all this useful to its decision-makers, the European Community will need a small new instrument or entity, to which the name of Europe Plus Thirty is given. This need not be its final name; but at the time of writing nobody, in spite of much thought, has come up with a better one. The word 'institution' is best avoided, because the Community already has, or rather consists of, four major Institutions with a capital 'I': the Council of Ministers, the Commission, the Parliament, and the Court of Justice. Since the word 'institution' already has a special connotation, it is better to use the less imposing word 'instrument', lest it be thought that there is any proposal to alter the constitution of the Community itself.

The new instrument must belong to the Community and be peculiar to it. There are at the moment proposals for forecasting or forward-looking instruments in various wider international organisations to which the nations of the Community belong – in the UN family of organisations including the World Bank, and especially in OECD. These, and perhaps particularly the last, are valuable initiatives. But it would not do if the Community had to rely on them alone. It must not be condemned to look into its own future solely through, for instance, OECD spectacles, since they will inevitably have North American and Japanese tints. OECD is an organisation for the developed world as a whole, of which the European Community is only a part; and although Western European interests largely coincide with American and Japanese interests, they do not always and entirely do so. Thus the Community, especially since it is a public power constituted under national and international law and the other organisations are not, must have its own forecasting instrument serving its own purposes.

Europe Plus Thirty must have a purpose, a method of work, and a structure. Its purpose can conveniently be set out in the form of Terms of Reference: the following are proposed.

TERMS OF REFERENCE FOR EUROPE PLUS THIRTY

(1) To provide the European Community with a comprehensive capability for long-term forecasting and other ways of thinking about the future as a basis for examining alternative policies and strategies for the Community, including

(a) a continuous output of long-term forecasting related to the planning needs of the Community;

(b) a scanning, look-out, or early warning system with regard to impending dangers or conflicts or new potentialities;

(c) an information centre available for use by the Institutions of the Community, by its member governments, by other organisations, and (through its publications) by the general public;

(d) a monitoring system for social and other developments, aimed at obtaining a satisfactory data base.

(2) To create worldwide links with other organisations carrying out related work.

(3) To carry out research relevant to the acquisition of this capability, including

(a) methodological development;

(b) post hoc policy evaluations.

(4) To carry out specific policy-oriented studies on request from the Institutions of the Community, member governments, or other appropriate agencies or organisations.

(5) To undertake technology assessments exploring as far as necessary the social, economic, environmental, and other consequences which contemplated technological policies or developments might have, and comparing alternative policies or developments.

(6) To undertake these functions not only on request but also as the Board of Europe Plus Thirty (see below) considers necessary.

We now turn to the method of work. The job of Europe Plus Thirty has been described above under the headings of 'methodology' and of 'sectoral content' and in the proposed Terms of Reference. It will be a job of enquiry, reflection, and synthesis: that is to say, a certain number of people will have to find things out, think about them, and put their thoughts together. And when that has been done, the whole will have to be put in a form which does in fact help policy-makers to make policy, as opposed to burdening them with yet more kilos of free-standing knowledge.

The Terms of Reference carry implications for the structure of the organisation. Many things must be reconciled. Europe Plus Thirty must have both adequate in-house resources and a flexible method of drawing in outside resources as required. It must also create working conditions in which people of ability and experience will be willing to spend part of their lives – people who will neither be prepared to bombinate in a vacuum, far removed from the reality of planning, nor wish on the other hand to be absorbed into the day-to-day machinery of the Commission. It must ensure that what the Community gets is a clear-cut, custom-built account of the various possibilities and strate- gies open to it, related to one another in a consistent and comprehen- sive way, and not a mere catalogue of what various other people in other places have thought possible or desirable.

To meet these needs, three elements will be necessary for the management structure of the continuing instrument: they can be called the passive network, the active network, and the central team.

In the passive network, the central team would simply keep track of what was going on elsewhere and would reflect upon, and as far as possible synthesise, the work of others. It would keep itself informed of the work of all relevant forecasting and analysis institutions and teams: they would include the services and dependent Institutions of the European Commission itself, other international organisations, government departments, university departments, independent re- search institutes and workers, and firms, both inside and outside the Community.

This way of working is necessary but not sufficient. Neither the primary work nor the purposes for which it was done would be under the control, or even open to the influence, of Europe Plus Thirty as an instrument of the Community. The questions asked would be chosen by other social entities (national governments, firms, academic research boards, etc.), and the answers would be provided within the limits of vision of the primary producers (national, industrial, aca- demic, etc.). Europe Plus Thirty would only come in when the impor- tant part was over. It would be like someone listening to conversations between other people about things which might or might not be of interest. Europe Plus Thirty would be able only to report the conver- sations and comment on them; it would not be free to take part in them. Moreover, passive work attracts passive people.

In the active network a small central team would itself formulate the questions to be asked or the research programmes to be under- taken. It would then let contracts to existing organisations (research institutes, university departments, units of member governments, and so on). It would also call together groups of outsiders to grapple with ad hoc problems.

But this too, though necessary, is not enough; it would provide neither continuity of experience nor the ability consistently to adapt and present complex arguments year after year. No organisation relying entirely on contract results from outside, however high its quality, can serve policy-makers in a way really suited to their needs. It has also to have a precisely tailored capability for doing work itself. It is therefore essential to combine the network concept (both passive and active) with that of a strong central team.

It will thus not be enough if the central team merely formulates its own questions and designs its own research programmes. It must also answer some of the questions and carry out some of the research itself. Especially, it must carry out much of the integrated forecasting described in chapter I.4 above. This would be an in-house operation; the members of the team would work together in one place, an arrangement which would secure the advantages of cross-fertilisation and of multiple employment of individuals. Forecasting and technology assessment could be pursued side by side, by the same people. A given member of the unit could be working on more than one question at the same time, and that is a big advantage in an operation which should indeed be interdisciplinary and 'cross-sectoral'. The people would meet not only across the work-table but also in private life, and professional collaboration would be fortified by personal knowledge and understanding. The resulting humus of shared perception and common working methods would be fertile for conceptual breakthrough and methodological innovation.

If the Community were to decide to limit Europe Plus Thirty to an extended network structure, it would be able to point to the small number of people in the central team: 'Look, only ten professionals.' In a time of retrenchment and of scepticism about new instruments, that is attractive. But 'only ten professionals' implies many and costly outside contracts; a larger number of in-house professionals implies fewer and cheaper outside contracts. It evens out. Moreover, the Commission and Council of the Community are not alone in the world in favouring retrenchment. The greater its dependence on outside institutions, the greater the risk that the work of Europe Plus Thirty will be interrupted by someone else's retrenchment, over which the Community would have no control. Research institutes and departments do sometimes collapse. This is a reason to favour in-house work.

The right solution, then, is a mixture of all three ways of working: passive network, active network, and central in-house team. It is a question of proportion. In terms of cost these three parts should, when Europe Plus Thirty is operating at full strength, probably compare as follows.

Passive network: 10 per cent.

Active network: 30 per cent.

In-house: 60 per cent.

These are proportions of cost, not of man-hours. Much of the raw material of forecasting lies in time series and many other sorts of statistical data, and most of what will be necessary as statistical input is collected already by the services of member governments, of the Commission, and of other international organisations. The labour involved in that data-collecting is many times what would be involved in Europe Plus Thirty. But it is already done for existing purposes, and the extra demands made upon these services by Europe Plus Thirty will be relatively very small.

So much for the method of work. We now turn to the structure.

Any sizeable team of research workers needs a governing board to help to determine its general direction of work in accordance with broad priorities and horizons, to protect it from political attack, and to sift the demands which may be made on it. A research team needs a compass, a lightning-conductor, and an umbrella; and these three functions can be combined in one governing body, provided its members are rightly chosen.

Europe Plus Thirty should thus have a Governing Board consisting of perhaps ten members, plus a Chairman, plus the Director, making twelve in all. The Board should meet perhaps twice a year. It should settle the broad programme of work a few years ahead and the budgetary and staff allocations for different projects. It would approve contracts for work to be done for Europe Plus Thirty by other institutions, and with the advice of the Director it would screen requests from the Commission, the Parliament, and member governments for pieces of work to be done. This last will perhaps be particularly arduous in the field of technology assessment; there may be far more work requested than can be done with the money.

Three qualities have to be present among members of the Board. It must include people with political experience, people who understand forecasting and technology assessment, and people who understand the fields in which forecasting is done. If there were a lack of political experience, the work might become too academic and not so useful to decision-makers; if there were not enough understanding of forecasting and technology assessment, it might become short-sighted, too analytical, not synthetic enough; if there were a lack of sectoral expertise, it might neglect the need for hard and valid inputs.

To ensure this sectoral expertise, there should probably be one Board member who is strong in each of the following groups of fields of study:

(1) social, political, educational;
(2) resources, energy, and environment;

(3) science, technology, and industry;

(4) economics and finance.

Naturally, a reasonable balance should be observed among the nationalities of the Community.

The Board of Europe Plus Thirty should be appointed by the European Commission. This arrangement is open to criticism in that it might be held to make Europe Plus Thirty too much an instrument of one of the Institutions of the Community. But this disadvantage is probably outweighed by the advantage of convenience and simplicity.

The Director should be appointed by the Board. He should work full-time and should be the professional and academic head of Europe Plus Thirty. He should sit with the Board but should not vote. He should, under the Board, hire and fire staff members.

While in principle the right size for the central team of Europe Plus Thirty must be determined by the tasks which are laid on it, there are also professional considerations. Given terms of reference approximating to those above, the size must be sufficient to guarantee good links with the existing professional networks and to allow a level of internal debate high enough to maintain the quality of output needed by the institutions of the Community. These two considerations jointly set a lower limit. Though there are examples of teams of microscopic size which perform wonders, they often have narrow tasks and do not need to maintain competence over the years. The concept of a minimum viable size is clearly applicable to work of the kind we have been describing, and for Europe Plus Thirty it is around thirty graduates. There is also an upper limit, less sharply defined but nevertheless real enough, at which control of the quality of output begins to overload the directing staff. It lies at about a hundred graduates.

It is difficult to decide what figure, between these upper and lower limits, would be right for Europe Plus Thirty. Between thirty and fifty would be acceptable. If economy dictates the adoption of some figure in this band as the target to be reached after five years, it would be worth launching Europe Plus Thirty on the understanding that the final figure should be regularly reviewed and should be raised as soon as financial considerations could be held to permit it.

Over fifty, the thing is certainly worth doing. The results would be better as the figure approached one hundred, but the returns, though real, would then be diminishing. Over one hundred would be unnecessary and unduly cumbrous.

The situation, then, is as follows:

fewer than 30: probably not worth it;

30–50:	worth it, but likely to lead to rather sketchy outputs;
50–75:	good;
75–100:	better, but not all that much better;
over 100:	not necessary.

Many of the people recruited will be academics and civil servants. But industry and finance both need to be represented in Europe Plus Thirty, so that it can include some direct knowledge of how that world ticks. The point applies to all parts of industry: management, research, and unions.

Throughout Part II above, the need was stressed for task forces of outside people, brought together by Europe Plus Thirty for various lengths of time and at various frequencies, to identify problems, to analyse them, to discuss methodology, to find factual inputs, to concoct scenarios, for brainstorming, and so on. This way of working should be a regular part of life, and there should be budgetary and logistic provision for it. Some of these task forces might with advantage be composed mainly or even wholly of member-state officials, whether seconded or part-time.

There must be scanning and scouting. Members of the central team must travel to see what is going on in other forecasting centres, both inside and outside the Community. And they must also travel outside the Community so that their work on relations between the Community and the rest of the world should never become unrealistic or academic. There should also be much attention paid to maintaining a broad and up-to-date knowledge of world political trends. The sources for this are not hard to come by, but it requires thought and a little money.

As many as possible of the team members should be skilled in expressing themselves in writing, at least in their own language. This ability does not always accompany originality of thought. Some specialists undoubtedly have difficulty in expressing what they have to say clearly and concisely, and too many such people would be a handicap to Europe Plus Thirty. This would be true even in a national organisation, speaking one language; in a multilingual organisation it is even truer, since a poor translation of an infelicitous text can easily carry work backwards.

The staff of Europe Plus Thirty, if they are of the right quality, will wish to take part in the development of forecasting technique. But (depending on the recruitment of one or two really outstanding individual workers) it might be valuable to underline a commitment to methodology by setting up a small Methods Group to act as a focus for such studies.

If Europe Plus Thirty becomes a source of useful inputs to the Commission and the Parliament, it is also likely to be regarded, from time to time, as a possible source of unintended embarrassment – even as an object of suspicion. This is a problem which would not confront a purely academic research organisation, but one which needs to be faced up to, given the policy-oriented nature of Europe Plus Thirty's work. The practical solution to the difficulty has been found elsewhere to be complete openness between those carrying out studies and those who devise and administer the policies to which they are relevant.

The arguments for Europe Plus Thirty's publishing all its work are strong: they are that Europe Plus Thirty will be dealing with matters of public concern, about which the public has a right to be informed; that open publication provides a safeguard against error or prejudice; and that publication can be a bait to attract good workers.

The arguments against publishing absolutely everything are equally clear: much of the information used will have come from government or Commission sources, and some of it may be privileged; mutual confidence between Europe Plus Thirty and the Institutions of the Community would be forfeited if disclosures were made which afterwards proved embarrassing; and some of the reports made by Europe Plus Thirty will be no more than a step on a long road of policy-making.

The main output of Europe Plus Thirty's work would be of substantial public interest, as well as of scientific interest to other professionals. It would comprise a series of forecasting exercises expressed in terms of alternative futures and goals for Western European society: teleonomies, to use the language of the Introduction. It would also comprise a number of long-term studies of social and other developments within the Community, 'impact assessments' of technological and other aspects of Community policy, and studies of the relationships between the Community and the rest of the world. The publications should be explicit regarding the assumptions and value judgements built into the analysis, and the details of the technical approaches that are used. There should probably be a regular series of books, annual or biennial, together with occasional papers reflecting the changing priorities of the programme. The individual team members should also, subject to their contracts, publish specialised books and papers, as in any other healthy research organisation. Publication should be in as many Community languages as possible.

Publication, then, should be the rule, but unpublished studies should not be excluded if there is a good reason for non-publication. The decision whether to publish should be taken by the Board of Europe Plus Thirty before the study in question is begun.

Nothing is more important than the relationship between the continuing instrument of Europe Plus Thirty and the Institutions of the Community: the Commission, the Parliament, the Council, and the Court. It is important because, no matter how good the forecasting and technology assessment done by Europe Plus Thirty is, that work will be wasted if it is not available to the right people at the right time. Equally, if the needs of those people are not met by Europe Plus Thirty, the instrument itself will have no justification.

Contacts with the Institutions of the Community should be rather close and continuous, but they should not be so close as to deprive Europe Plus Thirty of the intellectual independence which will be its justification, or to prevent it from getting on with its job. The relations between a professional body and the executive or legislature it exists to serve are best regulated by close attention to what happens at the top. If that is rightly conceived, things will probably come right lower down. So the Chairman (and/or the Director) of the Board of Europe Plus Thirty should have access to certain people. It will not be enough for the written output of Europe Plus Thirty to be available to the decision-makers; there must also be personal contact. This right of access is of crucial importance, since Europe Plus Thirty will be finding things out which are not yet known to the centres of power, and which may or may not fit in conveniently with the current policies of those centres.

We recommend that there should be right of access to the President of the Commission and to each of the Commissioners severally. (This would not imply that Europe Plus Thirty had a right to make policy recommendations.) Conversely, the President of the Commission, and each Commissioner severally, should have the right to send for the Chairman or the Director of Europe Plus Thirty.

Individual staff members of Europe Plus Thirty would have their own contacts with those Commission officials who were most nearly concerned with their work, bearing in mind the complementary needs on the one hand for a free flow of information and on the other for the academic and professional independence of Europe Plus Thirty.

No less important than the relationships of Europe Plus Thirty with the Commission will be its relationship with the Parliament. If the European Parliament is to develop over the years to become a more influential assembly for general policy debate, and *a fortiori* if it is to assume (following the direct elections planned for 1978) some of the functions of a true legislature, then it and its committees should have the same access to what is going on in Europe Plus Thirty and the same right to affect what goes on in Europe Plus Thirty as the Commission has. Indeed, this should be so even if there is no increase in the powers of the Parliament. The relations should therefore follow the same pattern as that recommended above for the Commission. The Chairman of Europe Plus Thirty should have access to the President and Secretary General of the Parliament and they, conversely, should have the right to send for him. But the European Parliament works mainly through its committees, and most of the major debates in its plenary sessions take place upon a report from a committee. It may be that the committees would in due course feel the need to develop with Europe Plus Thirty a system of hearings, following that which is already growing up with other institutions.

We come now to the Council of Ministers. Relations between the Council and the Commission are quite likely to change in the coming decades; the whole matter is subject to continuing debate. If there is no change, Europe Plus Thirty would lay before the Commission the sort of teleonomies which have been outlined above, as well as its technology assessments and whatever special problem-oriented studies have been done. There would then be discussions between the Commission and Europe Plus Thirty, and the Commission would draw its deductions for policy: for instance, that such-and-such a possible goal or strategy should be adopted and the alternatives rejected. The Commission would then lay its conclusions before the Council in the form of proposals, including also the teleonomy or other backing material which had been provided by Europe Plus Thirty. If the Council wanted to have clarifying discussions, those discussions would be with the Commission, and the Chairman or the Director of Europe Plus Thirty should take part in them as part of the Commission's team.

If there is a change in the relations between the Council and the Commission, or if the Council makes a major change in its method of work, or if it acquires a powerful secretariat of its own, or if yet further-reaching institutional changes come about as a result of moves towards European union, then the matter should be re-examined. The Board of Europe Plus Thirty should, as part of its normal work, keep all this constantly under review. Europe Plus Thirty may, in any case, have a contribution to make to the studies which will have to precede any constitutional changes.

There should also be links between Europe Plus Thirty and the long-term planning and forecasting institutions of member governments, and those links should clearly be as intense and habitual as they can be without changing the nature of Europe Plus Thirty as a Community instrument. They will obviously differ from country to country, since the national structures themselves differ. The purpose should be to achieve benefits both ways, with Europe Plus Thirty doing work which is useful to member governments, and member governments providing the inputs which are useful to Europe Plus Thirty.

Europe Plus Thirty could also develop a subsidiary function as a forum where national long-term planners and forecasters can meet and informally discuss matters of common interest on the Community level; such a forum is lacking at present.

The question of who pays for Europe Plus Thirty is bound up with the question of who has the right to ask it to undertake work. Although all sorts of people and institutions would no doubt suggest work to Europe Plus Thirty and find its output useful, yet the need for it has been expressed specifically by the Council and Commission of the European Community. Europe Plus Thirty will be the Commission's baby, and the Commission should always consider it a legitimate offspring. First and foremost, then, it should entertain requests from the Commission and the Parliament.

It should also entertain requests from certain other bodies, and the qualifications for the right to suggest work should be reviewed by the Board of Europe Plus Thirty itself from time to time. To start with, as soon as there is staff enough, suggestions should be entertained from member governments of the Community and from the European Investment Bank (as was discussed in Part III above). Later they could also be entertained from other organisations and associations, so long as they were the *European* association or grouping of whatever it was. For instance, a European industrial association or a European association of trade unions should have this right, but a particular firm, a particular trade union, or a national association of firms or unions probably should not.

All this, though, ought to be subject to an overriding rule of financial proportion. The continuity and the vitality of Europe Plus Thirty will depend on its having absolutely assured funding for a reasonable period of time, from one source, and on its never accepting more than a certain amount above that from all other sources put together. It should probably never be allowed to depend for more than a quarter of its income on sources other than the European Community itself, and the greater part of that quarter should probably come from member governments. Only by the imposition of such a ceiling will it be possible to ensure staff security, an orderly workload, and the avoidance of financial anxieties and dangers.

Europe Plus Thirty should have as much financial and administrative independence as possible, since only thus can it achieve the necessary academic and professional independence. The money it receives from the Commission should come to it in a quantity negotiated and settled (with an inflation/deflation clause) for a reasonable number of years, so as to permit the development of long-term forecasting programmes in an atmosphere of confidence.

Technology assessments may be fairly quickly done, but forecasting work is long-term work by its nature. Europe Plus Thirty must be given time to prove its value, and the value of such long-term work as this is not quickly proven. A period of a year or two, or even five years, would not be sufficient; Europe Plus Thirty should be guaranteed a minimum life of ten years. Ten years would be enough for it to build up a procedure of integrated forecasting, to produce results, and even to allow a few years after their appearance during which the decision-makers can judge their utility.

The ten-year build-up of Europe Plus Thirty should be divided into three phases:

(1) a preparatory phase, probably of one year;

(2) a four-year build-up;

(3) a five-year undisturbed run.

At the end of this ten-year programme, the Commission, the Parliament, and the Council – or whatever at that time are the power centres of the Community – should assess the achievements and the utility of Europe Plus Thirty and decide whether or not to arrange for a new ten-year programme.

The right geographical place for Europe Plus Thirty will be that which best suits its functional place. It should have a close relation with the European Commission, but not too close. Ideally, Europe Plus Thirty should find premises which are not less than one and not more than three hours, door to door, from the offices of the Commission. Less than one hour would mean time-wasting and unnecessary contacts: people would be dropping in for no good reason, in both directions. Europe Plus Thirty would risk becoming an organ of day-to-day advice, which it should not. More than three hours would mean that every meeting required an overnight stay. Personal contact would mean an expedition, and that too would be wrong. It would tend towards remote and academic work. The time-for-travel slot of one to three hours places the whole of Belgium and Luxembourg, much of the Netherlands, and part of Germany and France within range by car or rail. Relying on air transport would place a number of more distant cities within range, but would cost more.

There is another important question: should the office of Europe Plus Thirty be in a city or in the country? A place in the country would have the advantage of peace and quiet. A place in the city, and especially in a great city, would have the advantage not only of that surrounding intellectual effervescence which is only found in a metropolis, but also of a wider choice of schools for the children and jobs for the spouses of staff members. Europe Plus Thirty should be staffed by people with broad and lively minds, and largely by younger people.

Such people are more likely to be attracted to work in a great city than to the calm of the countryside. There is also the danger of an integrated team becoming hermetic or eccentric: this danger would be less in a metropolitan environment. Accordingly, a place in a great city should be chosen.

One last factor: the number of beautiful old buildings which form part of the architectural heritage of Europe, and for which it is difficult to find a use, is so great that it would clearly be right to choose one of these, or several small ones if they are close together. The future grows out of the past, and this truth can be pleasantly symbolised by the use of a fine old European building or buildings for studies about the European future.

This, then, is the outline of the new human instrument which, in late 1975, was recommended to the Institutions of the European Community in answer to their question. If it is created, it will differ from all previous instruments in two ways. The first reflects the fact that the European Community itself differs from all previous institutions in certain well-known ways. It has certain powers and duties, and the Europe Plus Thirty outlined here has been devised to help the Community to exercise just those powers and duties and to think about others which it might obtain in future. All previous forecasting instruments have been designed either to help different (smaller, and more concentrated) institutions to exercise their powers and duties, or they have been addressing themselves to the general reader who has no particular powers or duties.

The second way in which the Europe Plus Thirty outlined here will differ from its predecessors is that in its work it will very consciously attempt broadness, globality, inclusiveness. It will tackle each sector of human activity only to relate it to the others, and only by relating it to the others. If it is to look at the more distant future – over five years – it must do this. The conceptual structure suggested here and dubbed 'teleonomy', consisting of the two interpenetrating cones, should help it to do this, since if the macro-frame is wrong the finest micro-work will go astray.

No doubt even with such a frame, and even with fine micro-work, Europe Plus Thirty will still miss things and make mistakes. It has been the thesis of this book, and of the report on which it is based, that long-term integrated forecasting is better attempted than left undone, and better attended to – even if sceptically – than neglected. If attempted and attended to, it is likely to decrease the incidence of foolish policies, to increase political, social, and economic well-being, and to save money.

APPENDIX 1

RECOMMENDATIONS OF THE EUROPE PLUS THIRTY REPORT

(1) A long-term forecasting instrument, Europe Plus Thirty, should be set up to serve the Institutions of the European Community and, so far as the latter may desire, its member governments. It should work to a time horizon of five years and longer.

(2) Technology Assessment should be carried out by the continuing Europe Plus Thirty instrument as an integral part of its work.

(3) The forecasting should be integrated, namely:
    (a) not limited to a single sector, but encompassing and integrating all sectors relevant to the long-term future of the European Community, or to the particular problem area under examination;
    (b) integrated with the Community policy-making process.

(4) The forecasting should be devised so that a range of possible goals and possible ways to reach them can be examined. No one goal or policy would be recommended above others.

(5) Europe Plus Thirty should adopt a flexible and adaptive method of work, employing a whole range of quantitative and non-quantitative methods.

(6) It should work in three ways: by assembling work done elsewhere, by letting contracts, and by in-house research.

(7) Europe Plus Thirty should have, as well as 'generalists', an in-house staff with knowledge of the following subjects:
    Agriculture, fisheries, and forestry
    Social structures and values
    Education
    Science and technology
    Industry
    Energy
    Materials
    The environment
    Transport
    Economy and finance
    Defence and disarmament
    Politics and institutions
    Technology assessment

(8) For the following subjects Europe Plus Thirty should primarily rely on outside advice:

Climate
Population
Health
Communications

(9) (a) The governing body of Europe Plus Thirty should be a Board of twelve members, appointed by the European Commission.

 (b) The staff of Europe Plus Thirty should be headed by a Director assisted by two Deputy Directors.

 (c) The staff should be gradually built up to between thirty and seventy-five graduate professionals.

 (d) Publication of work should be the rule, but unpublished studies should not be excluded if there is good reason.

 (e) Europe Plus Thirty should be at the service primarily of the European Commission and Parliament and also, if they wish it, of the member governments. The relationship of Europe Plus Thirty to the Institutions of the Community should be kept permanently under review by the Board of Europe Plus Thirty.

 (f) At least 75 per cent of Europe Plus Thirty's finance should always come from the European Commission.

APPENDIX 2

AN INTERACTION
BETWEEN EUROPEAN
PARLIAMENTARIANS AND
THE MESAROVIC–PESTEL
WORLD MODEL

On 24–6 February 1975, a meeting organised by the European Commission was held at the Medizinische Hochschule, Hanover, when seven members of the parliaments of Community countries, some of whom were also members of the European Parliament, were personally to 'interact' with the Mesarovic–Pestel World Model.

The parliamentarians present were:

P.-B. Cousté	France
G. Flämig	Germany
Lord Kennet	Britain
C. Meintz	Luxembourg
K. Helwig Petersen	Denmark
Senator Mary Robinson	Ireland
J. C. Terlouw	Netherlands

Professors Mihajlo Mesarovic and Eduard Pestel, certain members of their team, certain members of the Europe Plus Thirty Project Board and Team, and about fifteen other observers, some from the European Commission, were also present.

PRESENTATIONS AND ACTIVITIES

The structure of the model and its modes of operation were described by Professors Mesarovic and Pestel and members of their team.[1] The model is global in scope, disaggregated into ten geographical regions and nine economic sectors, and is highly complex, containing about 100,000 relationships. These relationships are contained in a so-called 'causal stratum' and, in operation, are supplemented by input values specified by the operator. Values which must be specified are of two types: 'policy' variables (i.e. allocation of resources between sectors) and 'parameter' variables (such as potential oil reserves, about which uncertainty exists). The specification of these variables constitutes the operator's 'scenario', the repercussions of which are to be

---

[1] See M. Mesarovic and E. Pestel, *Mankind at the Turning Point* (London: Hutchinson, 1975); and Mesarovic and Pestel, eds., *Multilevel Computer Model of World Development System*, extract from proceedings of International Institute for Applied Systems Analysis conference at Laxenburg, 29 April – 3 May 1974 (Laxenburg, 1974).

indicated by the model. These variables can be given in qualitative form (e.g. a choice made between high, medium, or low values) or quantitative (numerical) form.

The model was in a state where two particular issues could be explored: the world oil and food situations. On the first day some sample runs of oil scenarios were made and results discussed. On the second day, the parliamentarians were given the opportunity personally to operate the model, on-line via terminals in the conference room, which allowed them to study the repercussions of alternative scenarios directly.

REACTIONS OF THE PARLIAMENTARIANS

As far as we know, this was the first time a group of 'real live decision-makers' had carried out an interaction with a simulation model relevant to their work. The parliamentarians all felt that the operation had been useful, and also that computer models in general could form a useful input into the policy-making process and could help to reduce uncertainty in decision-making.

Obviously, the model did not address itself to the kind of problem with which the parliamentarians were often concerned in their day-to-day work. Firstly, the scale of the problems considered in the model was very broad; the parliamentarians were usually concerned with comparatively small decisions, while the model considered gigantic ones. Politicians were normally engaged in forming policy within particular sectors and were not used to discussing cross-sectoral policy. Secondly, the time scale covered by the model runs (up to fifty years) was far greater than that normally considered by parliamentarians, who were often forced to be concerned with short-term issues with an eye on the next election. On the other hand, one member of the Mesarovic–Pestel team, who had been sitting with the parliamentarians and coaching them in the interaction procedures, gave the opinion that they used the model 'better' than the average group of the same education, since they were 'already aggregated to the right level', i.e. were already used to thinking farther and wider than most people.

Most of the parliamentarians thought that the model had an indirect value, in that it helped them to step back and survey long-term issues. One compared it to a religious retreat. This view is in line with its makers' own hope, that it can help help to form conceptual guidelines for policy rather than to form specific policies. Some parliamentarians remarked that it forced them to think far and wide.

One parliamentarian wondered how long it would take, for instance, a parliamentary energy committee to understand the use of this particular model. Professor Mesarovic estimated that about six two-day discussion sessions would be required for a general understanding and intuitive acceptance of the uses and limits of the method.

One parliamentarian devoted considerable preparation and care to 'trying the standard solution of lower energy consumption and lower growth in the West and seeing if I inadvertently kill a few million Asians'. None of the parliamentarians was flummoxed by the interaction process, though some learned to do it much more slowly than others, and continued to do it for longer. Several asked searching questions about the relation between man, machine, and reality. The experiment confirmed what was already known: you don't have to be a computer professional to use a computer, or a systems analyst to understand a system.

CONCLUSION

The meeting was not to judge the Mesarovic–Pestel model or to discuss the place of computer modelling in forecasting. It was simply to try, for the first time, a direct interaction between a group of parliamentarians and a model. We sum up by quoting the words of one of them: 'It is hard to believe once a policy-maker has been introduced to it that he would just say thank you very much and walk away.'

Index

accidents, health and, 114
adult education, 127–8
agriculture: present forecasting by Community on, 50–1; and climate, 85, 90; forecasting on, 99–100, 101–5
Agung eruption, 84, 88
analysis by precursive events, forecasting through, 27
Arctic sea-ice, changes in, 89–90
Armytage, W. H. G., 37

Ball, R. J., 21
banking, and technology assessment, 213–14
Bariloche world model, 37
Battelle Institute eV, Frankfurt, 209
Belgium, present forecasting in, 58, 60
Bell, Daniel, 118
biosphere, environment and, 164–5
Bloch, Ernst, 200
Bourgeois-Pichat, J., 94
Box, G. E. P., 91
'brainstorming', forecasting by, 28
Britain, see United Kingdom
British Empire, decline of, 5
budgets, present Community forecasting on, 53–4
Bundesministerium für Forschung und Technologie, 208
butter 'mountains', 103

CAP (Common Agricultural Policy), 102–4
car ownership, 174
carbon dioxide and climate, 89–90
Cassandra, 10
Central Policy Review Staff, UK, 210
CIME (Intergovernmental Council for European Migration), 97
climate: forecasting of, 83–91; agriculture and, 85, 90; human modification of, 86–7, 89–90; see also energy
coal, 142; see also energy
COMET (Community Medium-Term Model) Project, 49, 184–5
Commission of European Communities: functions of, 1n, 44, 45, 46–7, 48; relation of Europe Plus Thirty to, 227, 229; see also Directorates General

Committee of Permanent Representatives, 47
Committee on Economic Policy, 142
Common Agricultural Policy (CAP), 102–4
communications, forecasting on, 178–81
Community Medium-Term Model, see COMET
Community Statistical Office, see Statistical Office of the European Community
computer solutions, forecasting by, 36, 37
conflict analysis, forecasting by, 33
consumption patterns, 19–21
cost–benefit analysis, forecasting by, 29–30
'COST 33' programme, 51
Council of Ministers of the European Community: functions of, 44, 45, 47; on migration, 97; and fisheries, 106; relation of Europe Plus Thirty to, 228, 229
Council on Environmental Quality (USA), 207
Court of Justice of the European Community: functions of, 44, 45; and technology assessment, 214
credit and investments, 53; see also banking
critical path method, forecasting by, 31
cross-impact, forecasting by, 34
Czechoslovakia, present forecasting in, 63

Dehrendorf, Ralf, vii
decision theory, forecasting by, 31–2
defence, forecasting on, 190–6
Délégation à l'Aménagement du Territoire et l'Action Régionale, 209
Delphi method, forecasting by, 28
demography, see population
dietary habits, 113–14
Directorates General of European Community: functions of, 48–57; and technology assessment, 214–15
disarmament, forecasting on, 190–6
disease, forecasting on, 111–13, 114

Economic and Social Committee, 47
Economic Policy Committee, 56
ECMT (European Conference of Ministers of Transport), 175